MADNESS TO MINISTRY:

A WOMAN'S JOURNEY FROM PSYCH UNIT TO PULPIT

NANCY BAUER-KING

www.ten16press.com - Waukesha, WI

Madness to Ministry
A Woman's Journey from Psych Unit to Pulpit
Copyright © 2017 Nancy Bauer-King
ISBN 978-1-943331-62-8
First Edition

Madness to Ministry
A Woman's Journey from Psych Unit to Pulpit
by Nancy Bauer-King

All Rights Reserved. Written permission must be secured from the publisher to use or reproduce any part of this book, except for brief quotations in critical reviews or articles.

For information, please contact:

www.ten16press.com
Waukesha, WI

Cover photos property of Nancy Bauer-King
Cover design by Kaeley Dunteman

The author has made every effort to ensure that the information within this book was accurate at the time of publication. The author does not assume and hereby disclaims any liability to any party for any loss, damage, or disruption caused by errors or omissions, whether such errors or omissions result from accident, negligence, or any other cause.

The author tried to recreate events, locales and conversations from her memories of them. In order to maintain their anonymity in some instances we have changed the names of individuals and places, we may have changed some identifying characteristics and details such as physical properties, occupations and places of residence.

For the "Ore" kids: Joan, Stephen, Julia, and Gerard, who called me Mom (and then Reverend Mother) and for Stan, whose support helped us all grow up.

Table of Contents

Introduction   1

I
From Christian Story to Psych Unit
1970

Chapter 1: Faith of our Fathers   3
Chapter 2: Chaos to Collapse   18
Chapter 3: Saved by a Name   30
Chapter 4: Rock-a-Bye Baby   40
Chapter 5: Playing No-tes   52
Chapter 6: Father God Father   63
Chapter 7: Inside the Outsider   73

II
From Psych Unit to School
1971-1976

Chapter 8: Loves Lost   79
Chapter 9: Back-To-Ward   93
Chapter 10: Descent With Demons   108
Chapter 11: Re-released   128

III
From School to Seminary
1976-1982

Chapter 12: Career Confusion   149
Chapter 13: Strike Three   164
Chapter 14: Breaks Through   178

IV
FROM SCHOOL TO SEMINARY
1982-1985

CHAPTER 15: BACK TO THE FUTURE	199
CHAPTER 16: RAPPED AND RAPT	217
CHAPTER 17: WOMB BEFORE WORD	229
CHAPTER 18: MISMATCHED	238
CHAPTER 19: PASTOR PRACTICE	246
CHAPTER 20: STEP OUT AND STEP IN	264

V
FROM SEMINARY TO SERVICE

CHAPTER 21: ORDINATION	280
EPILOGUE	285
ACKNOWLEDGEMENTS AND THANK YOUS	287

Introduction

Several years ago, a friend asked, "How did you go from the psych ward to the ministry?" I looked at my watch and quipped, "How much time have you got?"

Though my answer was flippant, her words became seeds that took root in my mind and quickly became *my* question: How *did* I go from psychosis to pastor? How *could* I tell the story that had too many scenes? Terrifying, life-giving, and redeeming scenes.

Yet, the story was one I wanted to tell. In truth, I had been writing scenes for years as an important method of healing my mental and emotional distress. Sometimes I wrote the same scenes over and over. Writing became like prayer for me. With each session at the page, I experienced a little more growth, a little more healing.

Madness to Ministry: A Woman's Journey from Psych Unit to Pulpit begins with my decision to attend a weekend religious seminar and my month-long descent into psychosis immediately following. The memoir ends with my ordination as a clergywoman in the Wisconsin Annual Conference of the United Methodist Church. Through the years in between, I learned to trust myself through counseling, academic achievements, important friendships, and theological insights.

Though my story of healing takes place over thirty years ago, mental distress and religious discord are at the forefront of our current social discourse. I offer *Madness to Ministry* as one account of how a break*down* can eventually be seen as a break*through,* how someone who experiences psychosis can go on to have a full and productive life.

A seminary professor once told me, "We ask two questions throughout our lives: Who am I? and What am I for?

I am still asking those questions.

I
From Christian Story to Psych Unit
1970

Chapter 1
Faith of our Fathers

Faith of our fathers, holy faith!
We will be true to thee till death.
-Frederick W. Faber, 1849

January, 1970

Two months before the rescue squad carts me off to St. Elizabeth's, I sit with my pastor at the shiny beige Formica-topped table in the church office. Reverend Holton hired me four months ago despite the fact that I shamefully disclosed in my interview that I was taking four little orange "crazy" pills a day and seeing a psychiatrist once a month in Madison. Diagnosis: Depression.

Reverend Holton didn't visibly shrink at hearing my medical condition and I began to work at the church two mornings a week answering the telephone, preparing the Sunday bulletins and monthly newsletters, keeping membership records up to date, and doing miscellaneous filing and correspondence for Reverend Holton. I typed bulletins on a new IBM electric typewriter, cut hymns and prayers into a blue stencil, painted my mistakes with a fast-drying blue goop and retyped. I fed viscous black ink into a drum of a mimeograph and hand-cranked each printed sheet through the machine. Every Friday my skin and sometimes clothing got stained with ink that oozed from the Gestetner or swung into my hip from a used stencil.

On the day Reverend Holton brings his coffee into the office and invites me to take a break with him at the table, neither of us has a clue that in a few weeks I'll be in a locked room in a psychiatric unit. As soon as he sits down with his mug of coffee, he begins to tell me about a workshop he wants me to attend.

"Religious Studies-1 is a weekend seminar offered by the Ecumenical Institute," he says. "I want all church officers to go." He describes the seminar, which will be held over the Valentine's Day weekend.

"For a whole weekend?"

"Yes."

"I don't know," I say, cupping my hands around the coffee cup I got from the church kitchen. "I shouldn't be away from Stan and my children all weekend."

He names other church members who will be going and continues to describe RS-1 and how his participation several years earlier changed his life.

"There is something at the Ecumenical Institute Nancy Ore needs to hear," he says, and raises his heavy black mug to his lips.

I wonder what he knows about me that I don't know.

"I'm afraid to go," I whisper. Ever since hearing the sermon "God on the Hunt," I've felt something stalking me.

"Yes," he nods, "a leap of faith is frightening." I picture the tourist attraction at Wisconsin Dells, the dog jumping off the edge of an ancient limestone cliff, sailing in midair over viewers who hold their breath until the animal lands safely onto another outcropping of layered stone. And I remember riding on the boat that delivers mail to the residents around Lake Geneva in the summer. I watched the girl jump off the moving boat, run down the dock, hurry back in time to leap back onto the boat without falling in the water and drowning. Over and over around the lake hoping not to fall.

"I'm afraid to jump," I say. "I'm afraid I'll fall."

"Here. Give me your hand." Reverend Holton stretches out his arm and I place my stained left hand into his long, smooth, unblemished fingers. I am ashamed of my fingernails "chewed down to the quick," as my father said when he dipped my fingertips in rubbing alcohol to keep my hands out of my mouth. And I am embarrassed at the sudden flush of heat spreading into my cheeks.

"See?" Reverend Holton says. "A leap of faith is just that simple."

Friday, February 13th

I am one of 24 students sitting at tables that have been shoved together in a U-shaped arrangement. Next to me is Reverend Holton's wife, Marie, beside her, Dr. Stein and his wife. Dr. Stein, my family doctor has driven us to this Ecumenical Institute seminar.

At the front of the room stands the teacher, short and stocky, dressed in a dull brown suit, white shirt and tie. His eyes peer out through horned-rimmed glasses that frame a square face. His hair, the same color as his suit, is cropped close to his head in a crew-cut. The teacher introduces himself as Mark and says he's the pedagogue. I wonder why he doesn't share his last name and I don't know what the word pedagogue means. Will I understand what he's teaching?

After introductions around the room, Mark launches into the topic for the evening: God-the-Father. He lectures for an hour, describing limitations we experience in life and then distributes "The Crisis of Faith," a paper by Rudolf Bultmann. He gives us instructions how to "chart" the paper.

"Number and organize the paragraphs into major ideas and then plot them onto a grid on your paper."

Bultmann's words sift like seeds into the fertile soil of my consciousness:

"God the Father is the one who gives you life—*and* takes your life away."

"God is the one who causes you to long for love—*and* takes love away."

"God is the one who drives you to know—*and* the one who keeps you from knowing."

Father God, according to Bultmann, seems to me like a cruel creator of a squeeze play at the depths of human experience. "Father God," says the teacher, "is when humans bump up against their limitations. Father God represents the '*I Can'ts*' in our lives."

I do not speak during the discussion lead by the pedagogue after we've read and charted the paper. Comments by the other participants sound important. No one seems troubled with Father God's ruthless behavior.

Dread takes root and begins to grow when the pedagogue repeats "This is the way life is!" He strides to the blackboard and illustrates Bultmann's divinely ordered Father God who gives and Father God who takes away, with quick swipes of chalk—punctuated with three sets of up and down arrows pointing accusatorily at each other with an empty space in between.

He steps away from the blackboard and stares at his artwork. Then he chuckles with disbelief and says, "This is an impossible bind. What are we supposed to do?"

He answers his question with a shrug, looks at his captive and stunned students and then uses his chalk to draw a wavy line between the opposing arrows, like the trail of a drunk staggering down a city street, dodging mail boxes and weaving around light poles.

With a flourish, he places the chalk in the tray at the bottom of the blackboard. Then he rubs his hands together to brush away chalk dust, turns again toward his students, and, after a pointed pause, asks quietly, "And, how are you going to live *your* life?"

His question echoes off the walls of the room and begins an all night Friday-the-Thirteenth Bad News Bounce in my head. I lie awake all night on the sagging mattress of an upper bunk in a second story room with several other women. I can hear the steady breathing of Marie in the bunk underneath me. The gray-haired woman across the room groans when she turns over.

All night I watch a red neon sign on a bar across the street flashing on and off, on and off, illuminating the awful way life is. Trapped between the quivering up and down, in and out, yes and no, of a capricious, callous Father God.

"Praise the Lord! Christ is risen!" At 5:00 Saturday morning someone walks back and forth through the hallway banging a large metal spoon on the bottom of an aluminum dishpan.

"Praise the Lord! Christ is risen!"

I don't need the wake-up call.

My pastor's wife notices that, unlike Jesus, I am not rising. "I couldn't sleep," I explain, looking down at her from my saggy top bunk. "I'm going to stay here and try to sleep. I'm not going to this morning's lecture."

"There's something this morning that Nancy Ore needs to hear," she counters, with the same mysterious imperative her husband said when he recruited me for this seminar. I reluctantly allow her to talk me into getting showered, dressed and attending worship before breakfast.

Most participants are already seated by the time I get to the class, and I have to take a place near the front of the room.

"Praise the Lord! Christ is risen!" the pedagogue proclaims to begin the session.

"He is risen, indeed!" we respond to a ritual we have been taught earlier during the morning worship.

"This morning, we will be discussing God-the-Son," the teacher says, and turns to the arrows still sharp on the blackboard. He immediately launches into a lecture about Jesus.

"God-the-Son, or Jesus-the-Redeemer is the one who saves us from the black and white God-the-Creator dilemma we are in," he says. "If God is the *I can't,* Jesus is the *I can.* Even in our human limitations, we have options."

I sit up straighter, suddenly awake, with my eyes and ears open to anything that will help me deal with a fickle Father God.

Again with quick swipes of chalk, the pedagogue draws a deep v-shaped chasm with a little white lamb on the left side of the precipice. As he recites lines from the Apostle's Creed, he points to the lamb, trots it on its stick legs down to the bottom of the chasm, and back up on the other side where he draws another lamb, puts a crown on its head and says, "There's the story we believe: Jesus crucified, dead, and buried … rose again and sits at the right hand of God."

He finishes describing the central creed of the Christian faith as a *story … a story*!? Is he saying it is only a *tale*? Does that mean I don't have to lurch a zig-zag path through life bouncing off oppositional arrows like a pinball?

The teacher quickly distributes another paper.

"Read and chart this sermon on sin and grace by Paul Tillich," he instructs. "And when you get to paragraph #12, number each sentence."

I imagine Paul Tillich as another white-haired, bespectacled, old preacher with a benign smile stooped behind a fat wooden pulpit. But I dutifully reach for another piece of 8½ by 11 paper, draw lines, and assign numbers as directed. I read paragraphs one through twelve with no noticeable reaction other than interest, but when I read and number paragraph #12, a strange suffusion of warm light begins to spread through my body.

...*(19) Grace strikes us when we are in great pain and restlessness. (20) It strikes us when we walk through the dark valley of a meaningless and empty life. (21) It strikes us when we feel that our separation is deeper than usual, because we have violated another life, a life which we loved, or from which we were estranged. (22) It strikes us when our disgust for our own being, our indifference, our weakness, our hostility, and our lack of direction and composure have become intolerable to us. (23) It strikes us when, year after year, the longed for perfection of life does not appear, when the old compulsions reign within us as they have for decades, when despair destroys all joy and courage. (24) Sometimes at that moment a wave of light breaks into our darkness, and it is as though a voice were saying: 'You are accepted. You are accepted, accepted by that which is greater than you and the name of which you do not know ... "*

You are accepted. You are accepted. The kindled flame squeezes between the black on white prison bar letters on the page and shoots the words on a beam of light to me, Nancy Ore.

I am accepted the way I am? Bitten fingernails? A-minuses? Black and white and staggered sin between? Nancy Ore is accepted the way she is right now? N.O. is O.K.?

Internal voices quickly oppose Mr. Tillich's comforting words.

You had sex before your wedding day. You hate your mother-in-law. You make secret visits to a Madison psychiatrist. You take four little orange happy pills every day. You scream at your children, you detest housework, and you don't finish projects!

I read again and try to believe the shimmering black and white print.

You are accepted ... You are accepted ...

As I begin to savor the taste of this February 14th Good News Valentine from Mr. Tillich, the pedagogue pushes his horned-rimmed glasses up higher on his nose and begins the discussion.

He says God-the-Son is the response to the impossible human

dilemma created by God-the-Father. He turns, picks up the chalk, draws a huge X across the blackboard, and begins to fill in the four angled spaces.

"The death and resurrection of Jesus means: All is accepted. All is forgiven. The past is approved. And, the future is open!" His X drawing tips the cross of Jesus on its side. His statements obliterate the polarities, the ups and downs, the rights and lefts of the wooden cross beams.

The pedagogue grins, throws his hands above his head and closes the discussion. I am left with an X-marks-the-spot of grace branded in my head like a new baptismal sign. I have never heard or felt this kind of Good News. This story *upends* the Jesus story I had learned from all those men in black robes and even blacker viewpoints. No more sacrificial lambs and bleeding hearts. With my sin X'd out I am *O.K. the way I am!*

The scriptures, the old symbols and rules begin to vibrate and disintegrate.

I arrive early to the room for the afternoon lecture. God-the-Spirit. I sit at the very front of the room in the chair closest to the right hand of the teacher, my pen in hand ready to take notes.

But when the teacher delivers the lecture on the third name of God, I am not listening. I know he is talking about God the *I will*, the human decisions to *act*—to choose among the possibilities one can do amidst limitations. I barely hear him because I am basking in the comforting light of being okay and looking out the window at the black and white patterns made by snow clinging to a bare tree branch. It is Valentine's Day, spring is near and my frozen-with-red-sin heart is melting.

The teacher's voice interrupts my daydreaming. "Even with terrible things happening, the past is approved, the future is open!" As I'm considering his words, I notice he is moving toward me. He stops and stands directly behind my chair and addresses the group.

"What about sin? What about this God-the-Father squeeze play and the fear it evokes? What about all the terrible things that happen to you? Where are you in the midst of war, poverty, a broken marriage, terminal cancer?"

No one speaks. He allows the silence to hover over the seminar participants like a thick shroud.

"Where are *you*?" he says suddenly and leans over my back. "Where are *you* when terrible things rain down on *you* like Noah's Flood?" He wriggles his fingers as he moves his arms down and through the air over me like a heavy cloudburst drenching my head. Uncomfortably conscious of others watching, I bend my head down and look at my papers.

"Where are you?" he says again and gives a gentle shove into my back. "Where are *you*?"

"I am still here," I whisper, jolted into a soft awareness.

"Again." The pedagogue prompts, with another push.

"I am still here," I say more loudly, surprised, as if I'm hearing the words for the first time.

"Again!" the teacher commands and shoves me forward toward the table.

"I am still here!" I obey. The sound of the words and their meaning seem to come from a locked shell cracked open inside.

N.O. N.ancy O.re hears her own words. I'm still here. I'm still here! The Good News Gospel is an eternal Y.E.S.! It's Valentine's Day, and my broken heart is fixed to eternal life. My new proclamation rushes in to take up permanent residence in my memory. Even in the midst of my father's terminal illness, my husband's silence, my children's fighting, a nation at war with itself in Viet Nam, and my upcoming 30th birthday—which will render me untrustworthy according to the signs of war protestors—I am still here.

Amazingly I am still here! It's February 14 and it's my Birth Day. Nancy Bauer born March 14, 1940. Nancy Bauer born again *today*. Nancy B. will *always be*!

That evening the class participants have popcorn and watch the movie, Requiem for a Heavyweight. The prizefighter, played by Anthony Quinn, is manipulated by his conniving manager to enter the ring dressed as an Indian. My eyes fill with tears when the fighter lets loose with a war whoop. Having decided to sacrifice his dignity for his manager, who is in danger of physical abuse, Anthony seals his decision with a loud celebration.

During the inevitable discussion that follows, when our leader asks which scene is most important, I say, "The *war whoop*. It has to be the *war whoop*!" But I can't explain why. Thankfully, the leader nods and another participant describes another scene.

After another 5:00 AM dishpan alarm clock rising with Jesus, another worship, and another breakfast, the class participants gather in the seminar room for our final lecture and paper.

I cannot concentrate on the lecture or the discussion on a paper about the church. Words, phrases of songs, and new ideas presented the previous two days are careening through my brain cells looking for new space to settle.

"What are you planning to do when you get home?" the teacher asks, and begins to move around the table with his question. This time I have my answer ready. I don't have to *do* anything. I don't get the chance to verbalize my answer. Sunday noon has arrived and the seminar is concluded. As I leave the classroom, I feel smug because I understand the Jesus story now and have the right answer. There is no one right answer. *The secret of life is there is no secret!*

Before I go to my room for my suitcase, I stop at the Institute's gift shop. Fascinated by a multi-colored candle nestling amidst books and crosses, I greet the man behind the counter, point to the cone of colored wax wound around a wooden dowel and ask, "How much is that candle?"

"Ten dollars."

I am disappointed at the high cost. There is never any money left in our check book at the end of the month and $10 will buy milk for my children for two weeks.

"How long will it last?" I ask.

"Forever," claims the salesperson and grins at me.

"Yes." I laugh. "Yes, forever." I grin back at him because I am now in on the golden secret … there is no secret each moment is the eternal one secret of life and through Jesus I can do anything I want. I buy the candle.

As I come down the stairs with my overnight bag, I meet the pedagogue walking up to the second floor. Neither of us says a word, but I smile knowingly because now we're members of the same "we know the secret" club.

For the first time in three days I step outside and into an overcast February day. As I open the back door of Dr. Stein's car to step in, I look down and notice a shiny object at my feet. Even with thawing mud clinging to its thin circle of wire, the single hoop earring pulses shimmering gold. I laugh out loud, pick it up, wipe it off and show it to my traveling companions. "This is a sign!" I announce. "A gift for the new me."

My fellow RS-1 participants and I continue in animated conversation all the way back to Appleton. As Dr. Stein pulls up in front of 126 South Alton Court to drop me off, I can see the lights are on in the dining room. My husband, Stan, and the children are eating supper. I hurriedly grab my bags from the trunk and wave a quick goodbye to my church friends.

"I'm home! I'm home!" I call as I burst through the front door. Stan comes into the vestibule to greet me. I throw down the suitcase and fall into his arms. "I'm ME! I'm ME!" I announce as I hurry into the dining room eager to tell my family about my weekend at the Ecumenical Institute.

Someone has already set dinnerware at my place and one of the children passes me a casserole my husband has prepared. My excitement is contagious.

"We baked a cake for you, Mom!" Jerry says, and Joan and Julie hurry into the kitchen. Everyone is grinning as the girls return and place the creation in the middle of the table. Bright red, blue, and green frosting letters on white icing flash a loving message to me from my children.

WELCOME HOME, MOM!

I stand up, pick up my dinner knife, quickly cut around the M-O-M! and lift the large chocolate square out of the center of the cake.

"This piece is for ME!" I shout. "ME, MOM! Mom, Me! Mommy!" I shriek at my wordplay. Still standing, I cut the remaining cake in the shape of God-the-Son tipped on his side cross, four straight lines to the four corners of the pan. I serve Stan and my children from the X. I am pleased with my behavior. Yes. I'm saying Yes. I've changed from No. Eternally changed from NO in the world of black-white rules to the YES keys-to-the-kingdom of color. Yes. Yes. Yes.

"Mom, you've changed!" Steve says, his mouth wide open in a happy grin.

"Yes, I have changed," I agree and quiver with excitement.

Later, after the dishes are done, I show the children the rainbow swirls of wax I bought at the Ecumenical Institute shop.

"How much did you pay for *that*?" my husband asks when he sees the candle. His words poke a tiny hole into my conscience.

"Ten dollars," I say. Even his disapproval does not snuff out the flame dancing in my heart.

I flash my 'I've-got-a-secret smile,' and say, "The man who sold it to me said the candle would last forever." Stan does not respond. I go into the kitchen to find a match.

Ecstatic all evening, I am still awake at 4:00 AM. I don't want to sleep. This is my first day home from the Ecumenical Institute—the place that gave me new eyes to see, and I don't want to miss anything. I do not want to miss the sound of the cars on the College Avenue Bridge, the pulsing of the gray-green wallpaper flowers in the bedroom I share with Stan, my children's blue eyes. Coffee. Crisp toast. The smooth feel of peanut butter on the roof of my mouth.

As soon as my children leave for school, I drive to my job at St. James. I am there before Reverend Holton. When I see his car stop in the parking lot, I rush to the front door, push it open and throw myself toward Reverend Holton for a big hug. He jerks back, eyes wide with surprise, and raises his arms for protection.

The sting of rejection is brief and during our regular devotional time he gives me a handwritten card.

Good Morning! It's the day after Christmas. There is one difference from our usual Christmas observance. This tree won't die. It may change shape. It may grow and cause discomfort in its growth, but die it won't…even when you have lost touch. So Happy New Year, Nancy, and many more to come.

I clutch the card close to my chest and giggle. Yes. Yes. It's Merry Christmas! In the middle of February, I am born into the secret. There is no secret. Only a story with an "X" in the middle. I am free. Free. I can do anything.

Reverend Holton wants me to start typing the March newsletter, and, though I find it hard to concentrate, I fix my mistakes with the sticky blue goo and hand-crank the copies on the Gestetner.

"Look! Look!" I holler to Reverend Holton when I carefully peel the inky black stencil off the drum, place it briefly on a piece of white paper and lift it up again.

"It's a picture!" I carry the blot to the pastor's office door. "What do you see in the picture?" I ask. "I see mountains and a valley! Mountains and a valley!" Reverend Holton just smiles. I start singing Red River Valley.

In the afternoon, still in love with life and my life in particular, I drive over the Lawe Street Bridge and south on Oneida Street to Food Queen for groceries. As I push a full cart out of the store, I see the pet shop. I've always wanted to go into the pet shop but have told myself I'm too busy to take the time.

But I'm in eternal life now. I can do anything. I say no to black and white tasks and yes to a burning impulse. I enter the store and watch tumbling balls of fur. I hear fluttering wings and a deep squawk of a large bird with red, yellow and blue feathers. Nervous hamsters. Darting fish. I take deep breaths of cedar shavings and cracked grain, and then hurry home before the ice cream melts.

At supper, I light the forever candle and after grace is said, I ask my family one of the questions I learned at E. I. Questions to provoke reflection and a conversation. "What was the highlight of your day?"

No one answers. I am a new me and eager for conversation, but there is only silence. Then into a lull, and holding his fork mid-air, Stan asks, "What was yours?"

Excited to talk about my improvisational play, I say, "You know that Pet Shop in Valley Fair near Food Queen? I've always wanted to go in it, but I never did until today—this afternoon after I finished buying the groceries."

Stan and the children seem interested, so I quit eating and continue.

"It was wonderful. Like entering the Garden of Eden. An Old English Sheep Dog puppy, with a cute little pink nose, stood on its hind legs to greet me. I petted a kitten. Fur like velvet. And, they have fish … swimming rainbows of fish. I liked the smell. Fresh cedar shavings."

"Pet shops stink," Stan says.

Through a wisp of forever candle smoke, I see him wrinkle his nose.

I'm hurt. Confused. I thought pet shops were *yes*, but my husband who is always right (like my father) says pet shops are *no*. His pronouncement is the first black check, a dark blot in my neon heart light and casts the first shadow in a month-long darkening to come.

After supper I sit at the table. I get out the E.I. papers. I trace the X and stare through the forever candle's gray smoke swirls. I reread Reverend Holton's Merry Christmas card. Yes. The evergreen eternal yes born-again tree is the root of my life.

I set my teeth. I will say Yes. I will follow JesYes. I will stop biting my fingernails. I will stop taking the little orange happy pills, and because no one else at church volunteered, in a few weeks I will clean the house, make a fancy dessert, and host the Kum Dubble Klub's progressive dinner. For the next several days I keep silently repeating the E.I. mantras I have learned:

"All is forgiven. All is received."

"You are accepted."

"Praise the Lord! Christ is risen! He is risen, indeed!"

Throughout February and into March, I keep lighting the forever candle every morning, but I forget to eat and don't sleep well, and, as the rainbow colors gradually melt, my eternal-yes-life goes up in smoke.

Chapter 2
Chaos to Collapse

Jesus walked this lonesome valley
He had to walk it by himself
Oh nobody else could walk it for him
He had to walk it by himself.
You must walk this lonesome valley
You have to walk it by yourself
Oh nobody else can walk it for you
You have to walk it by yourself.

-Gladys Jameson

Friday, March 13, 1970

The telephone rings in the middle of the night. Stan reaches over to the small wooden cabinet next to his side of the bed and answers. Listens.

"I'll be right there," he says, hangs up, throws off the covers and heads for his closet.

"What happened?"

"Someone bombed the Early American Room. They got Lawrence, too."

I'm wide awake. From the bed I see my husband pushing his arms through his shirtsleeves.

"Where are you going?"

"Janitors think East will be hit, too. They're arming themselves."

"But, where are *you* going?" Even as I repeat the question Stan heads for the stairway.

"No! Don't go! Call the police!"

I'm terrified with the brief news my husband relayed. I'm not as troubled with destruction at Lawrence University or the loss of historical artifacts housed at Appleton West as I am panicked about Stan's safety as the principal of Appleton East.

I imagine a crew of men armed with brooms, mops and rifles, anxious to shoot at anything that moves. I see bombs exploding, shotguns fired, and my husband's body flung against a student locker, a hole blown through his gullet, leaving a shower of blood behind him on the twisted wreckage of metal and smoldering books as he slides to the floor of East High. Dead. All in slow-motion.

"No! Don't go! No!"

There is no response to my pleading. I hear the back door close, the garage door go up and the car back out onto South Alton Court. I curl up in a fetal position at the foot of our heavy walnut Victorian bed, hold my stomach, and wait.

I stay at the foot of the bed for what seems like hours until I hear Stan return.

"What happened?" I ask when he moves stealthily into the bedroom and begins to undress. I have to force my words through thick cotton batting that has settled in my head.

"Nothing."

"Nothing?" *No thing?*

Stan gets back into bed. He turns toward the wall away from me. He won't talk.

The next day, my 30th birthday, the Appleton Post Crescent carries the account of the bombing.

Fire Bombs Hit LU, West High
No Solid Leads Found

By Bill Knutson – Post-Crescent Staff Writer

> Authorities still are searching for the first solid lead into fire bombings early today that extensively damaged Lawrence University's Reserve Office Training Corps (ROTC) building and Appleton High School West.
>
> Local Federal Bureau of Investigation agents were called into aid Appleton fire and police officials. An agent said that although government property was not damaged, the FBI will work in liaison with local authorities in attempting to determine if today's fire bombings are tied in with similar disturbances in other parts of the nation.
>
> ...Although damage estimates were not available as of late this morning, the loss at Appleton High School West is expected to run into the thousands of dollars. ...Fire ignited by Molotov cocktails heavily damaged the Early American Room ... and there was minor damage to a classroom...

The tv coverage of the bombing includes young Viet Nam war protestors, carrying signs: NEVER TRUST ANYONE OVER 30!

I am 30 today. Am I untrustworthy?

I light the $10.00 candle. It is clear to me now that neither the candle nor I will last forever. Objects that shimmered in gold light a month ago as I left the Ecumenical Institute, appear waxy and warped by heat.

I look at the clock. 4:48. I look several hours later and it is only 4:50. I can't believe only two minutes have gone by. I can't remember what I was doing during all those hours.

That night the 10:00 news includes taped footage of more protestors as well as protestors noisily protesting the protestors. The U.S. is at war. U.S. Us. We're at war with ourselves.

Sunday night, the day after my birthday, Stan and I drive to St. James. Reverend Holton has invited graduates of the Ecumenical Institute's February weekend to a reunion, and my husband, who refuses to attend one of the weekend seminars, comes along. We are sitting with about a dozen other RS-1 "grads" at a U-shaped arrangement of tables in a classroom.

Reverend Holton leads the group in singing and praying. He summarizes the Religious Studies-1 course. The way life is. He goes to the blackboard and draws a stick man with a huge bubble around his head. "We're surrounded by our illusions," he says. Using the chalk as a saber, Reverend Holton punctures the bubble with several quickly drawn thrusts. "Only God's grace can break through this prison of our illusions."

In that moment, I realize his picture, his words, the blackboard and white chalk, as well as the people sitting entranced in this Sunday School room are all illusions in my bubble head. Constructs of my own limited creation.

Reverend Holton looks at me. And, in his gaze, I know that he knows that I know the secret. There is no secret and that's a secret. The secret must remain secret. I must not tell. I'm in a trap. My turned-on heart is a cruel trick, a dirty joke played by God-the-Father who, like my "own" father, balances my life like a card table on his whiskered chin. Just for laughs. To follow Jesus, I must not tell the secret, and I must eternally say "Yes" to Father God.

Reverend Holton grins at me and shrugs as if he is sorry he has to be the one to point out the absurd and horrifying trap. Suddenly, his face sprouts hair. A monkey tail appears behind him and uncurls itself into a question mark. Startled, I look at Stan, sitting to my left. His face is flushed, eyes winced into slits. Saliva seeps from the side of his mouth. He, too, is being squeezed into agony by the secret snare.

Panicked, I look across the room. Everyone around the table begins to blur into a fiery red haze. Horns sprout through the foreheads of my church friends and fangs press creases into their lips.

I'm still dizzy with a buzzing terror when Reverend Holton gives the benediction and Stan drives us home. Quelling a rising panic, I do not speak. Neither does my husband.

In bed, I can't sleep. I hold my belly and try to comfort myself by rehearsing the lines I heard at the Ecumenical Institute.

X = All is accepted. All is forgiven. The past is approved. The future is open.

X = You are accepted, just as you are.

X = The Cross on Which Jesus Died for Me.

And XOXO = Kisses of love.

But a kiss on the cheek of a gangster signals an imminent mob killing.

Kiss of Death.

A Kiss on the lips of Snow White by the prince brings her back to life.

Kiss of Life.

I'm certain now I don't have the Snow-White-narrow path through the arrows of this life figured out after all, and I'm in this birth-death battle *all by myself.*

Maybe the secret of resurrected life is the prince's kiss of his loved one. Jesus-the-Prince-of-Heaven was kissed by Judas and then kissed alive by God-the-Father-King. But Judas' kiss, like a GodFather kiss on the cheek, seals one's violent death. Maybe the white/right answer to the white/rite of death and resurrection is that an enemy must kill me and then a lover must kiss me. Does anyone hate me enough to kill me? Does anyone love me enough to kiss my stiff corpse?

Maybe when I die, I won't go into the next life unless I'm kissed by someone who loves me. Yes. If I need to be kissed when I'm dead, I need my husband to kiss me. I don't want to wake him up now, but I can't quell the squeezing and gnawing.

I have to know. I lean over and whisper, "When I'm dead, will you kiss me?"

Stan is lying on his back, his face illuminated by the dim light of the street lamp out on South Alton Court. He doesn't move. He doesn't open his eyes.

"Will you kiss me when I'm dead?"

His eyelids squeeze tight and his mouth twists into a grimaced knot as if he is being stabbed. He doesn't answer.

I'm desperate.

I cry, "Will you *kiss* me when I'm dead?"

He shakes his head, slightly. Back and forth. Back and forth across his pillow. No. No. No.

Monday I drive Stan to his principal job at East High, and on my way to my secretary job at St. James, drop a book off at the library. A revolver on the cover of the murder mystery pulses and shines. Going north on Oneida Street, I play with the traffic lights, willing the red ones to turn green as I approach. They turn just for me. I know now that if I look anyone in the eye, they will die. I carefully avoid looking at people walking on the sidewalks. I do not want to kill anyone.

I park the car in the St. James parking lot. I try to create joy by dancing my way across the asphalt into the church, singing the refrain of the hymn *Lord of the Dance*.

I know I have lived through a born-again Merry Christmas. But now it is Lent. Good Friday is coming up.

Reverend Holton, sitting behind his desk, looks up at me two-stepping into the office. He says good morning to me, but, by now, gray shrouded figures have arrived and warned me not to speak, so I don't answer. I sit at the typewriter waiting for Reverend Holton to give me work. He walks toward me with some papers in his hand and asks me how I'm doing. I put my hand over my mouth and shake my head. He reaches over and slowly traces the mark of the X cross on my back.

Yes. The brand of my baptism. There is no escape. I am marked to die. Yes, follow Jesus. Jesus not only walked on a deep water abyss, he danced tipsy alleluia circles through the arrows slung by his Father God.

Jesus said, "Lose your life, you'll find it." Do this right, Nancy Lu. Lu's your life. Dance right this way. Follow Jesus. *All* the way to the cross.

I am at home now. Standing in the bedroom. I'm no longer alone. Ephemeral specters are aiding me. "Follow Jesus. Jesus died. You MUST die. Jesus was killed. You must be killed. Don't tell anyone. It's a secret. Death is just a big joke. Just play along with the trick. We will tell you what to do."

"Call Reverend Holton," they instruct. "We will tell you what to say."
"Hello."
Say, 'will you kill me?'
"Will you kill me?"
"No, Nancy, I won't kill you."
Hang up.

I'm lying on the Victorian bed. I've obeyed the voices. Maybe in this secret, *no* means *yes*. Maybe Reverend Holton has to say no, but he's on his way right now to kill me. But, I don't want to die. I want to live. Maybe his no means no. I want to believe his no means no, but then I wouldn't die and I have to die. Who else could I ask to kill me?

You. You must do it yourself!
"I can't!"

Yes, you can. You promised. You promised to follow Jesus!

I am standing in the shower of the upstairs bathroom, with my back toward the nozzle and a book in my hands. I am trying to read *Journey to the East* and find the shimmering answer that I saw a few days ago in the words of Herman Hesse. I hold the paperback out away from the hot water hitting my back and neck. Washing warm over me. Soothing. I can't keep the book dry. I can't find the magic words in Hesse's paragraphs. Water mingles with my tears. I can't do anything *right*.

Now. Kill yourself! Now. Take aspirin!

I open the mirrored medicine cabinet. With dripping hands I am shaking one aspirin out of the bottle and hold it between my thumb and forefinger. I have bitten my thumbnail until it bled. Red.

Pour out more aspirin. Now!

"I can't."

Yes, you can.

"No. I can't take aspirin."

Now I am holding a razor blade in my right hand. Not the thin replacement razor blade that pushes another one out of Stan's razor, but the large blade with the thick steel on one side. Gillette. With the oblong hole in the middle. The kind we use to cut the wallpaper.

I sit on the toilet seat, my wet legs sticking to the plastic lid. I curl the fingers of my left hand into a fist.

Now! Kill yourself NOW!

I lift the razor blade over my wrist.

"I can't. I can't." I grit my teeth. Squeeze my eyes shut. Tears slip under my eyelids and drip off my chin onto the floor.

Yes, you can ... You have to die to prove you love God.

I sob, ashamed of my cowardice. Yes I can. I think I can. I think I can. I hear my father's voice reading *The Little Engine That Could*. I think I can I think I can. I think I can make my fingers slice red life out onto the hexagonal black and white tiles of the bathroom floor. I lie down on the cold floor and curl my naked body around the base of the toilet. I hold the razor steady above my wrist.

"I can't."

Yes, you CAN!

"No, I CAN'T!"

You have no will power, Nancy Lu! No will power.

I have no will power.

Like my father said.

No will. Noel.

Noel. Merry Christmas. Jesus is the gift.

No-el.

No well.

N.O. well. N.ancy O.re is not well. I am dying.

I am lying dried off and dressed again on the Victorian bed. I will prove I love my father god and Father God. I will *will* myself to die. I close my eyes and push. Push and strain as hard as I can. I am trying to force myself head first down a long black velvet tunnel. I see with a pinprick of light at the end. I push and push. The circle of light grows bigger. Through a pulsing lens I see purple feathers, a plump pink knee of a baby, and legs of can-can girls, who are gyrating to deafening and dizzying calliope music. This must be the next life. I push harder and harder into the cacophony, trying to will myself to move from life to death and death to life. The spiraling merry-go-round makes me nauseated. I am assaulted by shrieking noise and light. I pull back into the tunnel.

I can't. I can't. I failed again. My father is right. I have no will power. No power.

I hear the back door slam. My children are home from school. I hear them in the kitchen, opening the cupboards and closing the refrigerator. I hear them clomp down the spiral stairway to the basement. They turn on the TV in the family room to watch cartoons. I remember I must fix supper.

I enter the kitchen. I walk toward the stove. I fold my body across and over the middle of the gas range. I squint trying to see the time on the clock in the middle of the control panel, but the numbers keep blurring and the hands jerk back and forth like spastic fingers.

Stephen, nine-years-old, is near the basement door. He looks scared.

"Are you going to die, Mom?"

You must not speak

Claws grip my belly and stab the reminder about remaining silent.

I don't look at my son. I lean up on my elbows, close my eyes, and nod my head up and down. Yes. The eternal Y.E.S. must crush the eternal N.O. The YES must destroy Nancy Ore. N.O. Nancy Ore.

Now I leave the children watching late afternoon cartoons and drive over the College Avenue bridge toward East High to pick up my husband. On Calumet Street, I successfully dodge light poles that are falling in front of me. When I see Stan come out of the school, I move to the passenger's seat. He says he needs to stop at the drive-through window at the bank on the way home. But I'm supposed to be dead. What if the bank teller sees me? What should I do? I put my head back on the seat and close my eyes, careful to stay very still.

Now I am crying and trying to throw myself over the upstairs railing onto the vestibule floor. Stan is grabbing my wrists and holding me back. My foot is twisted between the wooden spindles and my shoe comes off.

Now I am standing alone in the living room, between one of the love seats and the piano bench. I notice my breath and an accompanying chant.

One breath at a time.
One death at a time.
One breath at a time.
One death at a time.

I know I am dying. I know. One breath at a time I am dying. It will be soon. My death.

Now I am lying on the blue plush carpet between the love seats. Dee-O-Gee, our dog, runs past, jumps on the window seat and begins to bark. The sound ripples backward, each wave wakes a different dog I once knew.

Fussbutton, the chow that fastened his teeth into my five-year-old thigh.

Sally, my grandmother's farm dog that I loved.

Butch, the snarling dog that chased me down Blaine Street on my way to school and my boot fell off in a puddle in front of Schoenfeld's house and I just kept running and running and never told my father what had happened to my boot.

Now I see Stan lying on the floor on his back. His eyes are squeezed shut and a single tear escapes and runs down his cheek. I reach out for him, but am too far away to touch him.

Now Reverend Holton is sitting near my head. He says, "You are giving birth to your husband."

Is that what I'm doing? Giving birth. Okay. I am willing to die to give birth to my husband. My stomach begins to contract with spasms. Maybe I'm the Virgin Mary. Maybe I've already given birth to the next savior. Maybe it's Jerry. Jerry was born after Stan's vasectomy. Gerard Craig. Jerry Craig. J.C. initials.

"Nancy, the bottomless pit supports you."

I hear Reverend Holton's words from far away and discover that, indeed, I am floating. Floating free in a deep, dark, velvet bottomless pocket. Floating. Peacefully floating. And, then, suddenly, a crashing, blinding flash of lightning sizzles through every cell. I open my eyes and see Reverend Holton.

"Did you rape me?" I ask, still stunned by the explosion.

"No, Nancy," he says, softly, shaking his head. "I didn't rape you."

I am relieved. There isn't any spinning or shouting in my head. The lightning struck me, and I know my life is over. I did it. I am finally dead.

Now Dr. Stein is leaning over me. He takes my left arm and pretends to give me a shot that will kill me. I know he is in on the trick. I know I am already dead. Now I am being picked up and put on a stretcher. I know I am supposed to keep my eyes closed, but, on the way out of the house, I peek and see Dorothy, my neighbor friend.

Red lights flash circles behind my closed eyelids. I am riding. I am riding suspended through dark streets. Now I am riding in brightly lit corridors and hallways. Now I am being slid onto a stiff pallet. I keep my eyes closed, but I can hear people bustling around my body.

I know I have been successful in dying. I know I am okay now.

Chapter 3
Saved by a Name

*Take the name of Jesus with you,
child of sorrow and of woe;
it will joy and comfort give you;
take it then where'er you go.*

-Lydia Baxter, 1870

March 16, 1970
    ST. ELIZABETH HOSPITAL
    ADMISSION RECORD
    Patient: Ore, Mrs. Nancy L. (Bauer)
    Birth Date: 3/14/40
    Occupation: Part time secretary and housewife
    Responsible Party: Stanley H. Ore, Jr.
    Relationship: Husband
    Religion: Protestant
    Admission Time 7:45 p.m.
    Physician: Dr. D.B. Stein
    Consultant: Dr. T.R. Nagler
    Primary Diagnosis: Acute psychotic reaction, other

PROGRESS RECORD
    30-year-old housewife—6 year history depression relatively well controlled on Tofranil Tid. Psychotic depressive reaction in last 48 hours with overt suicidal gestures, garbled speech, memory regression

and marked feelings inferiority. Symptoms suggestive mania within last month after attending religious seminar. DBStein

DOCTOR'S ORDERS
General Diet
Restrain only if violent
Watch carefully—has exhibited suicidal intent

The shadowy specters that warned me two days ago not to talk didn't have to tell me to keep my eyes shut. Waxy lids on all the corpses I have ever seen don't even twitch. But when there is a sudden flurry of people, pushing and pulling at my feet and legs and someone slips off my loafer (the other one must still be caught in the banister) and someone else sits me up to reach the buttons on the back of my blouse (the white short-sleeved blouse with embossed designs on front) and someone else peels away my socks and red plaid pants, I break the rules and open my eyes.

I see three attendants bustling around a too brightly-lit room. All three are dressed in white. White pants. White shirt. White blouses. White skirts. Each woman is wearing a stiff white hat and a small white plastic nametag pinned over the pocket on the left side of her uniform top.

I strain to focus on a name: *Madsen*. I read in small, square, black print. I struggle to connect frayed wires in my head. Madsen.

I weave the letters into Madison, the domed building with a rotunda and four stiff concrete arms that reach out into the city like a cross. The depot where I am standing with Mrs. Johnson and three other eight-year-old girls who call ourselves the Giggle Club and save our weekly nickel dues for a year so we can go on this trip. And Elsie the wide-eyed Borden Cow that smiles on us from a billboard near the depot. We have toured the capitol, wandered through Vilas Park Zoo, and licked Babcock ice cream cones, the must of any trip to Madison. We are waiting for the train to take us home. Madison. Madsen.

And, Johanna. The other nurse's name. Johanna. Sounds like Joseph. Joseph and Mary. Joseph and Mary and Jesus. I string Johanna's name onto a necklace of names like beads on a rosary. Johanna-Joseph-Mary-Jesus. Johanna. A holy tether to Jesus.

The searing light in the room stings my eyes. Jesus-Mary-Joseph-Johanna. I cling to the sacred umbilical cord and float backward through amniotic waters. Backward.

Back into the Great Silence.

"Nancy. Wake up."

Another woman in white is standing over me. She is holding a white paper cup in her right hand.

"I have a pill for you to take."

Squinting against the overhead light, I lift my head and see a blood red capsule quivering at the bottom of the cup. I shake my head no.

"Your doctor ordered this," she says firmly, and pushes the cup closer to my chin.

I am afraid of her. I know the pill could be poison and her insistence that I swallow it could be another trick because Dr. Stein knows I am already dead. Dr. Stein and I go to the same church. Last month, he and I attended the same religious seminar at the Ecumenical Institute in Chicago. He and I heard the same shocking secret of life and secret of death.

There is no secret at all! Jesus' death and resurrection is a *story*.

Does Dr. Stein know I have to die like Jesus to be part of the story? When he and the men came with the stretcher to remove my body from the living room floor, Dr. Stein looked directly into my eyes, pulled my left arm straight at the elbow and pressed his index finger onto my wrist. I knew the lethal injection was part of the drama I fell into and needed to play out perfectly.

So why is this woman telling me my doctor ordered this pill? I thought I was already dead and waiting to be ushered into heaven. Who is this woman? Is she a part of the play? Is this a test? Didn't I follow instructions properly? If I take this pill, what will it do to me?

The woman in white is getting angry. I do not know what to do. If I swallow the pill, I could be failing a test and be banished to hell. If I refuse to take the pill, I could still be alive. Maybe I haven't sacrificed my life at all like Father God wants and I will still go to hell. How can I know what I am supposed to do now that I am dead?

I don't want to cry. I squeeze my eyes shut and break another rule. I speak.

"I will only take it if Dr. Stein gives it to me."

The woman shakes me awake. Dr. Stein is crouching at the side of my bed. He is holding the blood-red life-or-death capsule between his thumb and index finger. I sit up and look directly into his wide-open, gray-green eyes. He is staring straight at me. The raw white lights in the room form a halo around his head and highlight strands of his fine, gold hair. He doesn't speak. He holds his gaze steady with the pill pinched motionless, a few inches from my face. Not knowing if I am swallowing a bullet to my brain, I reach out and take a little red step into a born-again life.

March 16, 1970
NURSES' RECORD
7:45 PM Admitted per rescue squad stretcher to 518. Appears very sleepy but responds. Is not aware of being in hospital. Asks for husband. Dr. Stein with patient. Patient refused her medication unless Dr. Stein gave it to her. Aide with pt at present. R.Marx

Omit admission vital signs until pt is resting.

    Verbal Order: If won't take oral med give Nembutal gr ii IM
10:00 PM Sleeping soundly. Door locked. R.Marx

Tuesday, March 17, 1970
    NURSES' RECORD

12:00 AM Awake when checked. Crying a little for her husband. Cooperative. Given Tuinal. Patient took med well. "Be sure to tell Dr. Stein I took it," she said.

12:30 AM Patient weeping. Aide staying in room.

12:50 AM Patient asleep now—aide out of room. Door locked.

    I wake in complete darkness. Alone. I do not know where I am. I do not know where they have put me. A crypt? I know I am dead. Waiting. I must be in purgatory. A holding tank. Waiting. Waiting.

    But I do not know how long I have been waiting or what I am waiting for. Am I waiting for my husband? Stanley. Or Harry. Or Sonny. Or Stan. A man called by many names.

    Just before I died and was writhing between the love seats on the living room floor, I thought I was the Virgin Mary giving birth to my son, Jerry, but Reverend Holton said I was giving birth to my husband. Did I do the right things so Stan can join me?

    I am alone. I am lying on a slab in a cement vault. Waiting. Blankets of darkness roll over me in suffocating waves. Unanswered questions squeeze like a vise into my temples. I am lying here waiting. In complete darkness. Alone.

    Maybe they forgot me. Maybe I won't be able to go anywhere or talk with anyone for years and years and maybe the Catholics are right and a prescribed number of candles have to be lit and prayers said before I will be admitted into heaven.

    And, what if someone comes who doesn't know the secret way the

Jesus story is being played? What if they bring needles and knives and tubes and try to embalm me? What if the blood I need for the next life leaks out onto their stainless steel slab?

My legs shake. My stomach lurches with spasms. I can't breathe. I want to call my husband. But I don't want to do anything that will hurt him. If I ask for him, will the sound of my voice be a summons that will kill him? Is he ready to die, too? Maybe *he* is waiting, too. Maybe the rule is *I* have to call someone *I* love so they can die, too. Maybe I have to call my husband before he can die. But what if he doesn't want to die? Do I have to kill him? I don't want to kill him. I squeeze my eyes shut. Try to force the right answer. Tears slip down my cheeks and into my ears.

When I open my eyes again, I see a faint square of light coming through a small window a few steps away. I roll off the side of the hard pallet and hurry toward the dim glow. I bump my left arm against something cold and hard. A doorknob! I grab it with both hands and try to turn it. Locked! Trapped. In the dark. Locked in a cell between heaven and hell. Alone!

Then suffocating panic squeezes a name through the cracks in my memory. Jesus. The name, Jesus. Just the name, but a name that is one of the beads tied to the sacred necklace of names I saw when they took off my clothes. Jesus-Mary-Joseph-Johanna. *Johanna.* I remember her name! Only the name Johanna. As if her name all by itself, like Jesus, is some magic open-sesame word.

Then through a small window that is reinforced with wire woven into hexagonal designs like Grandma Field's chicken coop, I can see a dimly lit, empty hallway. I scream and rattle the doorknob and cry, "*Johanna. Johanna!*" until suddenly two wide-open eyes peek in at me through the threaded wire. Johanna. She stares at me for a second, then disappears.

Bright lights snap on.

"Stop crying, Nancy!" Johanna, my first midwife in this next life, has returned with someone else. I am not alone. Another woman wearing a white uniform steps in front of Johanna and asks sharply, "What do you *want*?"

"I want to call my husband," I whisper.

"You can't talk with him now," the woman is frowning.

I am scalded with shame. I am causing more trouble. I am not following the rules and have asked for a sinful thing. I begin to cry because I can't see my husband. And, because of my weakness and disobedient sinfulness my husband will die.

The angry woman in the uniform brings me another red pill. I swallow the capsule.

Obediently.

Tuesday, March 17, 1970

NURSES' RECORD

5:00 AM Patient slept very well until 5 am. Crying for husband again. Very noisy.

Aide with patient again. Calling for husband and asks when Dr. will come. Took oral med well.

5:30 AM Sleeping again. Aide out of room. Door locked.

I wake and cry out again. Lights go on again and I am told again that I cannot talk with my husband. I whimper. Why won't they let me talk with him? Has something terrible happened?

"He's a busy man," says the woman in white. I can tell she is still angry by her clipped words. "He has an important job. He needs his sleep. You don't want to bother him now."

Maybe the woman means that he is not ready to die. Maybe she is part of the charade, and she can't reveal the answer. I close my eyes. I remember the gray-shrouded figures who flitted through my consciousness for two days before I died. They warned me not to talk about the secret. I am being bad. I resolve again to keep quiet.

"Do you need to go to the toilet?"

I nod.

"Wait here. I need to get someone to help you."

I nod.

Two women, each taking one of my arms by the elbow, hoist me out of bed. I stumble into a large, green-tiled room with toilet, tub, and chrome bars.

"We need a urine specimen, Nancy," one of the women says. She hands me a clear, plastic container. The women lift the edges of a light, cotton gown I'm wearing so that I can urinate without getting my swaddling clothes wet.

Do your duty, Nancy Lu, Grandma Field said as I perched on the red-rimmed edge of the white enameled slop jar. Duty. As if peeing in the right spot as a three-year-old was a patriotic act.

I am trying hard to be good, but I am awake again. I am afraid and I cry and ask for my husband again. This time, another woman promises she will call him for me in the morning.

Tuesday, March 17, 1970

NURSES' RECORD

6:00 AM Urine specimen to lab. Sleeping again-aide out of room. Door locked again. G.Kuenzl, RN

When I open my eyes, daylight is creeping through the small window and brushes the face of a young dark-haired woman sitting in a chair at the foot of my bed. She is wearing a navy blue sweater. There is no nametag and no white hat. She is knitting something with fuzzy, yellow yarn that falls in soft folds over her torso. The woman's eyes meet mine.

"Good morning," she says. "My name is Julie. I'm one of the nurses here."

"You aren't wearing a white uniform."

"I know. Some of us wear street clothes now."

"Did someone call my husband?"

"I think so."

I am comforted by the information and then offer information of my own. "I have a daughter named Julie."

The woman smiles and asks, "Do you have other children?"

"Yes, I have three others."

"I'm expecting my first," she says and points to her belly with one of the knitting needles. "I'm making a baby blanket."

"Oh. I never learned to knit."

I wanted a knitting bag like my third grade classmate, Ellen. Her case, made from fake red alligator skin, was shaped like an oatmeal box, had a zipper that went all the way around the top, and when Ellen unzipped it and flipped open the top, the inside was shiny metal and her knitting needles made a hollow clink when she dropped them into the canister. I begged my father, but he scolded, "We can't afford it. You can't knit anyway, and I am paying one whole dollar every Tuesday for you to take piano lessons!"

"Do you live in Appleton?" the woman asked.

"Yes."

"Did you grow up here?"

I wonder why she is talking with me. Is she dead, too? Is everyone in this place already dead? She keeps knitting and asking questions. She seems friendly, and I am glad I am no longer alone in the dark.

Tuesday, March 17, 1970
NURSES' RECORD

10:00 AM Ate fairly good breakfast. Talked continuously about her father and mother always telling her what she couldn't do. States she can't say "no" to people—greatly resents people telling her what to do because she can't refuse. Quite weepy on awakening—insisted on husband being called. Dr. Stein visit. Husband visit. Patient fell asleep after husband visited. Rested and slept soundly. G.Johns, RN

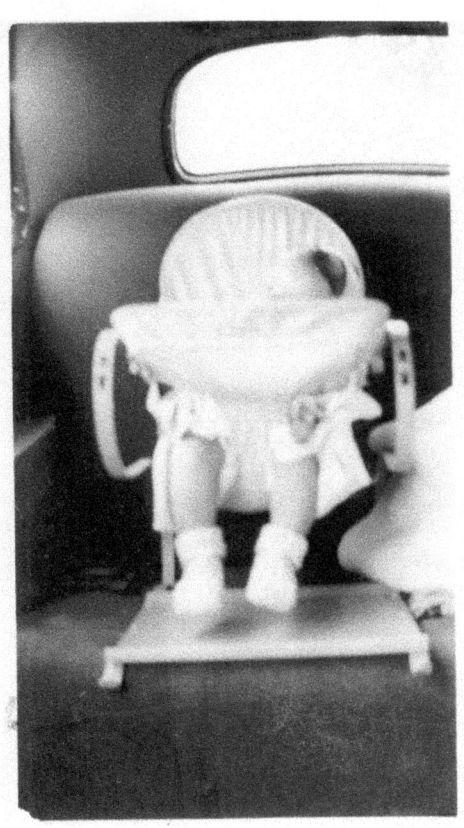

Chapter 4
Rock-a-Bye Baby

*There is nothing in this world so easy to silence
as the authentic voice of the child.*

-Alice Miller

1940
Diary of Russell Bauer

March 14: Thursday. Phoebe had her first pains this morning at 2:00. I was all for calling the Dr. but she held me off until 3:30. He got here about 4:00 and we left for Edgerton about 4:20. The baby daughter arrived sometime around 9:55.

March 15: … Phoebe says the baby has a temper and is hungry all the time. It weighed 7 lbs. 1 oz. when born.

March 24: Sunday. Well, I've got my family home but it has been a pretty hard afternoon. Margaret Olson is here and she sure knows what to do and how to do it. Hospital bill for the baby cost $55.25. I paid it by check.

March 29: Friday. The baby seems to have a crying spell again tonight and we aren't experienced enough to tell whether it is in pain, or just spoiled.

April 1: Monday. Some day when Nancy Lu is big enough I'm going to give her a spanking for the past 2 nights, and from all indications, tonight is going to be the same.

April 3: Wednesday. Our baby has us just a little bit worried. She cries altogether too much. We gave her an enema hoping it would help. But I don't think it did.

April 4: Thursday. Margaret took the baby down to the Dr. this morning and he advised a change of formula and another one Sunday if this didn't help. As a further resort he suggested going to Dr. Hartman in Janesville.

April 11: Thursday. We certainly haven't got a settled baby yet ... We gave her an enema tonight and sure cleaned her out. The fighting in Europe is getting furious. Hitler has occupied Denmark and is now in Norway.

April 13: Saturday. Nancy Lu is getting us down. She cries <u>all</u> of the time. I honestly don't see how she can stand it. I don't know how much longer Phoebe and I can stand it.

April 15: Monday. They took Nancy Lu to Hartman today and he pronounced her hungry. He increased the strength of her formula and after 2 feedings she is crying as hard as ever. I didn't expect anything else.

April 29: Monday. While Nancy was crying tonight I went over to Dr. Davis and he suggested peppermint in the water. We tried it but it didn't help any. It is now 9:15 and she has cried steady since soon after 7:00.

April 30: Tuesday. Last day of April. Nancy cried all month. Hitler took Norway and Denmark.

Tuesday March 17, 1970
   NURSES' RECORD
   7:00 PM Supper—ate well. Requesting to take bath; assisted. Large emesis in bathroom. M. George

She sits on a squat metal chair next to the tub I'm in, her hands resting on her lap. She is watching me carefully. Why can't I take a bath by myself? I am too embarrassed to wash between my legs, and I don't want her to see the tiny hairs around my nipples.

"Lots of women have those," Stan said on our wedding night.

"How do you know?" I asked and was not comforted by his answer. What if there was a child in the Philippines without a father? What if a Japanese woman showed up at our door wanting money?

I wonder if the nurses are afraid I'll try to drown myself. I wonder if they are afraid of me. Whether by my own gritty will or by a crash of lightning that sizzled through every muscle, bone and cell, I know I am beginning a new life. And, I know I am in Saint Elizabeth's Hospital. In a psychiatric unit. I know I am being watched by a nurse's aide. I pull my knees up under my chin to scrub between my toes and run the washrag down my legs.

Grandma Field's voice ripples across the bathwater.

"Look at your skinny legs," Grandma says, pointing at my scrawny legs dangling from her kitchen chair. "They look like dry cornstalks. You don't eat enough to keep a bird alive!"

Grandma hovers over me while she slaps a piece of white bread on a chipped porcelain plate, covers it with fresh, warm, milk from the barn and dusts it with scoops of sugar. The tiny soaked sponges of my favorite food drip off my fork, slip easily through my beak, and down my craw. She wipes my mouth with a sour dishrag.

Grandma eats enough for a whole flock of crows. In the morning, she straps in her ample torso with hooks and elastic and hurries to feed Grandpa eggs collected from the day before. She whaps the reins against the backs of the horses that are hooked to ropes, pulleys, and forks of hay. As the horses step forward, the hay swings up, up, and into the mow and Grandma and the horses stop to wait for the next load. In the afternoon, she shaves flakes off the pig skull for headcheese. On Saturdays, she plucks feathers from chickens and scoops out their innards. She smashes potatoes and adds the butter she has churned on the back stoop. She rolls out piecrusts from scratch and throws a few gooseberries in with the apples, for "just a little tart." At night she smells of stale sweat and rubber.

"I'm ready to get out," I tell the woman watching me bathe.

"Okay." She pulls a cord hanging on the wall near the toilet.

Another woman comes in to help me step out of the tub, dry off, and dress in a clean hospital gown. The women are guiding me back to my room, when my gullet convulses and erupts, splashing a pale soup across the green tile floor. Still holding me by an arm, one of the aides grabs for a towel to wipe my mouth.

"You vomited *constantly!*" my mother said. "You didn't keep anything down. Dr. Davis called it projectile vomiting. You weighed less at six weeks than when you were born. We quit feeding you. We thought you were going to die!" Mother sighed and added, "And, you cried all the time. Grandpa Field wouldn't visit."

"I'm sorry!" I cry to the women and reach for the towel. "I'll help clean it up."

"No. No, it's okay. It's okay. We need to get you back to your room."

They each take one of my arms again and stepping carefully, lead me around the mess I've made. My steps are halting and deliberate. I think I am learning to walk all over again. We walk slowly down the hallway.

And now I am in another hallway. I am three years old and playing in an upstairs apartment on Catlin Street. Mr. and Mrs. Krohn, the owners, live below. We have just moved from Milton to Edgerton, and my father is a science teacher at the high school. I am on my knees pushing a squeaky little wooden train back and forth by the stairway. The downstairs door opens. Mrs. Krohn is standing at the bottom step.

She is in her gray, speckled dress. She is holding her hands against the sides of her head. She is crying. She hollers up at me. Mother, drying her hands on a towel, hurries out from the kitchen and takes my train away. She says I am giving Mrs. Krohn a headache. Now my mother is crying, too.

The two aides steer me back to my room and help me into bed. I wonder if a requirement in purgatory is to repeat and repent of all the times I have caused trouble.

I am sorry I have hurt Mrs. Krohn and my mother. I am sorry I have made such a mess for these two women on 5 South.

Wednesday, March 18, 1970
NURSES' RECORD
8:00 AM Patient in better spirits this a.m. Stayed in bed resting. Patient apparently has a good memory. Can remember things that happened during her hysterical episode. Dr. Stein in. Dr. Nagler visit. G. Johns, RN

3:00 PM Patient still very unsteady when up. Visited with husband. Found returning from bathroom—had taken bath by self; had been told to wait for assistance. Patient spent time writing. "I've always wanted to write a book."—3 pages written.
M. George, RN

The nurse is angry with me. I don't remember anyone telling me I can't take a bath alone. Even in this born-again life I can't seem to keep from breaking rules.

"May I have some paper and a pencil?" I ask when an aide comes into my room. A few minutes later she returns with three pieces of ragged-edged paper torn out of a spiral notebook. She hands me the paper, but furrows her eyebrows when I reach for the pencil.

"I promise I won't stab myself," I say, making a joke. She gives me the pencil, but doesn't give me a smile.

I am eager to begin. I sit on the edge of my bed and roll the hospital table toward me to use as a desk. I remember the funny little picture sketched on the blackboard by the teacher at the Ecumenical Institute. Jesus-the-Slain-Lamb falling into a chalk-drawn canyon and trotting up the other side to sit on a throne and save the world. Now that I have survived the journey to the other side, I have a responsibility to make a map for other pilgrims. I must tell the Jesus Story through *my* story.

Once upon a time there was a little girl named …

What name should I call myself? I know everything in the Jesus Story has to be disguised. Jesus didn't ever come right out and say, "The secret is there is no secret." Jesus told open-ended stories that challenged people to search for their own answers. He provided signs that pointed to The Way. He said that the kingdom of God is hidden, like Narnia, or Alice's Wonderland. My job is to point to the rabbit hole or the door in the back of the wardrobe for folks to fall in or walk through.

So what name shall I use? I don't like my name, Nancy Lu. Although when I was at the Ecumenical Institute, I learned my name meant "grace."

"Amazing grace, how sweet the sound that saved a wretch like me." I will call myself Grace.

… Gracie stood beneath the sign where Randall Street angles into Blair Street. When she looked across the street, she could see her house and her neighbor's houses. Townsend's to the north. Schindler's to the south …

I'll have to change their names. My mind wanders to Mr. Townsend, who was fat, bald, smoked cigars and drove a beer truck.

Get-get-Gettelman Beer. Drink Edelweiss. It tastes so nice.

And, his wife, Mrs. Townsend, who dropped her basket of flowers and ran to pull Fussbutton's teeth out of my left thigh. And, their cream-colored linoleum with the aptly named chow dog silhouetted in black. And, Fussbutton's demise in the road in front of their house on Blaine Street. No. Blair Street. And, I shouldn't use the real name Fussbutton, but what better name can I come up with? And, if I call Blaine Street Blair Street, then I can't write about the townspeople calling it Brain Street because so many teachers—like my father—lived on the street. And how will I get my father into this story? Like God the Father, I thought God was like *my* father—distant, punitive, demanding perfection.

My *father god* plays a major role in my story.

I am confused because I don't where I am going with these names and street signs. Writing this story is hard work.

Thursday, March 19, 1970

NURSES' RECORD

11:00 AM Seemed to sleep well. Dressed in street clothes. Up and about ad-lib in room, writing most of the morning. Appears in good spirits—converses with other aides and nurses who enter her room. B Hartzheim, LPN

"Dr. Nagler wants you to take this," the nurse says and hands me a booklet, as if she is dispensing pills. "Can you read the directions?" she asks without a smile.

I nod and notice I am being given a test.

"You fill in the answers with this pencil."

"I already have one."

"You need to use this one."

"Okay."

"Let someone at the nurse's station know when you are finished."

"Okay."

When the nurse walks out of Room 518, she leaves the door unlocked and open.

I have always done well on tests, but I have never taken a test like this one, and I am afraid Dr. Nagler will use this test to poke through my mind and pluck out answers in my brain that I don't even know are there. Terrible answers. Like maybe I'm dangerous. Or on the day I died, during one of those fits and starts of time, I lost my mind altogether and did something horrible. I haven't seen or heard from my children yet. What if I killed my children and no one is telling me? Tears start pushing into my eyelids. I can't stand the thought even. I could not go on living.

What if I am crazy and have to be locked up forever?

I pick up the number two pencil and begin to fill in little holes in my memory. I promise myself I will answer the test questions honestly and keep my vow until I come to the questions about hearing tunes in my head. Sometimes while I peel carrots or empty the dishwasher or iron Stan's dress shirts, a song drones around and around in my brain like a lazy carousel. Songs I sang at the Ecumenical Institute: *Free men live in responsibility.* Or the haunting folk song from the library book I played on the piano and sang over and over like a stuck record a few days before my thirtieth birthday: *The cuckoo is a pretty bird, she sings as she flies…*

Ani. A three-letter word for cuckoo in crossword puzzles.

Nuts. A four-letter word for Nancy.

That cuckoo flew the coop right along with me into this locked cage. I hesitate over the question about hearing tunes in my head. I decide hearing things that aren't there must indicate a terrible abnormality. I break my oath of honesty. I lie. *Only* on that one question, *but I lie.*

My eyes begin to burn, the print blurs, and when an aide enters the room to refill my water glass and interrupts my concentration, I realize I have a headache. When I finally finish, I stumble out to the nurses' station and hand the test to a sane woman with a stiff, white-winged hat perched on her head.

This is my first trip into the day room on my own. People are shuffling past the desk and bustling up and down the hallway. A low hum of fluorescent lights blends with the mumbling of a man standing against the far wall. A small group of people sits silently in front of a television set. A woman screams she can't take it anymore. A door slams. I know I am in the psych ward at St. Elizabeth's. The funny farm. The loony bin. I know I am crazy. Cuckoo. A cuckoo bird. Ani-Nanny-Nancy.

I stop at one of the round pillars holding up the day room ceiling, wrap my arms around its cool support and press my cheek against its pale green side. I hear footsteps behind me and turn to see Dr. Nagler walking down the hallway toward me. Tall, blond, and blue-eyed, he is tanned even at the end of a Wisconsin winter. As he passes behind me, he lifts his left hand and pats my right shoulder. Only a brief touch as he passes, but a golden touch.

Thursday, March 19, 1970
PROGRESS RECORD
Severe chronic depressive disorder with severe ob-comp personality problems. TRNagler

NURSES' RECORD
6:30 p.m. Visited by husband. To day room with him. Made telephone call. Quiet. Appears hard to express herself orally. Working on writing project. Is willing to move to double room. N. Madsen, LPN

I am lying on my bed that evening when Stan comes into my hospital room. He pushes an ad for women's slacks at me. "Pick two," he says and sits in a chair to my left.

I look at the women modeling bright summer slacks. At first they smile at me from shiny pages, but soon their frozen grins begin to melt and slide across the page. I get dizzy. I don't like the two-for-$11.95 pants, but I don't want to hurt my husband. I hold up the ad and point to a pair of bright blue pants that are printed with wide, white swirls, and another pair that looks like they were made from men's red bandana handkerchiefs. Stan nods, takes the ad, folds it and puts it in his pocket.

When I ask about the children, he suggests we walk out to the telephone in the day room. I am anxious to hear their voices. To know I didn't kill them.

Stan says his parents have come to care for the children. I am filled with shame because Stan, Sr. and Marian had to come rescue their Sonny from his crazy wife. My mother-in-law answers the phone.

"Hello?"

"Hi. It's Nancy."

"Yes?"

"Are any of the children there?"

"Joan is." Her words are snipped and thin.

"May I talk with her?"

"Just a minute. I'll see if she will come to the phone."

I untwist the phone cord while I wait and breathe again when I hear a "Hi, Mom." I talk briefly with Joan, who tells me Julie is at her friend's house. She hands the phone to Steve and then Jerry. I assure each one that I am okay, that I just needed "a little rest" and isn't it nice to have Grandma and Grandpa there to help?

Stan, who leans against the wall three feet away from me for the entire conversation, accompanies me back to my room.

I tell him I have started to write my life story, and I give him the three pages I have put in my nightstand drawer. Anxious to hear his approval, I watch him carefully while he settles on a chair against the wall to my left, reads, then leans over and places my story at the foot of my bed. All without comment.

A few minutes later, when he gets up to leave, he gestures at the pages I have written and says, "Your story?"

I nod and wait expectantly. He wrinkles his nose and says, "It is terrible."

He doesn't kiss me goodbye. And, I don't ask the nurses for any more paper.

Friday, March 20, 1970

NURSES' RECORD

8:00 a.m. Up and dressed early—in dayroom working on puzzle. Transferred to Room 502. Spending more time out of room. B Hartzheim, LPN

The jigsaw puzzle is a picture of brightly colored flowers in a vase. There are several straight pieces missing from the border. I can do a Guild 304 piece in 56 minutes if I'm not interrupted. But the day room repose is pierced by a young man walking back and forth, back and forth, hollering "Hey mah man! Mah man! Hey mah man!" His belt droops unbuckled, his wrinkled plaid shirt is half-tucked in, and his hair looks like Grandma Field's gooseberry bush.

Thin fingers of cigarette smoke crawl into my nose from two women puffing nearby. A man with food stains on his rumpled robe shuffles over to the table, looks at the puzzle, and then stabs me with a pinprick stare. Someone down the hall screams, "Go fuck yourself!"

I am still working on the puzzle in the day room when Reverend Holton steps out of the elevator. He is wearing his long black coat. He has taken his gloves off and holding his fur-lined hat with unblemished fingers.

"Hi Nancy," he says, walking over to the table where I am working on the flower vase puzzle. I am glad to see him and eager to talk about what happened to me on the living room floor just before the rescue squad arrived and deposited me in St. E's.

"I'm here to see your doctor," he explains.

"Oh."

"I have an appointment with Dr. Nagler now, but I will stop and see you afterward."

"Okay."

I am hesitant, but decide to ask anyway, "Will you tell me what you talk about with Dr. Nagler?"

"Yes, I will," he promises with a nod.

He doesn't keep his promise. I don't see Reverend Holton again until after my release from St. Elizabeth's.

And I quit working on the jigsaw puzzle.

Too many pieces are missing.

Chapter 5
Playing No-tes

The death of one god is the death of all.

-Wallace Stevens

Saturday, March 21, 1970
   NURSES' RECORD
   12:30 p.m. Patient out in dayroom all A.M. Socializing well

The telephone designated for patients' use rings while I am eating my lunch alone in the dayroom. Conversation skids abruptly into an expectant silence. A young girl in jeans and navy blue T-shirt jumps up and hurries over to the phone, which is sitting on a small table pushed against the wall.

"Is there a Nancy here?" she asks.

"Yes." I raise my hand.

"This is for you." She points the receiver in my direction. I slide my chair back away from the table, get up and walk to the phone. I have been here five days. This is the first time the phone has been for me.

"Hello?"

My father's voice slices into the late morning. "Nancy, your mother and I drove up this morning. We have time to come up to the hospital and see you."

Children should be seen and not heard. Seen and not heard...

No. No. No. I do not want to see my father and mother. No. Dr.

Nagler told me I don't have to see anyone that I don't want to see. I do not want to see my father.

I do not want hear him either.

"You'll thank me for this someday, Nancy Lu," my father hollers at me from the kitchen doorway at 707 Blaine Street. I'm sitting at the piano that pushes its upright spine tight against the north wall of the dining room.

My father is wiping the supper dishes. My job. Practicing the piano is my job, too, but tonight a deal has been struck. My father will wipe the dishes if I practice the piano. My mother is up to her elbows in Ivory Flakes, and my father is drying plates with brisk, circular swipes.

My parents are keeping their part of the bargain, but I am whining and twisting my eight year-old body in semi-circles on the piano stool. When my father steps into the doorway and decrees his idea of *someday* into my future, I know from the tone of his voice, I'm one degree of whine from getting hit. I quickly reach for *Technique is Fun*.

Weekdays, from September through May, my father wears a suit, white shirt and tie. He uses chalk, a microscope and sense of humor to interest Edgerton High School students in Newtonian physics. He measures with a slide rule.

Questions have answers. Right ones and wrong ones.

On Saturdays and summer weekdays, he wears bib overalls. He builds barns with Uncle Harold. He carries a hammer, pencil and nails in loops and pockets. He comes home smelling of sawdust and sweat. He measures with a wooden folding ruler, insuring straight edges and precise corners.

Questions are problems to be solved. Solutions always appear.

Every Sunday morning year 'round I ask my father, "Why do we have to go to church every Sunday?" He answers precisely and scientifically,

"Because I said so." Every day of every year, my father is the ruler and measures my behavior by commandments the color of the piano keys:
No drinking.
No smoking.
No swearing. (including the word "poop")
No card playing on Sunday.
No biting my fingernails.
No boisterous behavior, tears, anger or sass.
No play until everyone's work is done.

No questioning God the Father, and
NO "No's" to father god!
I try hard to play the "no" tes just right.

No. No. Dr. Nagler said I don't have to see anyone I don't want to see. I do not want to be seen *or* heard by my father. I grip the hospital's day room telephone, take a deep breath and say, "No."

I am shocked at my outburst. I can't remember ever saying no to my father. I remember pouting and whining. I remember complaining and crying until I was grabbed and slapped into shape, but I can't remember refusing his demands or ever saying the forbidden word. On the other end of the line, my father is silent for a moment, too. He clears his throat and quickly recovers.

"Nancy, you are doing entirely too much. Your mother and I came up to see if we could be of any help, and we found all sorts of unfinished work."

My father has metastasized prostate cancer and has driven 96 miles to clean up after his irresponsible daughter. My father must be talking on the phone in the kitchen, the almond-colored wall phone with a thirty-foot stretchy cord that allows me to do dishes, flip pancakes, or scrub cupboards while talking with my friend, Dorothy. If Father is standing by the oven, he can also see into the dining room and is disgusted with the clutter on the built-in buffet that runs fifteen feet along the wall under the windows. The buffet hides the radiators and is a convenient repository for library books, unread magazines, old mail, catalogs, announcements from Edison Elementary School, papers from my secretarial job at St. James, and the lumpy blue compote that holds a bouquet of plastic flowers.

Somewhere in the scattered debris of my old life, my father has learned that our house is the dessert stop on a Progressive Meal being planned by the Kum Dubble Klub at St. James. He mentions the upcoming party and then scolds, "You have too many irons in the fire, Nancy! You need to stop some of the things you are doing!"

"No," I say again and swallow. "That is what *you* think I need. What I need is to decide for *myself* what I need!"

I am surprised at the rush of words like weapons from some hidden arsenal. I am surprised at the flush of strength accompanying this strange victory. Embarrassed at my vehemence, I look around and am relieved no one seems to have heard my outburst. I am 30-years-and-one-week-old, and I have finally said no to my father.

I'm not being seen *and* I'm being heard. An entirely new me. ME M.E. M.y. E.go.

I'm rising up on ego's wings. Eagle egg. Ego egg. Nancy Ore has cracked through her shell. A new N.ancy O.re ... N.O. NO has been born!

I hang up the telephone feeling battle fatigue and decide what I *really* need right now is a nap.

Saturday, March 21, 1970
DOCTOR'S PROGRESS RECORD
Ecumenical Institute—several weeks ago. "heard the word—OK to be me—a work of art" " then got idea could do anything—then got back, felt like failure." Multiple phobias developed—likely acute psychotic episode. Dr. Nagler

Monday, March 23, 1970
DOCTOR'S PROGRESS RECORD
Fears Virgin Mary—upset husband's vasectomy—distrust and paranoid core still prominent—emotionally labile "playing like happy so can get out of here." TRNagler

November, 1962

Stan stands in the kitchen doorway to announce his decision. "I just saw Dr. Erickson. I'm going to have a vasectomy. He said I could have it done during Christmas vacation and I would be all healed up by the time school starts again."

I can't speak. I don't even know exactly what a vasectomy is.

"It doesn't affect sex," Stan explains after he describes the procedure. "I knew a lot of guys in the navy who had it done. They just didn't want any more kids."

I hug my arms around my belly, ashamed at crying when Dr. Erickson told me I was pregnant again. I am ashamed that I am not coping well with three toddlers, ashamed my weakness is causing my husband to sacrifice his manhood, and even more ashamed at a sweet, flush of relief at his decision.

"Four children are enough," he proclaims as if the discussion is closed.

"But, what if something happens?" I argue plaintively. "What if the children are all killed at a railroad crossing?" I see tiny lifeless arms and bloody legs sticking out from a wad of crumpled steel.

Stan doesn't answer and my words float around the room sifting silently back to me like dust. I can't imagine losing this baby I'm carrying. Two weeks ago, I was shocked when Dr. Erickson said my vomiting was caused by a three-month-old fetus. Now the child is already part of our family. What if something happens to this baby after Stan takes his holiday trip to the doctor's office?

The specter of being crippled for life by guilt grips its fingers into my belly.

My husband remains resolute about his decision and is irritated with me when I ask if I can talk with our pastor, Reverend Jensen.

"This has to be kept secret," my husband insists when he reluctantly gives me permission to make an appointment. "I don't want you to tell anyone else."

Late the next afternoon, I leave the children with their father, drive to the church, and knock at the door of the pastor's office. Reverend Jensen greets me, indicates a chair for me and returns to his place behind his desk.

Reverend Jensen is a short man with a pasty complexion and almost completely bald. He has a gap between his upper middle teeth and enunciates his words with sharp staccato punctuations. He peers at me over wire-rimmed glasses. "How can I help you?" he asks.

When I finally mumble that my husband is planning to have a vasectomy, Reverend Jensen places his elbows on the desk and presses his fingers together into a tent as if ready to offer prayer. I break an uncomfortable silence.

"I'm not sure…" My words trail off.

"Why not?"

"Well, what if something happens? Like, one of the children dies?"

"You can't replace a child!" Reverend Jensen pronounces, sitting up straight.

I nod in agreement with his logic and then whisper the question I am afraid to ask out loud. "But what if God wants me to have more children?"

Reverend Jensen throws the top half of his body across his desk and points an accusing finger at me. "God didn't make you pregnant!"

I start to cry. Isn't God involved in my pregnancy somehow?

Reverend Jensen seems certain that if God is involved, it is in a minor role. As I fumble for another Kleenex in my purse, Reverend Jensen names a couple in the congregation who made the decision for the surgery and says they are doing fine. I know who this couple is, and I know Stan said his vasectomy has to be kept secret. What if

Reverend Jensen tells other people about us? I wish I hadn't made this appointment.

Stan's sacrifice is scheduled for two days after Christmas. The surgery will be performed in the doctor's office after the last patient has been seen, the doors locked, and the sun completely set. We sign the papers required by the state and prepay the doctor bill in full. $75.00.

We have no savings. Stan gets a bank loan for the entire amount.

I cancel my Thursday piano students and stay home with the children while my husband keeps his clandestine rendezvous. I am feeding the children supper when he rushes in through the back door, pushes past me, and hurries upstairs to the bathroom. I find him lying on his back next to the claw foot bathtub. His pants are down around his knees, his shriveled penis quivering over an oozing red scrotum, and thin streams of tears slipping down his temples into his ears.

"What can I do?" I cry, and sink down on my knees next to him.

"Nothing," he says, angrily, his lips twisting in a grimace.

You've already done enough, another voice scolds.

I remember the Modess box of 48 in the hall closet and quickly get up to grab one, kneel on the cracked blue linoleum floor, tie together the tapered ends that are meant to be pinned to an elastic belt, and fashion a gauze sling for the wounded sac.

Then I leave him lying next to the tub and hurry back downstairs to children I can hear fussing in the kitchen.

"You sure haven't used those rags for anything else in the past five years," Stan says later, making a weak attempt at humor. He heals as expected and returns to his classroom at the beginning of the New Year.

In mid-February, we drive to Edgerton to celebrate my mother's 47th birthday. After cake and ice cream, Stan and I stuff the three children into their snowsuits, boots, hats, and mittens for the hour's drive back home. He takes the children and heads for the car, but Mother stops me at the back door.

"Stan's parents were here last night," she says, looking at my protruding belly. "Marian thinks you should go on the pill, but I told her I thought they were too dangerous. They say they cause blood clots. They say that's why Sandra Cunningham died." Mother leans in, lowers her voice, and says, "I told Marian I heard about a little operation a man can have."

A *little operation*? As if the procedure is no more difficult than cutting toenails?

I look at the down at the diaper bag I am holding, hoping my face doesn't reveal my guilty secret.

"They say it isn't permanent," Mother continues. "They say it can be reversed. But when I told Marian, she said, 'No one is going to touch my boy!'"

My mother's words taste sweeter than her birthday cake. I put this delicious information in an arsenal for use in some kind of growing war I'm having with my mother-in-law, who has tried to be in charge of my reproductive behavior since I married Stan.

"Too late, too late!" I'll scream at her someday. "Your baby boy has already been touched!"

Wednesday, March 25, 1970
NURSES RECORD
Up and showered. Spent most of morning in Rec room. Somewhat demanding and hostile. R. Tillitson
PROGRESS RECORD
May be out 7:00-10:00 pm with husband. TRN

Stan parks in the driveway and I follow him along the low brick wall in front of our house. This is my first visit home since being carried out on the stretcher. This time, instead of being carried, I walk in through the heavy wooden front door and into the vestibule.

My husband's parents are standing in the living room to my left. Marian, her hands clasped in front of her, looks at me with a blank stare. Stan, Sr., wearing his typical gray suit, white shirt and tie, is turned toward the east wall, his arms down at his sides. His head is bowed and eyes downcast, studying the plush blue-carpeted floor beneath his feet. He doesn't move.

I am whitewashed with shame. They have come 150 miles from their home to help their son keep his four children safe, clean, fed, and on time for school. I have not only abdicated my job as a housewife and abandoned my husband and children, I have brought disgrace on my family.

Holding back tears, I walk slowly toward Stan, Sr. I reach out, encircle him with my arms, and lean my head into his chest. He doesn't move. He keeps his arms stiff at his sides. He doesn't touch me. He doesn't speak.

I quickly let go and move to one of the flowered loveseats in front of the fireplace. Nine days earlier, I had collapsed on the floor between these upholstered couches. This time, I sit down carefully. I lean into the padded upholstery. Stan sits motionless beside me and talks with his parents who have settled together on the loveseat across from us. No one is touching anyone else. I keep my hands folded in my lap so that my sleeves don't brush against my husband.

My children are not there. I am afraid to ask where they are. Someone must have decided that I'm not ready to see them. Or they aren't ready to see me.

The conversation is polite. Stilted. We do not talk about my hospitalization or when I will be coming home to stay.

At the front door, as I am leaving, Marian steps closer for a whispered scold. "Don't hug Stan's dad. He doesn't like it."

Thursday, March 26, 1970
DOCTOR'S ORDERS
Mood lighter on Dexamyl. Plan transfer to MAO Inhibitor TRN

"I'm starting you on Parnate," Dr. Nagler informs me in our twenty-minute session. "No cheese or Chianti," he warns, "or you could have a stroke."

I laugh and he looks up quickly from writing in my chart.

"I have never tasted alcohol," I explain. His eyebrows go up in surprise, and he turns to write again in my chart.

I no longer question all the pills I'm swallowing. I no longer am frightened of Dr. Nagler's nonchalance at playing Russian Roulette with the loaded gun he prescribes for my brain. I have been in St. Elizabeth's psych unit for ten days. I want to go home. I want to do whatever I have to do to be released. I will not eat cheese. I will not drink Chianti. I will neither complain, nor cry. I've been following rules since I was a little girl, and I'm good at it. I will swallow the rules along with the pills.

I just want to go home.

Thursday, March 26, 1970
NURSES' RECORD
7:30. To day room—conversing freely with other patients about their problems. Frequently mentions her new med (Parnate) and states she feels she needs "a happy pill." States parents set "heavy limits when I was a child—no smoking, drinking, or sex. I obeyed and that's why I'm here now." J. Koepke, RN

Chapter 6
Father God Father

Not to call God "Father" is unbiblical.
To only call God "Father" is idolatry.

-Anonymous

Friday, March 27, 1970

DOCTOR'S ORDERS

Occasional paranoid, grandiose ideation—flighty and hypomanic. Up Parnate on 3/28 to 10 mg b.i.d. 8:00 + 2:00 TRNagler

"What is this Ecumenical Institute?" Dr. Nagler asks. He sinks into his cushioned tan leather chair-on-wheels and rests his left ankle on his right knee, providing a makeshift desk for his notepad.

I do not know how to tell him about my weekend conversion.

I could begin with the lecture on the grace of God the Son given by the short, stocky man who called himself a pedagogue. I could describe his coffee-colored crew-cut, horned-rimmed glasses, and his chuckle as he took the stub of chalk, went to the blackboard and scribbled a wavy line between opposing arrows that was supposed to represent the human trek through the "slings and arrows of life." I could include his story about the funny little metaphorical lamb he sketched, and how he threw the fuzzy sacrifice off the side of a cliff, trotted him across the deep chasm of this life over to the other side of the blackboard, and hoisted him up on top of a high throne.

But I get confused. How am I going to explain this to Dr. Nagler without going into all the details? Did the pedagogue draw his wavy line and lamb *after* the paper I read by Paul Tillich? When did the teacher tell us to number the paragraphs and number each sentence of paragraph 12? And, when did I read the words in sentence 24 that launched me into a trip that I'm still trying to make sense of?

You are accepted.

I could tell Dr. Nagler how I believed the Ground of Being—Tillich's term for God—*accepted* me. Even with all those flaming red sins, I was not damned to hell.

I could tell him about the soft warm light that flooded my body and bathed each cell into a strange calm. The Ground of Being *loves me*. Ground of Being. G.O.B. I had *never* heard that I, Nancy, was *loved*.

"You look all dreamy," Dr. Nagler says, breaking into my rapture. "What's happening with you?"

"GOB," I say, grinning at the acronym. Dr. Nagler's eyebrows furrow into a suspicious squint.

"G.O.B. The Ground of Being," I try to explain. "G-O-B, an acronym of Paul Tillich's term."

Dr. Nagler stares at me as if studying a bug under a magnifying glass.

"God," I say quickly, hoping that G-O-D is the magic code word that will prove I am in on the secret of life and Dr. Nagler will let me go home.

But he wrinkles up his nose and shakes his head in disapproval.

"No. I don't want you to talk about God."

1945

My daddy looks just like Jesus. When my daddy folds his hands and kneels by the side of my bed he looks like the picture that hangs on the wall over our telephone. Jesus, forever in agony, draped over the rock in the Garden of Gethsemane. Forever waiting to be kissed by Judas, hauled away by the Romans, and nailed to the cross. When Jesus' prayer was over, his daddy walked him out of the garden and into death.

When I am done singing my bedtime prayer, my daddy pushes himself to his feet, walks out of the upstairs room and turns off the hall light, leaving me in total darkness.

I beg my daddy to leave the hall light on.

"Big girls aren't afraid of the dark," he says, ignoring my pleas.

I try hard to be a big girl. But I am afraid of the dark. And I am afraid of Japanese bombers. When I hear the whine of an engine, I hold my breath until I know the sound is only a pick-up truck, slowing down as it comes into the city limits.

I am afraid of thunderstorms. The sizzling flash of lightning and crack of thunder feel like the smack of my daddy's hand. I am afraid a bolt of lightning that splits the sky in half will split the earth, too, and the end of the world will come just like the story in *The Janesville Gazette* about the people in South Dakota waiting for Jesus on the roof of their house and not worrying about being hungry or cold.

And, I am afraid of Jesus' daddy.

Mrs. Greenwood, my first grade Sunday School teacher, says, "God is watching you all the time. He knows everything, everything you are doing, so you better behave." Having my complete attention, she adds, "God even knows what you are thinking."

At night, I lie on my bed in the dark, panicked by my thoughts. Right now. Right now, there is someone, somewhere, slipping into my head. Someone, somewhere, who knows just what I'm thinking right *now* as I'm thinking it. What if I think a bad thought? Will God get angry and make me die right now? And, if the darkness is safe like my daddy says, why do I have to ask Jesus to stay with me until the sun comes up?

Neither my daddy nor Jesus answers my prayers.

My father insists we all go to Sunday School and church every

Sunday. Though the Methodist Church is less than a mile from our house, we get into the '46 Chevy, and he drives my mother, little brother and me to the sturdy yellow brick building. Mother sits in the front passenger seat and my brother, Butch, and I on the stiff, prickly, upholstered seat in the back. We stop two blocks from home to pick up Auntie Lockwood, an old gray-haired lady that pats her sagging cheeks white with a layer of velvety powder.

"Auntie Lockwood never had any children of her own," my mother explains when I ask if she had kids that could give her a ride, "but she delivered hundreds of Edgerton babies."

Auntie Lockwood lumbers off her porch toward our car, pushes herself in with her cane, and lowers our car by several inches. Heaving with exertion, she spreads out her ample hips, and squashes Butch and me against each other into the other side of the car. Five minutes later, my brother and I scramble out the car door we've been jammed into and are in the church doors before Auntie Lockwood has her cane on the pavement.

Mrs. Newman, the Superintendent of the Sunday School, meets us in our classroom near the sanctuary, lines us up in our classroom for our opening song and plays the piano as we sing.

> Step. Step. Step. Step. We're going to our church.
> Step. Step. Step. Step. We're going to our church.
> We're going there to work and play.
> We're going there to sing and pray.
> Step. Step. Step. Step. We're going to our church.

Our small class listens to stories about Jesus and memorizes Bible verses. We build a Galilean village out of a salt mixture to learn how Jesus lived. The village has to dry for a week. At harvest time, we learn about a Jewish custom and make a Succoth booth from a cardboard refrigerator carton and hang gourds and ears of dried field corn over the entrance.

My mother helps Mrs. Newman. Mother's involvement in the planning gives her the opportunity to insert me into all the programming. Though my father insists that children should be seen and not heard, he suspends the rule for performances at church. I sing for Christmas pageants and baptisms. And I sing a duet with the other Nancy on Children's Day:

>Little feet be careful where you lead me to.
>Anything for Jesus I would gladly do.

The other Nancy is taller than I am and her mother gives my mother hand-me-down dresses that I can wear.

One Sunday morning, while Mrs. Newman is lining us up to sing the closing song for Sunday School, the other Nancy tries hard to move her careful little feet out of the classroom.

"I need to go to the bathroom," Nancy whispers to Mrs. Newman.

"Just wait until after our song," Mrs. Newman says and slides across the piano bench.

"But I don't feel good," the other Nancy complains, her dark curls quivering under a red felt beanie.

"Just wait!" Mrs. Newman insists. "It will just be a minute" And, Mrs. Newman begins to play.

>Our Sunday School is over and we are going home.
>Goodbye, Goodbye, be always kind and good.
>Goodbye, Good…

We never sing or wave the last goodbye. Nancy, *her* hand clasped over her mouth, tries in vain to stop the contents of her stomach from oozing through her nose, sliding off her fingers and plopping onto the grass green carpet like chunks of rotten cottage cheese.

Mrs. Newman jumps up from the piano bench, sends Donnie Wentworth to the restroom for paper towels, and sends the rest of us out of the primary department. While I wait for church to begin, I can hear Nancy crying. And the dress Nancy is wearing that Sunday, a light blue one with bodice pleats that catch some of the sour curds of vomit, becomes mine a few months later.

Sunday worship begins fifteen minutes after Sunday School. My father insists we all stay for the hour-long service. I sit by myself in a padded pew right under the stained glass window of Jesus, whose unblinking eyes see every move I make. My father directs the church choir, and my mother sings in it. She leaves my little brother in the nursery and sits in the front row of the choir loft with the other altos, so she can keep an eye on my behavior in case Jesus misses something.

During the interminably long service, I study Jesus' feet, which are at my eye level and perched effortlessly on a rainbow. His toes are outlined with a black inky swirl of glass. I count his toes. Four on each foot. I count again. Still only four toes and both malformed feet are standing on a rainbow. Not only can he walk on water with only four toes, but his careful little feet can balance on a rainbow.

"Jesus died for you," Reverend Anderson says during the sermon, speaking in a deep, lugubrious drawl. Reverend Anderson is taller and skinnier than my father. He towers over the pulpit and peers down at the congregation through round wire-framed glasses. The few strands of gray hair strung over his bald head almost meet the loose jowls that droop along his thin face. When he prays, he bows his head, stretches his arms out over the pulpit, and leaves his long, thin fingers dangling as if he is reaching for the people in the front pew rather than his Father God.

I sing the hymns and try to listen to Reverend Anderson, but one Sunday morning when I am bored and filling in all the o's in the bulletin with the dull pencil I took from the back of the pew, Reverend Anderson stands tall, waves his arms, flapping the sleeves of his black robe like a crow taking off, and proclaims, "Father God loves you." While his startling words are seeking a place to make a nest in my head, Reverend Anderson, smiles, looks directly at me and repeats his pronouncement.

I discount the novel proclamation. The only father I know is distant, punitive, and demanding. I am afraid of my father, and I'm afraid of Jesus' father, too.

Some Sundays, my father speaks at church about the evils of alcohol. A lifelong teetotaler, he carries temperance literature in his shirt pocket and is ready to cite dire statistics "whenever the occasion calls for it," as he says. He warns often about the depraved power of liquor. "Hundreds of brain cells die with just one drink!" he claims. He describes their futile gasps for oxygen before shriveling up and succumbing to death.

The only time I miss worship is the Sunday my careful little feet are hopping in the grass in front of the church during the fifteen minutes between Sunday School and worship, and I step my new white summer sandals in dog grunt. My mother lets me go home. I figure Jesus probably never squished dog grunt into his sandals. He probably never missed worship either.

Most Sunday afternoons we drive to Milton to visit Grandpa and Grandma Bauer. Sometimes we have dinner with cousins, aunts and uncles. One Sunday my father's relatives gather for a picnic on the lawn of the Rock County Insane Asylum. My Uncle Archie, the superintendent, and Aunt Myrtie, the matron, live in the big building closest to the circle driveway. I like my Uncle Archie, who smokes fat cigars, and I like my Aunt Myrtie, whose chin is lost in a goiter, but I'm afraid of the building at the edge of the lawn.

After ham sandwiches, potato salad, beans, red Jell-o with bananas, cookies, pies, and cakes of every kind, and talk slows to a sleepy drone, my father picks up my little brother and announces he is taking his kids into the tunnels, a system of dark, wet underground veins that connect the buildings of the County Farm.

I do not want to go. My father tells me the adventure will be good for me. I do not like what is good for me: cod liver oil, sleeping without the hall light on, and practicing the piano a half-hour every day. I'm afraid my father will take Butch and me into the building that holds its sides together with iron bars. The building that moans. The building that Alice lives in.

My mother says Aunt Myrtie invites Alice to our family gatherings because Alice doesn't have a family. Mother says Alice works for Aunt Myrtie, sweeping floors and folding laundry. Alice is not much taller than I am. She has dirty gray hair braided and wound around the top of her head into a bun. She wears a plaid housedress and black shoes with little holes poked into a design. She rolls her thick, brown, stockings down to her ankles and when she sits on the lawn chair her feet don't touch the ground.

Alice knits through after-dinner conversations, a ball of yarn twitching at her feet. She doesn't talk much and never makes sounds like the ones I've heard coming from the building she lives in. But she has a large purple mole on her lower lip that stretches like a leech when she grins and glistens when she caresses it with her tongue.

I do not trust my father, who insists I follow him and my brother through the damp tunnels with weeping walls. I stop walking when I see a dim light shining on steps leading up to a closed door. My father, still holding my brother, continues toward the door and then, suddenly, to my relief, turns around and leads us back toward my relatives, who are still dozing and digesting.

1947

Dream

I see the man at the end of the weeping, fiery red tunnel. He is coming for me. He is bald, thin, and a wide moustache covers his lips like Andy Gump in Grandma Bauer's Sunday newspaper comics. A blinding light shines on slippery tunnel walls. The man steps closer and closer. He is coming to get me.

The first time I scream, my daddy comes in and tells me the man isn't real. I beg him to leave the hall light on. But my daddy says no. He says I am a big girl, and big girls aren't afraid of the dark.

On the nights that Andy Gump stalks me, I open the thin white door by the side of my bed, crawl into the closet and hide on the floor under my shirts. I pretend the sleeves of my jacket are soft arms. Holding me in the velvet dark. Until I feel safe enough to crawl back into my bed.

Saturday, March 28, 1970

NURSES' RECORD

Up and about dressed. Appears friendly. Visits with other patients in dayroom. Out on pass for week-end.

Monday, March 31, 1970

NURSES RECORD

8:00 AM Returned from pass in seemingly depressed mood. Seemed to snap out of it when she started socializing. Dr. Nagler visit. G. Johns

Wednesday, April 1, 1970
NURSES' RECORD
Playing piano in music room. Home with husband for p.m. States she is reading "child rearing" books and trying to apply this to raising her children. A Geske, RN

They fight. They slap, hit, and kick over who gets the last cookie, gets to hold the dog, or gets to sit in the front seat. When Steve's view of Gilligan is blocked by Julie, he whacks her head against the built-in bench in the family room. When Jerry hollers, "Fart Face" at Joan, she chases him out the back door and slams him into the garbage cans.

Joan is ten years old, Stephen, nine. Julie, eight, and next month Jerry will be seven. My threats do not stop the ongoing battles, and I can't stand the sound of my own shrill screams. I am the mother. I am supposed to fix it, but I am caught in the middle, between children I love. I want to go home and be a good mother, but I do not know what to do. I take parenting books out of the Appleton Library.

"This child rearing book doesn't help," I tell Stan.

"Apply it to their backsides," he advises.

Chapter 7
Inside the Outsider

You can't see the picture if you are in the frame.
                                            -Walter Wink

Thursday, April 2, 1970

DOCTOR'S ORDERS

Discharge tomorrow AM. Discharge should be cleared with Dr. Stein. Plan follow up group therapy and individual—couple counseling sessions every 2-6 weeks. TRN

"You can go home tomorrow," Dr. Nagler says, smiling at me over the top of my chart.

"What did you find out from that test I took?" I ask. I don't want to go home if I'm not okay.

Dr. Nagler winces at my question and looks at the bound sheaf of papers propped up against his knee. I wait. He flips through my records and then, as if the information is of no consequence says, "It indicates you could become an alcoholic."

Doesn't he remember? I already told him I've never tasted the evil brew. I wait for Dr. Nagler to share more of my diagnosis. I want to know what's wrong with me so I can work to get better, but he looks at his watch.

I know my time is up.

Friday, April 3, 1970
NURSES' RECORD
Up and dressed. Husband here. Discharged. Left with husband. 4/3/70 9:30 AM.
Discharged with meds. R. Marx

DISCHARGE SUMMARY
This is a 30 year-old married mother of four who is admitted with acute psychotic episode following an intensive group experience. She improved rapidly with rapid clearing of her hallucinations and delusions and reverts back to her chronic depressive state. She was discharged on Parnate 10 mg. t.i.d., Meprobamate 200 mg. t.i.d. with meals, Sodium Amytal at h.s. and Stelazine 2 mg. t.i.d. with meals. Plans for follow-up psychotherapy visits. TRNagler

Stan picks me up at the hospital eighteen days after the rescue squad carried me in. I initiate the only conversation we have on the way home. "Are your parents still here?"
"No. They left early this morning."
Why didn't they stay to say goodbye to me? Were they afraid of me? Ashamed? Stan picks up my suitcase as I get out of the car. Uncomfortably aware I might be seen by neighbors, I quickly follow him past the low red brick wall in front of our solid stucco battleship of a home. I wince at the irony of the yellow Dead End warning sign at the edge of our property, continue my hurried pace past the trashcans propped against the spiked wooden fence, and through the back door into the kitchen. I am armed with a new determination to be a good wife and mother. My arsenal is stocked with a sackload of medication and an appointment with Dr. Nagler.

I put my purse and pills on the kitchen counter and walk into the dining room.

My children are lined up against the set of French doors that opens out onto the porch. They are staring at me. Stan sets my suitcase down at my feet and walks over to stand with the children.

The morning sun rushes in from the east like a wide ribbon and binds all five of my family together into a single bow. Without me. They continue to stand silently in front of the doors—one set of doors with windows that need to be cleaned.

While I was in St. Elizabeth's trying to glue broken shards of my brain back together, Stan's mother, Marian, has kept the household from shattering. There is no dust on the buffet. Our Kirby vacuum cleaner has left its tracks across the blue plush carpet. The giant spider web over the buffet that I was saving to show my friend, Dorothy, is gone.

Shortly before my marriage to her son, Stan's mother tried to train me in good housekeeping practices. "I wash my stainless steel Choreboy every two months and hang it on the clothesline," she said, then pointed to the floor under the dining room windows and added, "and every seven years I strip the varnish on the baseboards and refinish the woodwork."

I nod in disbelief. I'm 18 years-old and have never seen my mother clean a pan scrubber.

The lesson continued in Stan's bedroom. She showed me his Victorian bedroom set. "This will be yours, soon," she said, and waved her hand at the walnut bed and marble-topped commode and dresser.

"We bought this set at an auction when he was only six years old. Stan, Sr. had to cut several inches off the bottom so he could crawl into it."

The headboard of the bed, carved in intricate scallops, knobs, and curlicues, stretched seven feet toward the ceiling. It looked like the prow of a Viking ship sailing through the bedroom. A removable panel in the headboard allowed a landscape or portrait to be inserted. Years later, in the half-light of dawn, the grained slices of wood twisted into the horns and eyes of a leering demon.

"At least once a year," Marian said, "you'll have to clean the headboard of the bed and dresser with Q-tips and furniture polish."

"How?" I asked, sinking with Marian's ballast of household chores.

"Oh, I'll show you," she said and hurried to the hall closet. I watched her dip the cotton swab in Pledge and twist it into one of dozens of carved wooden dimples.

"You'll have to clean the marble, too," Marian added. "And, you can have those crystal lamps," she said, pointing to the two antique glass globes, each one dangling crystals and perched across from each other on walnut pedestals that framed the dresser's four-foot mirror.

"I got those lamps with the set. You can wash the lamps with hot sudsy water. You can wash the marble the same way, but if the marble gets stained, you'll have to look for some kind of an acid that will take the spot out. In all these years, though, the marble has never been stained."

Marian is as fastidious in her grooming as she is with her house. Her permed dark hair is tinged with gray and never out of place. If she uses any make-up, it is not noticeable and her fingernails are emery boarded smooth. She wears sensible dresses that are carefully pressed and belted at her waist and wears slacks only to garden or paint. The only visible flaws are white blotches on her arms that are caused by disappearing pigment. She dismisses the condition with a sniff. The same sniff of disapproval she gives when she sees Joan's hairstyle or hears me say the word "crap."

In my first minutes home from St. Elizabeth's my husband and children continue to stand motionless in front of the French doors. Doors with tiny windows. Like tiny windows throughout the whole house that Marian told me I would need to clean, using a razor blade to scrape out all the ancient built-up scabs of dirt in the four corners of each of those windows.

The set of French doors behind my motionless family has forty windows. That's 160 corners on the inside and 160 corners on the outside. 320 corners to be cleaned. Behind me, over the built-in buffet that hides the radiator, there are three sets of windows, with 60 small panes, each. 360 + 480 corners. There are over 800 corners to be scraped in just this one room.

There is another set of French doors to the porch in the living room and a set in the vestibule. There are four more sets of windows in the living room, added to three sets in the hallway, bathrooms, and four bedrooms.

Count the storm windows, and the total number of corners doubles. The math is dizzying. Factor in two batches of river flies that hatch each spring and drag their muddy feet across the glass, the spiders who spin tunnels between the windows and screens and lie in wait for river flies, the Foremost Condensery Factory down the hill to the south that belches a milky mist year round, and I haven't even considered the other household tasks: walls, floors, beams, toilets, laundry, mending, shopping and cooking.

"Cleanliness is next to Godliness," my mother-in-law's voice croons through my head. But which god wants the windows shaved and the oil changed in the headboard?

From their tableau in the dining room, my husband and children watch me warily. Stan puts his hand on Joan's shoulder. They are as frozen in place as the people printed in the blue toile paper on the walls. My children seem afraid of me now. Our letters, phone calls and visits did not begin to mend family fabric rent by my breakdown.

Later, Stan takes me to the basement to show me how to use the new automatic washing machine. While I was hospitalized he replaced the old Maytag wringer and tubs.

"We're walking on eggshells," he says.

We are … he says. *We are*. He and the children. Not me. I'm the problem. As I begin to try and wash the craziness out of my clothes and memories, I don't feel as if I belong anymore.

I try to forget my "little spell," as my mother calls my three-week hospitalization, and resume my roles as wife and mother. But I can't forget my three-day experience at the Ecumenical Institute, nor the shimmering, searing, and shattering light.

II
FROM PSYCH UNIT TO SCHOOL
1971-1976

CHAPTER 8
LOVES LOST

The greatest human problem is our deep sadness
And our greatest human need is to be consoled.

-Abbe Huvelin

January, 1971

For the first several minutes of my appointment with Dr. Nagler, I avoid the haunting issue. Then, ramping up courage I mumble, "My father is going to die soon."

Dr. Nagler does not respond, but I see his narrowed eyelids and know his silence means he is waiting for more information from me.

"The cancer has spread throughout his pelvis. He is in University Hospital in Madison now."

"Have you seen him recently?"

I nod. I keep Dr. Nagler informed about my father's physical condition, but I don't describe the scenes that stick needles into my consciousness.

I don't tell Dr. Nagler about our recent Christmas dinner—how my father in his pajamas and robe struggled from his bed and, with my mother's help, took his place at the head of the table. I don't tell him that when my father tried to say grace, he choked up, left the table, and limped back to the bedroom with only the help of his cane. I don't tell Dr. Nagler that all the rest of us sat like statues in our chairs. The turkey and dressing stuck like sawdust to the roof of my mouth.

I don't tell Dr. Nagler that students and teachers took out a full-page Christmas Card in the Edgerton Reporter. Dozens of personal signatures and greetings declared their love for my father. "We love you, Mr. Bauer." "You are my favorite teacher!" "Merry Christmas!" "Get Well, Mr. Bauer."

The names of the admirers, many of which I knew, were like a wake up command to me from insistent voices in my head.

"You must tell your father you love him before he dies."

"I can't."

"You must!"

"I can't!"

Dr. Nagler is silent, waiting.

I can't hold it in anymore and blurt out the strangling pain. "I think I'm supposed to tell him I love him before he dies," I say and begin to cry. "I can't tell him."

"Who told you that you have to do that?"

"Nobody, but I think that I have to." Since Christmas, the injunction that has troubled me has increased in its urgency.

I don't tell Dr. Nagler that I think I will go to hell if I don't reconcile with my father before he dies.

"You don't have to tell him you love him if you don't want to."

"I don't?" I am surprised at Dr. Nagler's response.

"No," he says, shaking his head back and forth. Relieved, I interpret his words as both prescription and permission. I wait out the next soul-sick weeks in silence.

March, 1971

Reverend Holton sits at our dining room table, his winter coat thrown over the back of another chair. He puts his briefcase on the table between us and asks, "How are you doing, Nancy?"

He is referring to my father's death a month earlier.

"I'm doing okay," I answer and try to ignore the buzzing in my head. I have not told anyone about my determined refusal to tell my father I loved him before he died. I have not told anyone about the visitation, or the funeral, or the burial.

I only cried once. The day after the funeral. Back home. For about two minutes. Stan held me. On the Viking Bed.

Reverend Holton waits for me to say more, but when my silence gets too loud, he opens his briefcase and pulls out a paper.

"I got this paper from the Ecumenical Institute," he says. "I think you might find it interesting."

As he pushes the paper across the table toward me, I'm flooded with memories of my week-end seminar and my hospitalization a month afterward. Afraid I might drown again if I slip into Ecumenical Institute material, I hesitate to look at the paper, but the title yanks me into deep waters: *Schizophrenia-The Inward Journey,* by Joseph Campbell. I've never heard of Joseph Campbell, but I've heard of schizophrenia.

Was my experience schizophrenia?

Reverend Holton's offer to pray, indicates his pastoral call is over. After a prayer that God will help me heal my grief, he stands up, reaches for his black wool clergy coat, and leaves. With the Campbell paper, still in my hands, I go to the dining room windows over the buffet and watch him get in his car and drive away.

Still at the windows, I prop my elbows on the buffet and begin to read the paper my pastor has given me. I am hooked by paragraph three:

... the imagery of schizophrenic fantasy perfectly matches that of the mythological hero journey ...

I move to the kitchen, sit at the counter and read through the entire paper.

... sense of splitting ... terrific drop-off and regression ... dangers to be met ... and, if one has the courage to press on, there will be experienced finally, in a terrible rapture, a culminating overwhelming crisis ...

I begin to cry. Someone else knows what I experienced. Someone actually knows. I am not alone. What happened to me is real!

... for instance, a person who in childhood had been deprived of essential love, brought up in a home of little or no care, but only authority, rigor, and commands ... will have been seeking in his backward voyage a reorientation and centering of his life in love ...

I finish reading the paper for the second time just as Stan comes through the back door.

"Read this!" I say, with excitement, waving the pages. "This is what happened to me! I've underlined important parts."

"Oh?" Stan says, and walks through the kitchen to the closet to hang up his coat. "What's the mail?" he asks. "Anything important?"

"No. A couple bills," I answer. "The mail is on the buffet." I follow my husband into the dining room and wait while he opens the MasterCard bill and bank statement. When he picks up the copy of Newsweek and walks toward the living room, I put the Campbell paper on the buffet and go back into the kitchen to prepare supper.

September, 1971

I'm sitting at my son's desk in his classroom at Edison Elementary School's Open House when Dr. Nagler's wife enter the room. She is willowy thin and wearing a cable knit sweater and rust-colored corduroy slacks. Her long brown hair falls in gentle curls onto her shoulders as she leans over, smiles and greets someone. I wish I were pretty and could look people in the eye like she does. She seems to float as she passes me and slips easily into an empty chair in the front of the room. I wonder if her husband talks about me.

Mrs. Nagler sits down a couple of rows away from me and near two women I don't know, one in a turquoise blouse with silver buttons that I like, the other in a plaid Pendleton jacket. They are laughing and chatting and as we wait for Jerry's teacher to greet us, I overhear part of their conversation.

"That's Stan Ore's wife over there."

"Where?"

"Two rows over from us … toward the windows. She's wearing that blue knit top and skirt. You've heard about her, haven't you?"

"Yes. Poor man … saddled with a crazy wife."

As soon as I hear them identify me, I look down at my hands resting in the folds of the homemade skirt I'm wearing. Their comments tear into the top-stitching of my carefully dressed ego, and I am reminded how my hospitalization has irredeemably hurt my family. I swallow my shame during the teacher's presentation and follow other parents to the next classroom.

When I get home, I tell the children how nice it was to see their schoolwork. All four are anxious to get to the television in the family room and don't respond.

The next morning, after the rest of my disgraced family leaves for school, I lean over the dark oak buffet that stretches beneath the fly specked dining room windows, look down Alton Street and remember the conversation between the two mothers *before* they expressed their sympathy.

"Did I tell you I am back in school?" The turquoise blouse woman asked her friend.

"No. What are you taking?"

"I'm going to update my teaching certificate and see if I can get a job. I decided I didn't want my tombstone to read 'She pushed dirt around for 80 years!'"

While looking down Alton Street through dingy windows, I realize I've been pushing dirt around this three-story, four bedroom, four bathroom, huge family room house every week for five years. And, these stupid windows? In addition to fly crap and spider webs, each tiny pane has wrinkles and bubbles that distort my view down the street.

Suddenly, I see clearly through the pain and my cracked character that I am ultimately alone. For the first time, I know I must make decisions about my future.

Alone.

Summer, 1975

"What are you interested in?" Mrs. McCory asks. I am sitting in her spacious office in the administrative wing of the Fox Valley Center - University of Wisconsin.

For two years, Harriet McCory, a thin, wiry, middle-aged woman who dresses in sensible shoes, has helped me navigate through the overwhelming hallways and two courses of a part-time return to college. Today, no longer sweaty and shaky when I get out of my car in the parking lot, I am ready to enter Fox Valley Center as a full time student.

"I like music," I tell her. "I've been looking at the catalog. What about Music Appreciation?"

"That's a good choice," Mrs. McCory says. "Ralph Schumacher is the professor. He teaches all the music courses. If you're interested you might want to consider one of these other offerings as well."

She points to several other courses in the music department, and I decide to include Music Theory and piano lessons in my 16-credit load.

On the first Monday of the fall term, I show up for my first piano lesson in over twenty years. Professor Schumacher greets me with a warm smile. He is a short, impeccably groomed man with a full head of salt and pepper hair and a neatly trimmed beard. His square face is deeply tanned. In addition to silver-rimmed glasses, he is wearing a charcoal suit with a pale green shirt. Green paisley swirls in his dark gray tie match the shirt perfectly.

He ushers me to the spinet at the front of the music room and I sit on the bench. He stands at my left.

"Have you ever had any piano lessons?" he asks after we exchange brief introductions.

"Yes," I answer. "A long time ago. I quit when I was in eighth grade."

I do not tell Professor Schumacher I took piano lessons for eight years, organ lessons for three, won state contests with the clarinet, and played snare drum for the high school marching band. I do not tell him I am currently the organist at St. James, and I do not tell him I can sight read most choral music and any hymn Reverend Holton picks out for worship.

Professor Schumacher places a Grade One piano book on the piano in front of me and stretches over my shoulder to open it. His hands are wide, with short thick fingers. He has a wedding ring on his left hand and a gold ring with a large green stone on his right.

"How about this?" he says. "Does this look like something you could play?"

I nod. I hear my father's voice from the grave. *Don't toot your own horn!* he commands in fortissimo. I am too frightened to tell this man how easy the music is.

"Okay. Why don't you practice these first four pieces for your next lesson?"

I agree and my first piano lesson in twenty years is over.

April 1951

"You're going to forget this piece!"

I'm memorizing Mendelssohn's "Spring Song" for my piano recital when the frightening words burst from a hidden room inside my head. "You're going to forget your piece," they whisper like the rippling rills of Mendelssohn's composition. They convince me. I am going to forget the piece.

Mrs. Newman, my piano teacher as well as the Sunday School Superintendent, reserves the sanctuary of the Edgerton Methodist Church for the recital. On the Sunday afternoon of the recital I am sitting in the choir loft waiting for my turn to play when the voices predicting disaster begin their crescendo in my head. As the person before me finishes, I open Scribner's Music Library, Book Number One, to page 178 and with trembling hands give it to the girl sitting next to me. "If I forget my piece," I whisper. "Will you hand me my music?" She nods.

I walk down two steps to the piano, slide onto the bench and begin to play. The first two or three staves of notes trill like warbling birds on an April day. Then from nowhere a stun gun shoots a spring shower silence and my fickle fingers won't move. Black and white and red all over with shame, I lean around the piano, ask for my music, finish the song, manage a bow and return to my place near the altar.

After the recital I get my three-inch sized plaster statue of Mendelssohn—a reward from Mrs. Newman for finishing a grade in my music. I meet my father at the back of the sanctuary. I am afraid to look at him. We ride home in silence, my music and reward on my lap. When I try to wash the dust off Mendelssohn's head, some of his hair rinses off in pieces small as grains of salt and swirls down the drain.

The next day, while I am doing the breakfast dishes, the fourth finger on my left hand suddenly goes numb. I jerk all ten fingers out of the soapsuds. The paralysis spreads quickly past my knuckle, jumps to the next finger, creeps up my arm. I touch my cheek and the skin I touch tingles to numbness. Nose. Forehead. Scalp. Everything I touch goes numb. A wave of white panic washes over me. I holler for my mother. She runs up the basement stairs, pulls me through the dining room into the living room, stretches me out on the antimacassared mohair couch, and leaves me alone. Stiff with terror.

When Mother finally comes back, she kneels at the head of the couch. She doesn't say anything. She just looks at me. I look straight up at the ceiling. After several minutes of silence, I can feel prickly couch cushions on the back of my legs, arms and scalp. My hands and fingers work again. Mother returns to the basement. I finish the dishes and go upstairs to my bedroom closet where I keep the 8-Ball I got for Christmas.

"Am I going crazy?" I silently ask the oracle. The answer floats up through a murky mist. "Without a doubt."

"Am I going to end up in an insane asylum?"

"It is a certainty."

Professor Schumacher is standing behind me as I play the first assigned piece at my second piano lesson in twenty years.

"Good," he says. "Go on to the next."

I play the next simple one-page piece.

"Good," he says again and then adds with some puzzlement, "Did you have to practice much?"

"Not really."

Professor Schumacher opens the book to the middle. "Can you play this?"

"I think so."

"Go ahead."

I play the piece without a missed note or beat. I put my hands in my lap and sit stone still, staring straight ahead at the music.

"Hmm."

The professor turns to the last piece in the book. I sight-read it flawlessly.

Before the end of my second piano lesson, I am the new accompanist of the school choir and the rehearsal pianist for a fall production of *A Funny Thing Happened on the Way to the Forum*. I also have the phone number of another piano teacher, a woman who teaches advanced piano students.

By the beginning of my second full year at the Center, I have a schoolgirl crush on Professor Schumacher. At first, I am attracted to his hands. During choir rehearsal, I watch the way his fingers curl around the baton, wave it like a magic wand and pull pure sounds right out of the air. From my spot at the piano, I see him turn the pages of the music, and his diamond ring cuts rainbows through the black and white semi-quavers.

He buys me coffee in the school cafeteria, and, unlike my husband, Professor Schumacher talks to me. As we sit across from each other at a small table in the lunchroom, he talks to me about a talented student who is composing serious music. He talks to me about accompanying *Mikado*, the school's Gilbert and Sullivan production for spring. He talks to me as he reaches inside his suit coat with his right hand for his cigarettes, and he keeps talking to me while he taps the pack against his other hand, pulls out a cigarette. He lights up, draws in, and talks to me about his marriage going up in smoke.

Fantasy as a nine year old child.

I am at the top of the wooden steps by Miss Gardiner's fourth grade schoolroom. It is late afternoon. All the children have gone home. I have stayed after school to help Miss Gardiner clap the erasers and clean the blackboards. Only Miss Gardiner and I are left in the building. She thanks me for helping and looks back down at the work on her desk. Now I am going down the stairs toward the large glass doors that lead outside. I trip and fall and break my leg. Miss Gardiner hears my cry, runs to my side and picks me up. I curl into her arms. She begins to carry me to the nurse's office. These few moments of cradling are the sweet climax of my script. Miss Gardiner lays me on the thin, stiff cot, hurries to the telephone to call an ambulance, and the fantasy is quickly over.

The cast of rescuers changes as I grow into a teen-ager. All the roles are filled by men who are kind to me—a teacher, pastor, doctor. The man playing the part of my comforter changes, but the plot and my dream to be gently held remain the same.

In my fantasy, I just want to be held.

Gently held. For a few minutes.

Just held.

Until Professor Schumacher.

Now when Professor Schumacher leans over me to tap out a rhythm during choir rehearsal, I am ashamed of the tingling at the back of my neck. When he brushes against me in the cafeteria line, I blush. And, at night, when my husband reaches for my breast, I see my professor's hand.

My childhood Jesus scolds from Matthew's Gospel as if he is speaking in red lettered quotes, "If your right eye causes you to sin, pluck it out. It is better to be maimed than to have your whole body go to the unquenchable fire."

I am blinded by sin, but I don't know which body part to excise. I know the little swollen button between my legs is offensive, but what about my hands or my brain that spits out these uncontrollable, imaginative fantasies? Increasingly distressed, I use my still attached index finger to dial my psychiatrist's office.

"I haven't seen you for awhile," Dr. Nagler says a few days later when I'm sitting across from him in his office.

I shake my head.

"What's happening?"

"I'm depressed."

"What is your depression about?"

"I don't know."

"Yes, you do." Dr. Nagler's words are tinged with frustration. He doesn't like 'I don't know' answers, but I do not *know* how to confess. I talk about playing the organ at church and the piano at the Wednesday worship service at Oakridge Gardens nursing home. I talk about school, my grades and my schedule as rehearsal pianist for the *Mikado*.

Dr. Nagler listens and nods. I run out of trivia and after a long silence he asks "Did you and your husband ever do any couple therapy?"

"No," I whisper, feeling like a naughty, disobedient child. Dr. Nagler had prescribed marital counseling when he released me from St. Elizabeth's five years earlier.

"How is it between you two?"

"It's all right."

"Just all right?"

I take a deep breath, look away, and answer, "Well, he wants sex more than I do."

"Oh?"

"I get tired early, and I just want to go to sleep."

"You don't have to make love if you don't want to," Dr. Nagler advises. "If you don't want to make love, just lie there very still. Don't move at all. He will quit."

Stunned with Dr. Nagler's strategy, I quickly discard it. I know from one April afternoon early in our marriage that my husband is too big to fight off. I picture Professor Schumacher. He is only a couple of inches taller than me. If we ever kissed, I wouldn't have to hurt my neck at all. Dr. Nagler is waiting for my response.

"I'm attracted to another man," I mumble.

"Someone at school?"

I nod.

"Have you told your husband?"

"No."

"Why not?"

"I'm afraid."

"What are you afraid of?"

"I don't know."

My shame is compounded. I'm full of lust. I'm too afraid to talk with my husband, and I can't answer Dr. Nagler properly.

I leave my psychiatrist's office with a new guilt, a new prescription for medication, and a new prescription for unwanted sex. I don't have a prescription on how to tell my husband that I am attracted to another man. But I know that if I am going to be a good wife, I must confess my sin to my husband.

A few days later, on my 36th birthday, I wake up in the early morning darkness with my husband's gift for me poking me in my right thigh. I remember Dr. Nagler's advice. I lie in the Victorian bed, stone still on my back.

Stan prods again. Reaches for my breast. Squeezes my nipple. I follow the doctor's orders.

"What's the matter with *you*?" my husband asks after a few more probes.

Squeezing my eyes shut, I confess in a whisper, "I want an affair."

Stan doesn't say a word. He rolls out of bed, gets dressed and walks out of our house into a three-week silence.

On opening night of the *Mikado*, while a few other students are folding chairs, picking up books, and grabbing their jackets, I am riffling through pages of the musical score, stalling until Professor Schumacher comes back from his room down the hall. Since January, I have followed cast, chorus, and my professor's hand into Titipu, a world of slanted eyes, brocade robes, and carefully enunciated patter. I am hoping my professor will invite me out for coffee and dessert somewhere.

One of the few people left in the building is a woman with her hands folded on her lap, waiting on a bench near the Fox Valley Center's north doors. She is the sweet, young, Vietnam War widow who is in one of my music classes. She has shoulder-length red hair, freckles, is pleasingly plump, as my father would say, and has large, sad eyes. I like her.

I run out of ways to procrastinate and step out into the hallway when I see the war widow smile shyly at someone to my left. I see Professor Schumacher walking toward her. She stands. They are the same height. He spreads his fingers like an oriental fan around her elbow and escorts her toward the exit.

I drive home and pour boiling water over my left wrist.

Chapter 9
Back-To-Ward

Within the body of every cynic beats the broken heart of a romantic.
-Scott Turow

Tuesday, April 6, 1976
4:00 p.m.

"Look straight ahead," Dr. Stein says and leans toward my face with his small black plastic probe. I hold my breath as the bullet of light shoots into my right pupil. I have wrapped myself in a stiff white paper gown for my annual physical. I don't blink as he moves over to take aim at my other eyeball. Dr. Stein steps away from the examining table, points to the gauze and adhesive tape wound around my wrist and asks, "What happened to your arm?"

"I burned it."

"How did that happen?"

I hesitate before answering.

"An accident in the kitchen."

"When?"

"A couple of days ago."

"Hmm. Let me see?"

I hadn't been thinking about my appointment with Dr. Stein when I poured boiling water over my arm. I had been thinking about the sweet release that would come after the searing punishment. As I tried to lift an edge of adhesive tape with bitten fingernails, I wondered how deeply Dr. Stein had seen into that tiny black tunnel in my eye.

He reaches for scissors, cuts away the bandage, and takes my left elbow in his hand. He gently rotates the sticky pink bed of weeping skin.

"This was an *accident?*"

I have never told anyone about the boiling water, the iron, the toolbox, the Maytag wringer, or the radiator next to my desk in Miss Jacobson's English class. Dr. Stein's eyes are a searing probe, and my eyes fill with tears. I shake my head and uncover the shameful secret I have kept since childhood.

September, 1947

During recess one Friday, while my second grade teacher, Miss Kruckenberg is crying in the cloakroom again, JoEllen Schroeder gives me an invitation to a party. I hurry home from school excited and eager to show my mother.

"Can I go to JoEllen's house after school next Tuesday?" I hand Mother the invitation.

"I don't know," my mother says studying the card. "I'll call JoEllen's mother and find out what kind of party this is."

I wait anxiously at my mother's side while she makes the phone call. When she hangs up, I ask, "Well, can I go? Can I?"

I can't believe my mother's refusal.

"Why not?" I whine.

"Mrs. Schroeder is starting a Brownie Troop. That's why you've been invited. She wants you to join the Brownies."

"Why *can't* I go? I *want* to join the Brownies." I crank up the volume on my complaining. "All my friends are going!"

"No, they are *not!*" my mother counters. "Only some of the second graders got invitations, and you can't go."

"Why not?" I start to cry.

"All of the little girls weren't invited, so you can't go!"

My mother's reason is in her "that's final" voice.

At supper, my mother shows the invitation to my father, and he strongly agrees with my mother's decision. They talk about the unchristian behavior of JoEllen and her mother.

At bedtime, Mother is in the living room ironing my father's dress shirts and listening to Fibber McGee and Molly. My little brother is upstairs in bed, and my father is at a church meeting. I am ready for bed and already in my pajamas, but before I head up the stairs, I ask my mother,

"Will you fix the hot water bottle for me?"

"No."

"Why not?"

"I'm busy. Your father's shirts would dry out."

"But I have a bad stomachache."

Mother ignores my argument and continues pushing the iron across steaming collars and cuffs.

"Please," I beg.

"No! I said, *no!*"

I start to cry. "Please…I…"

"Fix it *yourself!*" she screams.

Mother's command stuns me into silence. She has never allowed me to fix the hot water bottle by myself. I am still whimpering when I pass through the living room into the downstairs bathroom and lift the red rubber bag over the hook from its place on the closet wall.

And, I am still sniffling as I fill the aluminum teakettle at the kitchen sink. I turn on the left front burner of the electric range and watch the coils spiral a bright red under the kettle. When I see the cloud of steam spew from the spout in an angry cloud, I pick up the cauldron by its handle and pour boiling water down the front of my pajamas.

On purpose.

After I catch my breath, I pour the remaining water into the red rubber pouch, twist the black stopper a few turns into its mouth and push the slippery bag against my sticky wet flannel chest to burp out the extra air like I've seen my mother do. Then I tighten the top, hold the hard-to-get sweet comfort away from my stinging belly, creep through the dining room and tiptoe upstairs to bed.

The next morning, I lift my pajama top to look at the burn. The silver dollar-sized blister in the middle of my stomach is clover-shaped. I've branded myself with a Girl Scout emblem.

"This was an accident ..." Dr. Stein repeats as if trying to convince himself. I look at the shiny tile on his examining room floor as he finishes my exam.

"I am going to call Dr. Nagler now," he says, removing the stethoscope from his neck. "I'm going to ask him to see you as soon as you are dressed. He's in his office here in Doctor's Park. I'm going to ask him to work you in between patients. I want you to go over there right now."

My appointment with Dr. Nagler takes less than ten minutes.

"Dr. Stein thinks I should see you," he says, his eyebrows raised in a question.

I nod.

"He told me you've burned yourself. What's happening?"

"I'm depressed."

My psychiatrist looks at papers in a file on his desk, then spreads his fingers apart and puts his hands together with his index fingers pushing into his forehead. He stares at me past the fan of his hands.

"I think that you need to be hospitalized," he says.

Tears pool again at the lower rims of my eyes.

"When?"

"Now. Go home and get what you need for a few days. I'll call the hospital and let them know you are coming."

A half-hour later, when I come in the back door of 126 S. Alton Court, Stan is at the sink peeling carrots. He is doing my job. I should be fixing supper. I can hear the television in the basement and assume the children are in the family room, watching cartoons.

It is my job to feed my family. My job. Who told me that?

"Feed my sheep," Jesus said. "If you love me, feed my sheep."

My job. My job is to feed anyone who is hungry in the world. My job is to be a good housewife *She is always busy and looks after her family's needs ... Proverbs 31 ... her husband is well known, one of the leading citizens...* who keeps the toilets clean, the snot off her husband's white handkerchiefs and washes the hundreds of tiny, tiny panes of 72 year-old glass with ripples that distort the neighborhood on days when I quit cleaning and washing and changing beds and scrubbing long enough to look down Alton Street. Tiny, tiny pains, cutting me day after day after day.

When Stan turns from the sink and sees me coming through the back door, I tell him the only words I can find. "I have to go back to St. Elizabeth's." I don't tell him I am sorry I have failed again. I don't tell him I wonder if I will ever learn to be a good wife and mother.

"Always be part of the solution, Nancy Lu," my father said. *"Don't be part of the problem."*

Now Nancy Lu *is* the problem. Again. She must be shut away. Again. Until she can be happy while doing the housework, baking cookies, chauffeuring, and spreading her legs. Until she can be part of the solution of a dirty house, demanding children, and a distant husband. Until she can be grateful for all the things she has. Count her blessings. No longer complain and nag and bitch. No longer dump boiling water on her skin. She is sick. It is time for her to leave.

I walk through the pain and the kitchen and pack a suitcase for another try at growing up.

After supper Stan drives me to St. Elizabeth's. This time the children are old enough to stay home alone. This time there are no stretchers, sirens, or lights spitting bright red circles into a night sky. This time instead of lying unconscious on a rescue squad gurney, I am sitting upright in the passenger seat of our station wagon. This time instead of believing I am a success at being dead, I am convinced I am a failure at being alive.

I have been married to Stan almost 18 years. Stanley. Harrison. Sonny. Harry. I don't know who he is. His monogram S.H.S.H. Sh-Sh. 18 years of gaping silence, followed by this three-week punishment.

As Stan drives me toward my second confinement at St. Elizabeth's, I whimper, "I don't want anyone to know I'm in the hospital this time."

After a long pause, he spits an accusation back at me. "You can't keep a secret!"

Tears I have held back begin to spill over my eyelids. And he is wrong. I never told anyone about the afternoon Pete the parakeet escaped.

April, 1959

I am at the kitchen sink when Stan comes in from school. It is 3:00, and he has only a half hour to change into his work clothes, get in the car again and drive eighteen miles to his job in Edgerton. Stan and I have lived in this new 10' by 45' trailer since November. Our first baby is due in two months. I am nineteen years old, a novice wife.

I am at the light green enamel two-sided sink that is placed on a diagonal into the corner of the counter. I can't get as close to the edge of the counter as I want because my belly button is starting to push out, and, if I bump into the edge of the Formica and hit the inside of my protruding navel, the shock of the nerve endings takes my breath away.

Too sensitive. Like right after making love and Stan wants to touch me between my legs just one more time. Insists on touching me just one more time.

I have his lunch packed and ready at the edge of the counter. Two bologna sandwiches (white bread, lettuce, and I can't remember if it was mustard or Miracle Whip), an apple, some cookies.

Did I pack him something to drink, too? I can't see clearly this awful picture that keeps pushing pushing pushing like he did into my memory.

He wants me to go into the bedroom. I try to refuse, but he pulls me down the hallway and shoves me onto the bed. He grabs my wrists and squeezes them together with just one of his fists. With the other he unzips and rips and thrusts and stands up again and zips and stomps down the hall and grabs his lunch pail and slams the door, jarring the whole trailer.

I cry while I wash my legs and straighten up my clothes, but I can't seem to get myself together again.

Pete flies the coop later that afternoon.

I am properly dressed, wearing the nubby, striped, maroon maternity smock I made, when I take the blue and white feathered bird and his cage out onto the cement patio slab and begin scrubbing the cage with extra care. I go back into the trailer to that crooked sink to wash out and refill Pete's water dish, but when I return the parakeet's cage door is open and Pete is gone.

Mr. Watson, the man who owns the trailer court, greets me as he is walking past. I tell him the bird has flown away. He points behind him and says he saw the bird in the young maple tree in the back yard at his house. I pick up the empty cage and hurry up the hill, but there is no color in the midst of bare limbs.

I cry and cry that night because I keep seeing those sky-blue feathers stiff with cold or maybe strewn across our yard by the Watson's cat. Mr. Watson said to leave the cage outside with the door open and maybe Pete would find his way back home, but in another scene, I see Pete flying and free. I know he will never return.

Stan is mistaken. Though this secret often forces itself unwelcome into my memory, I have never told anyone.

Tuesday, April 6, 1976

7:30 p.m.

This time I walk into St. Elizabeth's carrying a suitcase I have packed myself. Stan accompanies me down the shiny tiled hallway toward the elevator: past a pink lady at her desk, past the bank of pay telephones, and past the five-foot white marble Jesus, who is blanching into his plaster niche, eyes rolled to the heavens in resigned disgust at my behavior. Jesus is still suffering and dying for my soul. A hard, black, shriveled bulb.

Stan pushes the elevator buttons. The psych unit has been moved to the southeast corner of the second floor. People at church call 2 South the "Funny Farm." They talk about the crazy people they know. They say they could never trust anyone who has been hospitalized in a psych ward. When the elevator stops and the sliding doors reveal the nurses' station, Stan holds the doors open.

"Call me when you get your act together," he hisses as the doors slide shut.

This time I sign my own admission form.

April 6, 1976

NURSES' RECORD

7:30 p.m. Received ambulatory to Room 201-1, accompanied by husband. Depressed appearing. Quiet—slow conversation. Oriented and admitted to unit. Has had suicidal ideation, which is more frequent lately. Giving herself messages but continues to feel guilty about feeling good. Settled for evening. S. Olson, RN

Wednesday, April 7, 1976
   DOCTOR'S ORDERS
   Parnate 10 mg TID 8-2-6
   Dalmane 30 mg H.S. with repeat of 15 mg
   Valium 5 mg every 4 hours. P. RN
   General diet with Parnate restrictions
   Routine lab

   PROGRESS RECORD
36 year-old mother of four admitted with depression. Previous psychotherapy 1965-68 Madison; Acute psychotic episode 1970. Therapy at St. E's with sporadic out-patient psychotherapy 1970-1971. Has rigid, perfectionistic, personality traits, relating to early perceived rejection in relationship with father. Recent intensification of guilt—psychotic and morbid in degree, relating to father—as well as heightening of approval-seeking behavior with compulsive pushing herself in over-adaptive manner. Has been on Parnate eight days. Suicidal push past two weeks, self-mutilatory scalding left wrist one week prior to admittance. On exam tearful, helpless, with morbid guilt themes predominant. Severe depressive reaction. TRNagler

   DOCTOR'S ORDERS
   Group therapy: Tuesday and Thursday
   Art Therapy with Mrs. McKenzie
   Occupational Therapy: consult with therapist
   Ask Jim Verick to see patient. TRN

SOCIAL SERVICES

At Dr. Nagler's request I will be working with patient on one-to-one basis. Met with her today. Patient depressed, displaying flat affect and expressing anger at having to talk with me. High degree of intellectualization apparent. Dealing with feelings of being on psych ward "people (my friends) disapprove." Discusses strivings and activities she is involved in to find self-fulfillment but describes feelings of emptiness.

Four children at home; husband successful executive. Marital relationship should be explored further. J. Verick

Dr. Nagler gives me permission to continue my activities at Fox Valley Center. He tells me to have someone at the nurse's station show tell me about day passes. A properly completed, signed and approved form each time I leave the hospital will allow me to attend classes, accompany the remaining rehearsals of the *Mikado*, and accompany vocal students once a week at Lawrence University.

I am surprised at the changes in the psych unit since 1970. In addition to moving three floors closer to the ground, there are more windows, the walls are brighter, and the day room is bigger. There is a social worker with chocolate-brown eyes and long lashes who smiles when we talk, and there is a piano pushed against the east wall near one of the two doors into the room. The upright is in tune, has an easy touch, and has no missing ivories. The piano's condition is important to me because my piano performance exam is in a few weeks.

I have finished practicing my three recital pieces for the exam, and I am playing the spiritual, "Nobody Knows the Trouble I've Seen," when a woman enters through the door nearest the piano. I stop playing as she approaches.

"Hi. Are you Nancy?"

I nod.

"I'm sorry to interrupt you, but I want to introduce myself. I'm Rusty. I'm an art therapist. I want to invite you to art therapy."

"What's that?"

"We use art supplies to help us talk about our feelings. We use things like crayons, markers, and pastels. Sometimes we use poetry or music."

"What are pastels?"

"They are like crayons. They come in different consistencies, but the ones I have are soft, like chalk."

"Oh."

I like Rusty, partly because she apologized when she interrupted me and partly because her eyes softened when she looked at me. She knew trouble, too. Rusty has a spattering of freckles on her cheeks and a few stray strawberry blond curls. She is wearing a pair of navy blue slacks, a knotted cord necklace with dozens of tiny gold medallions that rests on a navy blue turtleneck sweater.

She is just my height.

Rusty puts her hands in the deep pockets of a multi-colored striped vest and says, "We meet most Tuesday, Wednesday, and Thursday afternoons from 2:00-4:00. The Art Therapy Room is up on the fifth floor. I hope you'll decide to come tomorrow."

Thursday, April 8, 1976

NURSES' RECORD

8:30 am Continues weepy. Poor self-esteem. Feels a disgrace to her family by being here. T. Vandenberg, RN

Attracted by Rusty's personality as well as her invitation, I leave my crying bed, take the elevator to the fifth floor, and find the Art Therapy room. As I enter, I see four or five people already sitting on a carpeted floor under the windows, lounging against large, colorful, pillows that have been spread around the room. Healthy-looking philodendrons and spider plants, cradled in macramé hangers, spill over the sides of pots that are suspended from the ceiling. A blackboard covers most of the wall to my right. A large built-in cupboard in the corner is open and reveals several shelves filled with huge sheets of paper. A table near the door holds plastic buckets with markers, crayons, and colorful rectangular sticks that I assume must be pastels.

The small group sits quietly on the pillows. After two more people arrive, Rusty closes the door and welcomes us. We go around the circle telling our names and then Rusty puts paper, pencils and a bucket of pastels on the floor in front of us and invites us to draw our childhood home.

I reach for a brown pastel, but when the dusty color comes off on my fingers, I reach for a pencil. As I sketch 707 Blaine Street, I am careful to include the right number of windows and the front porch my father built with its decorative railing. I am trying to draw the curtains in the window of the front door that leads into the house, when the door opens and I step across the threshold into the dining room.

The small table holding the telephone is to my right, its spindly legs standing on the flowery linoleum. Our telephone number is 409-R. We share a party line with Olsons, Boerners, and Binghams. A picture of Jesus praying in the Garden of Gethsemane hangs on the wall just above the phone. Jesus' body is sprawled across a huge rock. He is sweating blood. He has promised to obey his father and his father wants him to die a gruesome death. Jesus is perfect. He is willing to die for his father if he has to. In the picture, however, Jesus is still begging his father to spare his life.

But Jesus' father has other plans for his son. Sacrificial plans.

Taking their cue from Jesus, my father and mother are experts at sacrifice. They offer their bodies several days a week for church work to direct the choir, count the offering money, preside at the Official Board, teach Sunday School, and bake for the Women's Society of Christian Service.

My mother and father also sacrifice me.

March, 1945

Mrs. Borgnis lives next door. She says if she is outside, I can come into her yard and she won't let Fussbutton bite me. I am riding the tricycle I got for my fifth birthday. When I pass Borgnis' hedge, I see Mrs. Borgnis in her flower garden. I get off my red trike and begin to walk down their gravel driveway. But Mrs. Borgnis doesn't see me, and I don't see Fussbutton until it is too late.

Diary of Russell Bauer

March 21, 1945 ... the important thing today is that Nancy was bit by Borgnis' d--n dog. We couldn't get a doctor, being Wednesday pm, but we finally contact Floyd Shearer and he told us to keep it soaked in boric.

I'm lying on our dining room floor and my pants are pulled off and the linoleum is cold on my butt and my daddy is on the phone. And, when Mrs. Borgnis comes over, my mother pulls down my pants again so Mrs. Borgnis can see my naked wound.

March 22, 1945 ... A.T. came out here to cauterize the wound, said it was nasty, cussed the dog, and wanted to see the bite two or three more times. Charged $3.00. Total $4.50.

My mommy takes my pants off again and puts me on the kitchen table and the doctor is stinging my leg with something hot that hurts and then winding crinkly paper all around my thigh and telling my daddy he needs to bring me into the office the next day and hollering that the dog should be shot.

My mother speaks up for the dog. She says, "Mr. and Mrs. Borgnis don't have any children. They just have Fussbutton."

April 14, 1945

...The scab from Nancy's dog bite came off in the bathtub tonight. There is still quite a scar there...Roosevelt's funeral today.

Rusty's voice breaks into the maw of my memories. She invites the small group to hold up the pictures we've drawn and talk about what we've experienced. I wait to hear everyone else's description. The troubles they have seen are so much worse than mine. I don't want to talk at all.

1976

Dream

I am walking across the railroad tracks south of Fulton Street toward the Edgerton swimming pond. My swimming suit is rolled up inside a towel from home. A huge black dog bounds out from behind a gray building on the other side of the tracks. I run back toward Wikum's Bakery, dropping my suit and towel. I wake up panicked as the dog catches me and bites me on my left arm.

Chapter 10
Descent With Demons

No noble and exalted life can exist without a knowledge of the devil and of the demons and without a perpetual conflict against them.
                                                            -Herman Hesse

Monday, April 12, 1976
ANCILLARY SERVICES PROGRESS NOTES
Social Services
Second session with patient. Presents herself as depressed; affect flat, monotone voice and positions herself in fetus posture. Much into herself; guilt, living/dying issues. Some discussion around marital relationship. Feelings of failure and no hope. Denies anger/resentment, but states "I don't care." Husband perceived as "strong" by patient and patient has difficulty communicating needs. I would like to meet with patient's husband and will present this to patient at appropriate time. J. Verick

April 13, 1976
Nightmare
I am standing next to a large white trunk that is secured with a black iron padlock. I see a scraggy paw with three claws poking through a hairline crack where the lid meets the lower part of the trunk. The sharp, crooked fingers slither toward the padlock, dripping red tears of blood. I wake up panicked.

Wednesday, April 14, 1976
PROGRESS RECORD
Flat. Depressed. Guilt-driven compulsive personality traits explored. Feels selfish and guilty when pleases herself. There is a "racket" quality to her depression, which she is aware of—"since father's death have found things to keep myself depressed." Feels "demons" locked in box in stomach. TRNagler

Thursday, April 15, 1976
NURSES' RECORD
9:00 am to Group Therapy.
10:20 in room-sobbing-very reluctant to talk. States she feels shame being here – emotional problems as a matter of immaturity. Takes care of self by crying. States she has been in and out of therapy with intellectual insight but not able to really pull things together. "There is a box locked in my stomach, a Pandora's box that I can't open." Seen by J. Verick. M. Scoville, RN

ANCILLARY SERVICES PROGRESS NOTES/SUMMARIES
SOCIAL SERVICES
Third session. Patient remains depressed, but affect not as flat. More tears today especially in discussing marital relationship and relationship with mother. Patient expressing concern about facing mother and relatives this weekend. I would like to meet with husband and patient agreeable to this, but became agitated about any conjoint work. J. Verick

Friday, April 16, 1976
PROGRESS RECORD
Fears of family encounters over week end and fears of husband discussed. Affect not as depressed today. May be out on pass Friday – Sunday PM. TRNagler

Saturday, April 17, 1976

Six of us, plus D-O-G, our schnauzer mix pet, pack into our three-seater Rambler station wagon and head 150 miles southwest to celebrate Easter with Stan's parents. Stan, Sr. changed jobs in 1964, and he and Marian have moved back to the unglaciated area of their birthplaces.

We stop in Edgerton long enough to say "Happy Easter" to my mother and give her a basket of fruit. An hour later, we pull into my in-laws' driveway. As usual, Marian greets us at the back door and ushers us into the kitchen of their raised ranch home. As usual, our arms are loaded with overnight bags and offerings of food and small gifts. As usual, Stan, Sr. is standing in the living room in front of a blank television screen. He says hello with his head down and arms crossed in front of him, so there is no danger of any physical contact.

Marian gives us instructions about sleeping arrangements and where to put our luggage.

"Joan, you and Julie will sleep in the room at the end of the hall. Steve and Jerry, in the bedroom with the green walls. 'Harry' (her preferred name for her son), you and Nancy go downstairs."

The children hurry down the hallway to deposit their things. Stan takes our suitcase to the lower level bedroom adjacent to a second kitchen that is completely equipped for additional use.

Marian immediately offers us cookies, homemade tea biscuits, cranberry juice, crackers and cheese. Several varieties of mixed nuts and candy are within easy reach on the coffee table, end tables, and on the top of the TV. As usual she is eager to share her recent projects with us: a crocheted tablecloth, a knitted afghan, a project for a church bazaar that uses yards and yards of stiff red net. And sometime during our overnight visit each of his parents will pull their son aside for a private chat.

Stan does not share these conversations with me.

This visit, I have my own secret. Tomorrow, Easter Sunday, April 18, 1976, marks the 18th year of my marriage to their son. I do not want his family to learn that my bed on our anniversary night will be 204-1 at St. Elizabeth's and not the conjoint, conjugal, con*trap*tion at 126 South Alton Court.

As usual, after a casserole supper, all eight of us pile into our station wagon to drive out to Governor Dodge Park. Since moving to Dodgeville in 1964, Stan and Marian like to check on the park's campsites, count the deer and comment on the progress of the park's expansion. As we drive into a newly developed area, Marian spots a doe a few yards from the road. "There's number seven," she says with excitement.

"No," I squeak from my squeezed in place between kids in the back seat. "That's number four. She loped over from the other road, so she could be counted again!"

No one laughs.

Before bedtime, Marian offers more snacks and takes me on a tour of her treasures. She lets me know one more time that her favorite antique has already been bequeathed to Mary, her only other daughter-in-law. She picks up the rose flowered porcelain heirloom about the size of an ostrich egg and shows me a tiny slip of paper nesting inside on the bottom of the bowl. My sister-in-law's name appears in Marian's handwriting. I force a weak smile and hope my pretended approval of Marian's choice masks my feeling. I am completely unlovable.

The next morning the children are up with the sun and looking for the Easter baskets their grandmother has hidden. They are soon blitzed on chocolate and jelly-beans, but join the adults at the small kitchen table for a light breakfast of homemade tea biscuits and sugared cereal.

Also up early, Marian has set the dining room table with her newest china. "This may be the last set of dishes I buy," she says, holding up one of the white plates. "I know I have too many sets"—she says she has 26—"but I can't resist." She runs her index finger on the gold rim around the plate before setting it down on the table.

At Marian's strong suggestion, we attend the sunrise service at the United Methodist Church. We sing the traditional hymns-*Christ the Lord is Risen Today* and *Low in the Grave He Lay*-and we're back at the house by 8:30, with plenty of time for Marian to commandeer dinner.

Tom, Mary and their two girls arrive around 11:00. Marian accepts help from her daughters-in-law, but she is not happy that I put her homemade watermelon pickles in the dish she planned for the corn relish, mixed the hamburger dills with the sweet gherkins, and forgot where she told me to put the three kinds of olives: black, green, and pimento.

"You can put the ice in the glasses," Marian says to me. "Just a minute. Let me get the tongs." I try to use the silver tongs to put the ice cubes in crystal goblets, but when the talon-shaped tines keep slipping off the ice, I just use my fingers, and, by the time Marian announces dinner is ready, I am holding back tears.

In addition to using her new best china and sterling silver, Marian has arranged candles and a nest of colorful eggs in the center of the table. At each place setting she has placed a small hand-knit chicken stretched over a pastel plastic egg. When I twist open my egg, mints and nuts spill out onto the linen tablecloth. I can't even open a stupid egg without making a mess. I push the peanuts and candy into a little pile near my plate.

With everyone seated, she orders Stan, Sr., at the head of the table, to say grace. The prayer always includes a puzzling reference to bluebirds that evokes laughter from the Ore clan. I bow my head along with everyone else and wait for the dreaded words that point to an inside joke.

"Come, Lord Jesus, be our guest," Stan, Sr. says in his long-suffering mumble, "and let this food to us be blest." As soon as he says amen, his younger son adds "and the bluebirds," and three others around the table laugh at the reference. I learned early in my marriage that my question about the bluebirds is answered only with secret smirks.

Marian scurries to stand between the kitchen and dining area at a counter laden with ham, turkey, potatoes, gravy, sweet potatoes, green beans, tossed salad, Jell-o salad, homemade saffron buns, potato rolls, and the assortment of relishes I have arranged. Badly.

While she passes food, my children, sitting with their two cousins at the small table in the kitchen, break into their annual hymn take-off, "Low in the grav-y lay, under the mashed potatoes."

The food, as usual, is delicious, and, when Marian sees our dinner plates are beginning to empty, she hops up and, as usual, starts passing the food again.

"Here, have some more ham," she says standing behind Stan.

"No," he says, "I've had enough."

"You can have just one more piece," she says and my husband dutifully takes another slice of ham and does his what-can-I-do shrug when his mother plops another spoonful of potatoes on his plate, too. Though I would enjoy a second helping, when Marian gets to my place and passes the platter of turkey in front of me, I refuse.

"Just a little bit more of this?" Marian asks.

"No," I say, shaking my head.

"Are you sure?" she presses.

"Everything tastes wonderful," I add, "but I have had enough." As Marian moves to her other son, I savor my success. A sweet, silent, victory.

After pies, ice-cream, cookies and more candy, someone remembers the anniversary and my four giggling children run around the dining room table singing another family tradition:

"Happy Anniversary. Happy Anniversary. Happy Anniversary. Haaappy Anniversareeee!"

Their brief burst of energy is the only acknowledgment of the day's significance. After dishes, more conversation and more insistence from Marian that we must be hungry, the six of us, plus D-O-G, pile back into our Rambler. Each child is given a goody bag for their long ride home. Jelly beans, chocolate eggs, cereal, raisins, cookies and gum will be spread throughout our three-seater wagon during the three-hour drive.

Back in Appleton, Stan stops briefly at our home to unload children and luggage, then drives me back to St. Elizabeth's and drops me off at the front door. As far as I know, my secret is safe. I have not had a howling Easter Egg Crack Up.

Monday, April 19, 1976
TEAM PROGRESS RECORD

Vented at length about panic she was feeling in regard to possible interview with husband. Relating this to feelings she had with father. Unable to clarify what she is wanting or needing. Describing husband as perfect and strong and discounting herself. Feeling suicidal. Stated she punished herself this evening because of the demon inside her. Scratched abdomen with fingernails. Observed many long red welts – some open areas on abdomen. Dr. Nagler notified of patient's behavior. L Koepke RN

Tuesday, April 20, 1976
TEAM PROGRESS RECORD

Self-mutilating behavior last pm. Upset with charting and staff awareness of this "have done this since I was a kid." Felt relief after self-mutilation and able to sleep. TRN

Friday, April 23, 1976
>TEAM PROGRESS RECORD
>SOCIAL SERVICES
>Appointment has been scheduled with patient's spouse for Monday 4-26-76 @ 10:00 a.m. Patient agreeable to this. James Verick

Monday, April 26, 1976
>SOCIAL SERVICES
>Conference with Mr. Ore today to discuss marital relationship. He does feel there has been long-term communication problems which he has attempted to resolve but without success and now describes his own position with spouse as being somewhat distant and relates to her in a guarded way. Not allowing himself to be absorbed into patient's depression as he once did. Patient's dependency needs in relationship also discussed. Sees wife as "perfectionist" being over demanding of self. Mr. O willing to become involved in conjoint therapy but expresses apprehension as to how to approach Nancy in these sessions. Mr. O aware of his own inhibitions in dealing with affective issues, but also concerned as to how Nancy handles more open and honest communication. James Verick

Stan stops at the hospital after supper. We walk down the hallway to the day room and find a place to sit.

"What did you and Jim talk about his morning?" I ask. I see the slight tightening twitch at the edge of his left eye, which means he is frightened.

"Oh. Nothing really."

He talks about what the children are doing in school and what's happening at Appleton East.

He tells me we are going to chaperone the German class for the annual exchange program to Bavaria in July.

What? What about me? How did that decision get made?

Wednesday, April 28, 1976
TEAM PROGRESS RECORD
Worked on dream and got into anger. Depression still manifest with much retroflexed anger. TRN

I have been on 2 South for over three weeks. I have cooperated with Dr. Nagler's orders: medications, therapies, and socializing on the unit. I have continued filling out day passes and leaving the hospital a few hours at a time to attend classes at the Fox Valley Center, to accompany a student at Lawrence University, and to practice for my piano recital on May 13.

I want to be completely released.

"Can I go home yet?" I ask again at the end of my 20 minutes with Dr. Nagler. He wrinkles his nose as if I have pig manure on my shoes. "It's not a good idea," he says, shaking his head while he writes in my chart.

The lights behind my eyes begin to flash, and the mantras start pricking into my pincushion brain.

"You will *never* get out of here!"
"You will *never* be well!"
"You will *always* be crazy!"
"You are a *terrible* wife and a *rotten* mother!"
"You are a *selfish* child. A *spoiled* brat."
"You are fatally *flawed*!"

TEAM PROGRESS RECORD
9:50 a.m. Ran into room, eyes red, appears weepy, and ran back out. Went into Dr. consultation room, crying and wailing loudly. Would not allow me to approach her or talk. RN notified. Linda Baylor, *SN-UWO*

The demons come after the student nurse puts me into a consultation room, turns out the light, shuts the door and leaves. The malevolent spirits come after I am worn raw from angry screaming, open my eyes and stare up into a blank universe. They squirm their way through the hairline crack of that locked nightmare-trunk and float in through the ceiling of the darkened room, like waves slipping onto the coastline of my consciousness.

TEAM PROGRESS RECORD
11:15 AM Talked with patient. Talked about demons in her body, on her father's gravestone, etc. Dr. Nagler consulted. Allow her to verbalize and cry to get it out. Crying lasted for over an hour. Now regaining control of self. In room. Quiet. Linda Baylor, SN-UWO

"What's wrong, Nancy?" Rusty asks. "Can you tell us what you are feeling?" I have been sitting in Art Therapy with others for almost an hour and have not said anything.

Rusty's words are soft, inviting, like Grandma Field's feather pillows. I take a deep breath and blurt out, "There was a box of demons in my stomach and they got out."

Everyone is quiet for a moment. Then Rusty breaks into the silence and my blanched panic at revealing my naked shame.

"Can you draw them?"

I like Rusty's suggestion.

While the rest of the group continues sharing, I walk away from the circle to a table with a pile of large white paper, pick up a ruler and a black marker, and quickly draw the sharp, straight lines of the demon that was the first to pop out of the consultation room ceiling.

I pick up another piece of paper and draw the second face, using the same marker. But a few minutes later, when I pick up a red pastel to draw the third demon, the red rubber demon, he begins to move. He shows up outside the dining room window of 707 Blaine, he crawls over the window sill, his clawed hands slither across the bottom of my drawing and stab their sharp nails into my belly.

I run.

I run to my room. I hide in the closet of Room 204-1

"Nancy, it's Rusty. Can you hear me? It's Rusty. I want to talk with you."

Rusty's voice throws a blanket of relief over me. Someone I trust has come looking in the mothering dark for me. I push the door open and see her standing in front of my hiding place. She is alone.

"Is it okay if I sit down with you?"

I nod and slide my body just far enough out of the closet so that I can lean against the door frame.

"What's happening?" Rusty asks. She sits down to my left and pulls her knees up into her chest.

"I'm scared."

"Of what?"

"What I was drawing." I bow my head in shame.

"The demons?"

I nod. "A red one."

"Can you talk with it?"

"NO!"

"Why not?

"I'm afraid of it."

"Why?"

I hesitate before answering. "It wants to kill me."

Rusty is quiet for a moment before breaking into my fear with a surprising idea. "It may have a gift for you."

I can't imagine the slippery red demon with bleeding claws giving me anything but death.

"You could ask it for the gift."

Before I can consider her suggestion, Rusty adds, "I'll stay right here with you. I won't let it hurt you."

But when I look up, I see that the evil menace has materialized right in my room! Next to my bed. Full-figured, standing about eight feet away. Slippery, fiery red, skin. Leering. The demon raises one glistening arm and takes a step toward me.

"It's coming closer!" I put my hands over my eyes.

"Tell it to stay there," Rusty says calmly.

"I can't. It's still coming!"

"Put out your hand to stop it."

I stick out one arm like a traffic cop and am amazed when the red rubber demon stops.

"Did it stop?"

I nod.

"Now, ask it what it wants."

"It wants to kill me. It is crawling outside along the big bay window of my house. It is coming into the dining room."

"Talk to the demon," Rusty says.

"I can't! It wants to kill me!"

"We know what the demon wants. Now tell it what *you* want."

"I want it to go away!"

"Tell the demon to go away. Tell it!"

"Go away," I am mumbling softly with my eyes closed and chin resting on my knees.

"Can you speak up ... so the demon can hear?"

"I want you to go away!" I say with more volume. Feeling stronger, I look up. The demon steps back and a ripple of sadness moves across his face.

"Before it goes away," Rusty adds, "ask it if it has a gift for you."

With no prompting, the demon stretches out his right arm and offers me a small box wrapped in white tissue paper and tied with a red ribbon. And, then he fades into the wall behind my bed.

"What is happening, Nancy?" Rusty says after a few moments of silence.

"He gave me a package, but I don't know what it is. It's still wrapped."

"Oh. Well, that's good. You'll have time to open it if you want to. Demons often protect hidden treasures. Maybe the demon has been guarding something important for you."

Rusty's words are both comforting and intriguing. She pats my arm with her hand and tells me she has to go. As she leaves she asks, "Instead of running away from the group when you're frightened, could you stay and talk about what you are experiencing?"

I nod.

TEAM PROGRESS RECORD

4:45 AT. Patient crying a lot—talking about her demons. R. McKenzie

11:00 PM Social Services. Patient wanting to talk about "demons." "I've opened Pandora's Box and can't close it." Patient describes herself as an "empty box" all torn and shredded inside. "Having nothing left to control the demons anymore." At this point observed signs of physical exhaustion with minimum mental energy level. Asked patient if she could give herself permission to praise herself for finally opening Pandora's Box and wanting to deal with the contents; also not to discount all the work she has done to reach this "starting point." Patient concurred and also realizing having no energy left to work further. T.A. Wezniack

Friday, April 30, 1976

TEAM PROGRESS RECORD

8 am—3 pm RN BP 100/64 P 88. General (Parnate) diet taken. States she is finally getting down to what has been bothering her. Happy she stayed—helpless feeling gone. L. Wescott RN

Rusty says I can keep drawing the demons, and she gives me paper and watercolors. I want to draw and paint them in the order they materialized: the fox, the goat, the red rubber demon, the wraith on my father's headstone, the four crows digging my mother's grave, the genie, the lion and the pink spongy creature that slithered out of the water.

I want to draw them, but, when I see them appear so close in front of me, I get frightened. Art Therapy won't meet until next Tuesday.

Dr. Nagler wrinkles his nose when I talk about the demons. He doesn't want to hear about them. He wants me to talk about my father.

Wednesday, May 5, 1976

"Tell me about your drawing," Dr. Nagler says.

"I'm painting the demons."

He is silent, waiting for me to say more.

"One really scares me."

He raises his eyebrows and shifts in his leather chair on wheels.

"I think it might be my father," I say. I know Dr. Nagler wants me to let go of my feelings about my father. I want to do the right things so that I can get out of the hospital, but he doesn't tell me what I need to do, and I don't know how to let go of feelings.

TEAM PROGRESS RECORD

Further work on owning her demonic side of herself—one particular "demon" to which she ascribes power and lets take over her when she is self-mutilatory—relates to father --refusal to let go of grieving—guilt, anger, confusion with him still. TRN

Dr. Nagler wants me to say "goodbye" to my father. He puts an empty chair in front of me.

"Picture your father sitting there," he says. "What do you want to say to him?"

I look at the chair and wonder where Dr. Nagler got it. The

elementary school has chairs in the library that look just like the chair my father is supposed to be sitting on—a gray metal frame with a wooden seat and two wooden boards in the back. I never saw my father sit on one of those kinds of chairs. I try to follow Dr. Nagler's directions.

"Goodbye," I say, looking at an empty chair. "Goodbye."

My father doesn't materialize.

"What else do you want to say?" Dr. Nagler prompts.

I shrug my shoulders and shake my head. "Nothing."

"Yes, you do," Dr. Nagler says. But I don't know what I want to say. I'm just learning from Rusty that it is okay to want something.

"Draw a picture of yourself and your family when you were a child," Rusty says and distributes paper to the small group sitting cross-legged on large pillows.

"You can use crayons or pencils or whatever you like. When you are finished we'll talk about your picture."

I reach into a plastic pail and select a pencil and several crayons. I draw myself first, right in the middle of the paper. I dress myself in the red dress with the little white sailor designs that I wore on my first day of kindergarten.

I draw my father to the right at the edge of the paper.

I am suddenly six years old, and my daddy is grinning into the camera.

"I want a kite like that," I say to my daddy, who shows me a snapshot of himself holding a kite he made. The kite towers over his head.

"No, you don't want a kite that big. I'll make you a pair of stilts, and, when you learn to walk on them, I'll make you a kite."

I see Margaret O'Brien at the Rialto Theater in Edgerton.

"I want to be a movie star when I grow up," I say to my mother.

"No. You can't be a movie star. Only little girls who mind their mothers get to be movie stars."

I see my friend's knitting bag.

"I want a red knitting bag like Ellen."

"No, you don't know how to knit."

"I want to go to Madison shopping like my friend Nancy."

"No, we have to spend our money in the town that pays your father's salary."

I used to know what I wanted. And what I didn't want.

I don't want my father to dip the tips of my fingers in rubbing alcohol to keep me from biting my nails. I don't want to play the piano for relatives. I don't want to ride to church in the back seat of our '46 Chev with smelly old Auntie Lockwood. I don't want to walk to school with Shirley Gretschmann, who is two years younger than me and slows me down with her built-up shoe and brace.

And, I *don't want* to kiss Peter Edmunds on May Basket Day.

On April 30, the day before the big day, Mother fills the dining room table with yarn, ribbon, paste, pastel shades of construction paper and those brass paper fasteners that look like tiny gold mushrooms. When she pokes them through two pieces of paper they spread out two stems and hold a May Basket handle tightly when it is hung over a doorknob.

Mother knows how to make three shapes of May Baskets: a plain rectangle, a rolled cone, and the much harder kind with four little pointed cups that look like part of an egg carton. She knows how to fill the baskets with popcorn and candy and she knows how to put the baskets in a cardboard box so that the popcorn and candy don't spill all over the dining room table.

Mother also knows the rules of the May Basket ritual. "You hang the basket on the doorknob and then you ring the doorbell and run.

Your friend has to run after you and try to catch you. If he does, he has to kiss you."

My mother instructs me that when I hear the doorbell, I have to run, catch, and kiss, too. I like the popcorn and candy part of the spring custom, but I don't like the running and kissing parts. I especially don't want to kiss Peter Edmunds. Peter is older than I am. Most of the time he has a runny nose and he doesn't use a handkerchief. He just wipes his nose on his sleeve or sticks out his tongue and licks the snot off his upper lip.

When I hear the doorbell and see Peter on the porch, my stomach feels like it does when my father forces me to eat at least one canned green bean. And, when Peter rings the bell, Mother is right there to make sure I follow the rules.

Peter leaps off the porch and begins running around the south side of our house toward Schindlers' back yard that leads to Peter's house through Mrs. Schindler's flower garden. I let Peter get a good head start. Maybe he will make it all the way home, and I won't have to fulfill the final act of the stupid ritual.

But when Peter reaches the corner of Schindler's back porch, he looks over his shoulder and sees that I am just stepping off my porch. Peter slows down. So I slow down, too. Peter goes even slower and so do I. The few yards between us become a few less. As the distance narrows, I drag my feet into a walk. So does Peter. The slow and slower motion May Day chase ends when Peter reaches the white wooden trellis that leads to Mrs. Schindler's flowers. He falls down. On purpose. I stand trapped under the arched white arbor. Not sure who is caught, I lean over and peck Peter's upturned cheek, avoiding his wet upper lip.

I don't know what I want anymore. I only know what I don't want. And, I don't want to kiss Peter Edmunds!

"Tell us about your picture, Nancy." Rusty says, interrupting my memory. I realize everyone else has finished describing their families.

I look at the picture lying on the floor in front of my feet and point.

"This is my father. He is dead now. My mother. My brother. My little sister. She wasn't born until I was almost sixteen."

"There is a lot of space between you and everyone else," one of the other people says.

I nod. "I wasn't close to my family. My mother and father forced me to do things I didn't want to do."

"What did you want to do?" Rusty asked.

"I wanted stuff like a kite and a knitting bag."

"Anything else?"

"I don't know."

"What do you want now?" Rusty asks.

"I don't know."

"It's okay to want something," Rusty says.

Dr. Nagler peers at me through narrowed eyes. I know he wants me to talk with my father. But all I can see in my uncooperative brain is a blank screen, as if someone turned off the movie projector and left me in the dark.

After supper when the lion demon leers from the paper, the rush of white heat washes over me again. I break my cup and use plastic shards to scratch welts across my belly. I know I am crazy, but, after I finish crying, I can comfort myself.

TEAM PROGRESS RECORD
SOCIAL SERVICES
Contacted by RN to see patient. Found patient lying under the bed in her room to "protect me from everyone" (meaning the world)

Eventually patient felt "safe enough to come out." Some preoccupation with unfinished business with father before his death. Also relates fantasy of someone to hold her since eight years of age. Still viewing herself through her father's eyes. T. A. Wezniack

Chapter 11
Re-released

You must have shadow and light source both
Listen, and lay your head under the tree of awe.

- Rumi

Monday, May 10, 1976

TEAM PROGRESS RECORD

7—3 Parnate (general) diet taken. Has sad and fatigued expression. Spent much of AM working on new dress. P. Harsch, RN

The large day room at St. Elizabeth's has a television set, a pool table and a sewing machine all arranged within a large L-shaped space at one end of the psych unit wing and several feet away from the tables and chairs for meals. I am sewing a yellow cotton dress with an ankle length skirt, puff sleeves, and a white lace bodice. I baste each piece carefully, matching notches and seams with long stitches. At home my Singer Touch-and-Sew in the basement family room is piled high with clothes that need mending.

The sewing machine in the day room does not have holes from my son's BB gun in its plastic face, nor an extended worktable like my Singer. This hospital machine is against a wall in a far corner, and no one bothers me as I use my fingers to fasten seams and gather puff sleeves into cuffs.

I plan to wear the dress for my piano recital at the semester's end. I have three days to finish my frock. I am worried I won't finish the fancy project in time.

Thursday, May 13, 1976

    TEAM PROGRESS RECORD

    3:00 AM At desk. Concerned about concert today—wants to sleep but wants to be alert. Valium 5 mg. Seemed asleep at 4:30 AM. Spent fairly comfortable night.

    L. Roderick, *RN*

My recital is at noon. I want to leave the hospital at 10:30. Pieces of toast I managed to swallow at breakfast are chasing themselves around and around in my scratched belly as if they are playing a Bach fugue. My new yellow dress covers the welts, physical evidence of my craziness.

I can't sit still. I wander out to the nurse's station. I decide to fill out my release form to kill some time. Except for Mrs. Johns, the nurses are busy sitting at the desk and writing in charts. Mrs. Johns is walking purposefully to and from shelves of books and carts of medications. I do not want to bother the nurses. I pick up a pencil and begin doodling on pamphlets that are spread out on the counter.

Suddenly, Mrs. Johns, holding someone's chart, turns and notices me. "What are you *doing*?" she scowls and quickly steps toward me. I drop the pencil and ask for a release form. Mrs. Johns reaches behind the counter, plops the paper in front of me, then turns and steps away to finish her work.

I pick up the pencil and begin to write my reason for requesting a temporary absence from the hospital:

… to entertain in a fantastic manner afficiandos (sp?) of the art (I run out of space on the form and continue writing in the margins as I have done numerous times when leaving the hospital for school or home or lunch with a friend) *of communication by the medium of piano— an interesting instrument not invented until the late 18th century, and*

not fully appreciated as a versatile instrument in its own right until the compositions of Fredric Chopin. (A Pollock, can you believe it?) However, I will entertain with Turina (a Spaniard) and Lizst—who though his name may suggest it, does not walk with one.

Signed: Jose Iturbi

When Mrs. Johns sees me still holding the release form, she rushes at me from behind the counter and grabs the paper. She glances quickly at my writing. She is not amused. With lips pressed together and eyes narrowed to slits, she glares.

"This is a legal paper!" she says angrily, her black hair and white nurse hat quivering.

"Well, then," I answer, "maybe I should see my lawyer before I sign it!"

"*I* will not sign this," she informs me. "If you want to leave, you will have to fill out another one. Properly!"

Mrs. Johns shoves a blank form in front of me and, with her own pencil, marks an X where I should sign my name. Chastened, I write my reason for wanting to leave:

Class at Fox Valley Center.

Nancy Ore

TEAM PROGRESS RECORD

7—3 RN Self-care—dressed. General diet. Did not go to group therapy. Said she was excused; standing at desk making weird pictures and notes on notices acting very strangely—asked for pass sheet, deliberately scribbled it with a lot of nonsense after being told it was a legal paper. Also said she should really see her lawyer before signing it. G. Johns, RN

The recital, my final exam for the semester, is held in a room just off the school's main hallway. About twenty people gather to hear one other student and me perform. I open with Kabalevsky's percussive

"Prelude" (Opus 38. No. 2). I move from the crashing chords to a Spanish dance by Turina. "Liebestraum" is my final piece. I play especially for the professor with whom I once-upon-a time fantasized an affair.

I see him sitting in the second row on the left. Earlier in the week, while I was practicing "Liebestraum" on the concert piano in the Center's all-purpose room, he approached me and told me the composition was one of his favorites. Liebestraum. Love's Dream.

My dreams of love are as ethereal as the feathery cadenzas under my fingers.

TEAM PROGRESS RECORD
3—11 PM In a lighter mood tonight. Anxious to do something fun. 4:30 left unit to go on pass for supper with friend. 7:30 returned to unit. In good spirits, had a good time. Read rest of evening. N. McHenry, RN

After supper with my friend, Alice, I decide to walk back to St. Elizabeth's. Cars rumbling over the Oneida Street bridge send tremors up my legs. I peek down at the Fox River, which is raging its way north to Green Bay. The river's roaring can't drown out my decision. I will not jump off this bridge.

Two days ago, when Dr. Nagler told me that suicide was bad for the children, I decided not to kill myself. I don't want to do *anything* that will harm my children. Anything more than I have already done.

My decision not to kill myself feels like a covenant. A commitment I made with some other part of me. But if I don't kill myself, then what? The answer bubbles up from the tumbling waters right there in the middle of the Oneida Street bridge. "You will decide to live. You will decide to *live!*"

Yes. I will not kill myself *and* Yes, I will decide to *live*. Two separate commitments. I walk faster to get back to St. Elizabeth's. I will work hard. I will work hard to be a good wife and mother.

Dr. Nagler thinks I need to do more work on my father. He thinks I should visit my father's grave. I will do what Dr. Nagler wants me to do so I can go home.

Friday, May 14, 1976

"What happened between you and Mrs. Johns yesterday?" Dr. Nagler asks me as I sit down for my twenty-minute consultation.

I am Eve, face flushed guilt red as the forbidden apple, and confronted by God.

I look down at God's carpet and confess, "I messed up the release form."

"She said you threatened to call a lawyer."

I nod.

"Do you think you owe her an apology?"

I nod. I am still a naughty girl.

TEAM PROGRESS RECORD

Some adolescent testing re rules, which is best ignored. Grief around father worked on further. Guilt re being in hospital, but able to agree to working further before discharge. TRNagler

7—3 am. General diet—self care dress—apologized for yesterday's behavior. States she had a rough night because of bad dreams—talked about her drawings stating that art therapist has helped her express feelings shown in the pictures. Seems more hyper today. Left on weekend pass with meds from pharmacy. G. Johns, RN

Sunday, May 16, 1976

Dream

I am walking in a rural area—along a road. In the distance I see lions. I am surprised. I feel very fortunate knowing it is a rare sight. I look closely. I see three males and one female. I realize they will pass rather close to a spot where I see Stan calling from a phone booth. I begin to be scared for my life. I think perhaps the lions will begin to chase me. I start running toward a farm house. I run fast. I look back several times expecting to see them starting after me. I think if I can just get a little close to the house I'll be safe. Now, I notice several big farm dogs. One—a German Shepherd—comes running out, snarling at me. I stop. I'm trying to get the dog to allow me to go to the house to safety. The dog is to my left now (the house and other dogs to my right) stops growling, but doesn't want to let me go to the house yet. The dog is spotted. Now, I get scared again by the fear of the lions, and decide I can't wait. My movement causes the dog to begin snarling. He runs around to my right. I put out my left hand to ward him off. He takes it in his teeth and moves it looking for a place to sink his teeth. I kick him in the face, but it isn't a very strong kick or well-placed kick. He grabs my left arm again. I kick him away again – not a good kick – but kick him off. Now, he is enraged! He bares his teeth and lunges for me. As he comes, I notice his front fangs. One is discolored and engorged with blood. He sinks his teeth into my left arm. I remember my "power" or centering or whatever, and I holler for him to STOP. The whole scene freezes as if I'm in a stop-film shot. I wake up.

Monday, May 17, 1976

TEAM PROGRESS RECORD

Indicated awareness of still withdrawing on week-ends—sounds very hurt that Stan doesn't react more … "don't want couple counseling while I'm the 'sicky.' Stan doesn't show any anger or resentment." L. Levittson, MD

Dr. Levittson is covering for Dr. Nagler. I like Dr. Levittson. He reminds me of Reverend Carr, the Methodist minister who dripped water on my three-month-old forehead and promised I would have eternal life if I believed in Jesus.

Like Reverend Carr, Dr. Levittson has a full head of hair that matches his silver-framed glasses. When he smiles at me, the floor lamp behind him throws a halo around his head. He looks directly at me and, unlike Dr. Nagler, calls my husband by name. He sits in a chair *next* to his desk, not *behind* it like he's afraid of me. I suppose the papers spread across his desktop are my records. He must have read how sick I was, and he probably read Dr. Nagler's suggestions on what parts of my brain he needs to poke in, but he doesn't write a word while I am with him. He just listens.

Wednesday, May 19, 1976
TEAM PROGRESS RECORD
Say goodbye to father. Fear of going to his grave—still fearful of "whole old family." L. Levittson, *MD*

Thursday, May 20, 1976
TEAM PROGRESS RECORD
11—7 AM Heard crying out at 1:45. Found upset and crying. States she had a nitemare.[sic] Out to dayroom with writer for coffee. Couldn't remember much about nitemare. Had something to do with father. Spoke of poor relationship with father especially before he died. Appears to have both guilt feelings and feelings of bitterness. Also spoke of someone whom she had much respect for remarking that she would never trust a mental or former mental patient. Not letting friends know she's here this time ... took repeat sleeper before going back to bed. T. VandenBerg, RN

I'm startled awake by a figure dressed like Robin Hood and rustling the covers at the side of my bed. A forest green felt cap, complete with a quivering pheasant feather, is perched on the top of the head. I recognize my father's face.

I scream and he vanishes. I don't know what to tell the nurse. I did not wake up from a bad dream. I certainly do not want to say I was scared by my dead father, that he had grown a goatee and his face was the color of split pea soup. I do not want my medication increased again.

TEAM PROGRESS RECORD
SOCIAL SERVICES
3:00 pm. Patient again expressing fears, frustrations, and confusion over unfinished business with father. Still plans to visit grave but "I'm scared." J. Verick

Friday, May 21, 1976
TEAM PROGRESS RECORD
7—3 BP 98/72 (L) P 92 General (on Parnate) taken well. Showered. Spent much of a.m. in room. Rather uncommunicative but is fairly pleasant. Left on pass unaccompanied to go to father's grave. Instructed to go to pharmacy to pick up meds. A little more pleasant. E.Henning/M. Scoville, RN

I wear the white gauze peasant blouse with the lace insert pulled tight across fresh belly scratches and the blue pants I made with tiny yellow flowers and spring green leaves. Checking out of St. Elizabeth's, I drive the two-tone green Ambassado (the "r" was missing when Stan bought the used car)—down Highway 26 south of Oshkosh all the way to Milton.

Today, my youngest son turns thirteen. How could I leave my child on his birthday? When did I turn into this terrible abandoning mother? When did I become this Amazon woman with a frenetic mission— determined to go to the grave of my father and kill him?

The cemetery is on the west side of the highway and two short blocks from the house in which Grandpa Field died. I drive a few yards into the cemetery and park the car in an area I remember from my father's burial five years earlier. The day is a bright blue-flowered moist spring heaven.

I walk past cracked and bleached tombstones, reading names and dates carved in calligraphy and script until I find my father's grave. *Russell Philip Bauer: June 14, 1913-February 23, 1971.* The wispy demon, who three weeks earlier perched on my father's headstone, covered the name with his slinky, black, cloak, and hissed a refusal to allow me near, is not here. Instead there is a welcome carpet of new grass—fresh and Easter basket green.

I sit down, close my eyes, and picture what is beneath me. Metal casket. Father's body. Gray. Pulpy flesh packed in purple satin bruises. I stretch out on my sore belly and cry. My dad—whose hands made a cloud in a bottle and balanced a card table on his chin. Whose hands built stilts and porch railings on which my feet could walk, a perfect balance. Whose hands never touched me except to hit. Whose mouth listed and preached evils, Cigarettes. Evil. Alcohol. Evil. Swearing. Evil. Lying. Lipstick. Anklets. Pinball machines. Carnivals. Circuses. Bareback Riders. Bare Backs. Boys.

Evil. Evil. Everything evil.

Oh, Dad. Six feet below me, your hands are folded across your smooth belly. Left over right. Right over wrong for eternity.

I'm sorry I never learned to balance on your carefully constructed rules.

I'm sorry I fell off my promise to go back into your yellow dying room. Sunlight brushing across your jaundiced skin and plastic urine pouch.

I'm sorry I rushed into the lobby, scooped up my babies, and hurried into the icy February.

I'm sorry I am so late to tell you I love you.

I cry softly to the grass and grave, turn onto my side, and open my eyes.

Amazing! I see pointed pine trees, arrows bordering the cemetery. Sparrows, darting and building nests in the boughs. Clouds pushing the day along toward late afternoon.

It is spring. It is warm. I am alive.

The only sound is the whine of a lawn mower in the distance. I turn back onto my stomach, my head a few inches from the granite marker, and begin to talk.

"I love you, Dad," I say. "I'm sorry you are dead. I'm sorry for all the pain you had. And, I'm angry. How could you have no regrets?

"Do you remember? I am standing with Stan and Mother, in the center of the living room, saying goodbye after a brief visit. The children, ages 11, 9, 8, and 7, are outside in the car, ready for the two-and-one-half hour ride back to Appleton. You are in the garage.

"Conversation stops when we hear the back door close and your footsteps treading across the kitchen linoleum. You enter the dining room. You are dressed in your carpenter clothes, blue, thin-striped farmer bib overalls with one loose buckle dangling. Flecks of sawdust dot your chambray shirt. Suddenly, you begin a fast, purposeful stride under the dining room archway, across the stiff green carpet, and past the lannon stone fireplace. You plant your feet in front of me and with your fists clenched at your side, look directly into my eyes and say, "I have NO regrets!"

You turn and stalk off into the downstairs bedroom without a further word.

"How could you have NO regrets?" I cry over his grave. "How could you die without telling me how sorry you were for things you did? How could you have *no* regrets? I have so many regrets as a mother and so many things I'm sorry for. Wasn't there *anything* you were sorry for?"

I listen, but all I hear is the lawn mower and low hum of cars going by on the highway. My father doesn't answer. He doesn't defend himself. He doesn't speak to me at all. I picture my words seeping into the ground. Slipping like worms through the seams of his casket. He is dead.

Dead.

I sit up aware of a shift inside me, like I have slid a book to a new place on a shelf and have lined its back up carefully with all the rest. I look south toward my grandparents' house. They are dead, too. Their graves must be nearby.

I stand up and begin to step over the bones of family stories. I find the graves of my German grandpa, John Philip, who kept one bottle of beer in the refrigerator, and my grandma, Margaret Inez, his wife, a member of the Women's Christian Temperance Union.

Further down the gravel path, I find the headstone of Florence Mabel, pregnant out of wedlock and, Arthur Marion, not the father of the child, but the man who married my great grandmother anyway.

"He made an honest woman out of her," my mother said when she finally told me one of the family secrets. Then, the grave of Bessie Azalia, the illegitimate baby, who grew up and repeated the scandalous family behavior.

I feel my grandma's spirit join me, and we walk along the rows of granite markers. She carries her list of suffering: a miscarriage, fire, drowned child, three dead husbands. We find other graves. I stop when I see Grandpa Field's name.

"He hit the cows with his three-legged stool," my mother said about her stepfather, "but he never hit me. And, he cheated at checkers," she added. I thank Grandpa Field for paying me one penny for each ten potato bugs I caught and for teaching me how to drive the Farmall tractor. I stop above Aunt Nell and Uncle Ed's resting place. I grin and thank Aunt Nell for her popcorn balls, her custard recipe, and for letting me play in her attic.

Having made room again for family stories other than mine, I get back in my car and drive past my dead ancestors' former homes. I am too ashamed to stop at my cousin's house. What reason would I give her for being in town?

Monday, May 24, 1976
TEAM PROGRESS RECORD
Visited father's grave over week-end pass with some lightening of depression ... marital conflict further discussed—gets upset with husband's ob-comp. TRNagler

Thursday, May 27, 1976
TEAM PROGRESS RECORD
7—3 RN Spent much of a.m. in room drawing "monsters." "If I didn't dream them, I wouldn't draw them." Snippy towards staff—apologized. E.Henning/F. Terrington, R

I'm scared again. Still scared of the lion demon I'm painting. But this time I don't crawl under the bed or hide in my closet. With encouragement and coaching about the demons from Rusty, I am learning how to identify what I need and want, and I am learning to ask for it. And I'm supposed to ask the nurses as well as the social workers.

But as I walk out of my room, I see Mrs. Terrington sitting at the counter, her head bent over her work. Mrs. Terrington is like Nurse

Ratched. I'm afraid of her. And I'm interrupting her. As I cautiously step to the desk, she looks up and scowls at me over her glasses. "What do *you* want?"

"I need to talk." My voice quivers. I hope she'll ask someone else to talk with me.

Mrs. Terrington heaves a deep sigh. "Go back to your room. I'll be in to talk with you in a minute."

I want to talk because I am afraid of the lion. The lion has curled his body around the thick, black elm in the backyard of 707 Blaine. He is angry and he is hungry. He is waiting for me to come back down the narrow sidewalk between our back door and the Schindlers' porch. His green eyes are fastened on the path. His teeth are dripping with blood.

My mother has sent me next door to take a pint jar of sour milk to Auntie Schindler, who is baking a devil's food cake. The milk has been sitting out on our kitchen counter for a few days. Mother keeps it for special recipes and sometimes shares the lumpy, clots with neighbor ladies. I see myself jumping off the Schindlers' porch and taking a couple of steps toward home. When the lion pounces, I quickly leave my room and head for the nurses' station.

I am ready to talk about my father. He's like the lion, biting me.

September, 1943

"Nancy. Nancy, where are you?" My daddy is walking around the people still sitting at the park's picnic tables eating their sandwiches and Jello. My daddy is angry. I am hiding. Trembling. Crouching behind some bushes at the side of the building that has a drinking fountain and toilets. The back of my dress is falling into the dirt. My mommy will be angry, too.

Now, other people are looking for me. Some of them are moving away from me toward the creek. Then I see that older girl's legs. She's close. Walking slowly past the bushes. I hug my arms tight against my knees. Push back against the building.

But she sees me! She hollers, "Here she is! Here she is!"

Now, my daddy is bounding up the hill. He reaches in. Yanks me out. Bites me hard. On my left wrist.

"This will teach you not to bite!" he says.

Mrs. Terrington brings her pack of cigarettes into my room, sits on the chair at the end of my bed and asks, "What's the matter?"

"I'm scared," I say.

"I should think you would be scared!" Mrs. Terrington says, lighting a cigarette and pointing to the watercolors of the demons I have taped on the wall behind my bed. "Look at all those monsters you put up." She takes another deep drag on her cigarette, blows out the smoke to the side of her mouth and says, "What are you doing here, anyway? You have a wonderful husband who is well-known and respected in the community. You have four children who need their mother at home."

Mrs. Terrington plucks a piece of stray tobacco off her tongue, looks out the window and summarizes her advice. "You need to get your act together, go home, and be a good wife and mother!"

I quell a strange mixture of shame and anger that surge like bile through my body. When I drop my head to my chest and begin to pick at the edges of my pillow case, the nurse leaves. Why do I feel attacked?

When he visits me that evening, Stan's words sound like an echo of Mrs. Terrington. "Your job is to get well," he says. He doesn't talk about my housewife duties-fixing suppers, washing clothes, grocery shopping. He talks about chaperoning the German class on their school exchange to Altotting in July.

"Seventeen kids are going," he says.

I am afraid I will not be out of the hospital in time to accompany him. I am afraid if the parents of the seventeen kids find out that I'm a crazy person they will not trust their children with me.

Friday, May 28, 1976

TEAM PROGRESS RECORD

11—7 Sleeper taken at 1:15. In music room drinking coffee and venting feelings of anger and frustration. Back to bed after about 20 minutes. Up again at 2:30 AM. Asked if there was somewhere she could go and just scream. Said she had a lot of hurt inside of her that she had to get out. Laid on floor in security room with face in pillow. At first Nancy sobbed. Screams that followed sobbing were animal like sounds. Brief rests followed by more animal like sounds. (sounds were taped for doctor to hear) Patient checked at intervals. When asked if she would like someone with her said she wanted to be alone to do what she wanted to do for a change. After about an hour Nancy fell asleep—awakened when checked—said she felt better and was going to write down the names of all the people she was screaming at. Gave the writer the impression she never spoke up to any of these people when they angered her. "I always held everything in." Appeared satisfied with self, somewhat brighter and less depressed and frustrated. Resting quietly short while later. Appeared to sleep remainder of nite. E. Belland, RN

The nurse, hands on her hips, is staring down at me as if trying to decide her next move. I am lying on the tile floor in my bathrobe, head on the pillow from my bed, and my knees pulled up into my belly. I just want her to leave, but, when she turns out the light and shuts the door behind her, I'm not sure what *my* next move will be.

I hear myself say, "Well, Nancy, you wanted someplace to scream. You have what you want. Now do your duty."

I recognize Grandma Field's voice and see her in the doorway of the unheated spare room where she keeps her wringer washing machine and tubs. I am three years old, squatting over the white enamel slop jar, trying not to let my butt hit the frigid rim of the pail.

I do my duty on that cold psych room floor. I turn my face into the pillow and scream at Grandma. For a moment, she hovers in the room like a dybbuk, the mole on her cheek near her nose quivering. But when I scream, "No!" she fades, and my father's face appears. I scream, "No!" and he disappears. I watch and scream *No* through a long line of ghostly faces, each one hovering a moment and then floating away. This time there are no sprouting horns, no drooling leers, just blanched faces. People dead and alive with whom I am still angry. Grandmother. Father. Mother. Mother-in-law. Husband. Methodist Youth Fellowship Counselor who put candelabra on the church piano, made me dress up in a tuxedo, and play a piece from my Liberace book for the talent show fundraiser. The doctors and nurses attending my babies' births who strapped my legs into stirrups and stretched them out too far like pulling on a chicken wishbone until it snaps ... and then shamed my cries ... No. No. NO!

Saturday, May 29, 1976

TEAM PROGRESS RECORD

8:00 am. Felt some relief with work in security last pm. Hostile this morning—focuses on husband's success, own feelings of failure—problems with passivity and resentment-collecting. TRNagler

"Do you enjoy anything?" Dr. Nagler asks.

I am thrown off guard with his question. During fifty-three days of a round-the-clock mission to get me healthy *no one* on 2 South has asked me anything like that. I've been trying to learn to enjoy the homemaker stuff. Scrubbing grass stains out of jeans and rotten fish off the dog's butt. Until now, no one has asked me about what I *like*.

Dr. Nagler is still looking at me with heavy-lidded eyes. Sleepy as if he were in another mental world sifting words like grain and picking out kernels that might sprout healing balm.

"Is there anything you like to do?" he asks again.

"I took an oil painting class."

"Did you finish anything?"

"No." Why is he asking me *that*? Is he going to chart that I'm incompetent?

"Is there part of a picture you like?"

"I did a still life with cherries. The cherries were okay." "Could you cut that part of the picture out, frame it, and hang it up?"

What is he after? I liked the way the cherries turned out, but they were lying at the feet of a Made-in-Japan figurine. If I cut out the cherries, the geisha's toes would be stuck to the side of the red blotted fruit on the right.

"No," I say emphatically. His suggestion is ridiculous.

He shakes his head and looks at his watch. My time is up.

I am confused when I leave Dr. Nagler's office. For fifty-three days I have cried, screamed, talked, taken pills, obeyed the rules, talked to an empty chair, attended group therapy, occupational therapy, art therapy, and visited my father's grave. Now he's talking with me about things I enjoy? Has he decided some other test to keep me here? What do I have to *do* to get out of here?

Monday, June 7, 1976
TEAM PROGRESS RECORD
3—11 9:00 pm. Returned to unit. On verge of tears. "I had a rotten time while home." N. McHenry, RN

"We'll be in Germany in July," Stan says.
"During the bicentennial?"
He nods. He has been working with the German teacher at the high school and with a nun at a Catholic girls' school in Bavaria. The arrangements are in place, including my ticket and passport.
"We fly into Frankfurt and then take a bus to Altotting. We'll sightsee on our way to the school and make a couple of overnight stops."
The "we" he refers to includes seventeen students we will be chaperoning on a school exchange.
"A couple of the parents are worried about you being a chaperone," Stan says. "But I think it's okay now."
"Who is worried?" I choke on the words. But he won't tell me and won't talk about it further.

Tuesday, June 8, 1976
TEAM PROGRESS RECORD
2:15 PM Crying—states she left AT early. Couldn't concentrate. "Things spinning in my head." "Father, mother, home, our trip." When gets more specific becomes angry. "I just don't know." Asked to see J. Verick. Notified J. Verick. M. Scoville, RN

SOCIAL SERVICES
Feelings of alienation from family; pressures; anticipating summer agenda. Self-disparagement. "People are afraid of me." Feeling nowhere to go "can't go home; don't want to stay here." Talks of discharge

tomorrow, but appears ambivalent about this. Felt last night pass did not go well—anger towards husband as well as self-condemnation. J.Verick

Wednesday, June 9, 1976

TEAM PROGRESS RECORD

7-3 General diet, on Parnate, taken well. BP 98/70 P80 Talking of going home today. "I just can't take it up here anymore." Up and about spending time in room. In f.g. spirits. Seen by Dr. Nagler. Happy about going home. D. Madsen, LPN

I'm sitting on the edge of my bed. Waiting to see Dr. Nagler for confirmation of release. Can't sit still. I'm scared. Think I'll panic at home. Mind whirls. Can't spin any faster.

I decide to write what is happening.

If I fall down they'll strap me to the bed. Force-feed me Valium with sweet soothing words.

I can't I can't I can't

Stand it stand it stand it

I'm so *hyper*

I'm hot I'm cold I see *everything*: dust in corner. Tuft on bedspread. Paint blob on door knob. Hair on Liz's chin.

Try to eat orange at lunch. Fingers tremble when I dig my nails into peel. Afraid to go home and *need* to get away from these people. Please hold me down. One foot on each side of slipping abyss. Slowly splitting up the crotch.

Nora is banging on door! There's remodeling on third. Nelda with the spastic lips jack-hammering the air. Crap! Jeff went by counting. 4-5-6. To beat of Nelda's door bang-bang-bang.

GOD! GET ME OUT OF HERE!

That felt good.

I'm calming down again. I feel quiet in my stomach. Go with that feeling, Nancy.

Keep writing what's happening.

Slow down ... Write nicely ... Quit scribbling.

Air conditioner hisses. Telephone rings. People at nurses' station chattering.

"David! You have a letter!"

"What's she doing down there?"

"Somebody said somebody wants to beat me up and I want to kick 'em in the ass."

Elevator bell.

Charlotte just took my temperature. "98 on the button," she said.

I don't understand. I am *so* hot.

Shit—here comes Jeff. Puking words. Spitting bullets into my brain

White panic is coming again now

I can feel it creeping up my spine into my rib cage

Through neck up back of head into my eyes

They hurt on their rims—Funny—all the way around

Hurt—just the edges hurt.

Why? If I go *off* an antidepressant do I speed up?

Shouldn't I be depressed and slow down?

Minutes drag. Where is Dr. Nagler?

I'm tired.

Perhaps I'll relax on bed.

Lounge like lady with bump on her forehead

From banging repeatedly on steel frame in bathroom

God save me from Nelda

From Jeff.

From me.

TEAM PROGRESS RECORD

4:05 p.m. Discharged amb. Accompanied by husband. Reminded to stop @ pharmacy for medication. J. Zuelke, LPN

DISCHARGE SUMMARY

… Patient has an extensive past psychiatric history with withdrawal tendencies dating back to early childhood. We worked during her hospitalization on her disturbed relationship with her father … also on some of her sadness and loneliness in her relationship to her husband. Shortly prior to her admission she had developed some self-mutilatory behavior and some of this persisted during her hospitalization. She also had several episodes where she felt that some "demons" overtook her and worked through psychotherapy owning her demonic-side of herself.

Her hospitalization was prolonged because of some refusal to let go of her grieving regarding her father, guilt, anger and confusion in her relationship with him …

PRIMARY DIAGNOSIS

Severe depressive reaction. TRNagler

Stan picks me up at St. Elizabeth's. Though I don't have my act together as he threatened when he dropped me off in April, he needs me to help chaperone the high school class to Germany.

In spite of being co-led by the principal's crazy wife, the trip goes well. During the summer, I am accepted at the University of Wisconsin-Oshkosh for the fall semester.

III
From School to Seminary
1976-1982

Chapter 12
Career Confusion

It takes a long time to become young.

-Pablo Picasso

August, 1976

Prior to matriculating, I study the University of Wisconsin-Oshkosh catalog. The tiny seed of light planted in me six years ago on Valentine's Day at the Ecumenical Institute pulses as I turn the pages. Having learned from my work with Rusty in Art Therapy to identify what I want, I know now that what I *really* want is to heal my split personality – the chasm I experience between religion and psychology.

Material that bridges the gap between the two disciplines is rare. I transfer from the Fox Valley Center as a junior and am still undecided whether to pursue religion or psychology. I consult the catalog in hopes that courses available in psychology or religion will help me choose a major.

In addition to the expected Introduction to Psychology, Abnormal Psychology, Personal and Social Adjustment, I see a course titled, "Psychology of Religious Experience." Briefly described, the class is a third-level course with no prerequisites. Sounds perfect. I check the course with my pencil and read the requirements of a major in psychology.

Then I flip back and look at the courses in religion: Introduction, New Testament, Old Testament, Myth and Mystery... *What*?! Myth and Mystery? The title alone is intriguing. *Mystery* is the best name for God that I know.

I read further that the Religion Department does not provide a major, but an individually planned major is possible through the department if it is approved by the Dean of Letters and Science.

During the first week of classes, I make an appointment with the chair of the Religion Department, who agrees to help me with a proposal for an individually-planned major and directs me to the dean's office where I pick up the necessary papers I need to apply.

Included in my rationale for an independent major is my intention to enter seminary. I'm surprised at what I've written. I don't even believe it myself. But I want the courses that interest me and figure the seminary idea will help sell my proposal. After completing the papers and obtaining the required signatures, my plan is approved.

With a full course load, I drive the round trip between Appleton and Oshkosh every weekday. Stan and the children support me by helping to maintain the household. The children are 17, 15, 14, and 13. Though they are busy with baby-sitting, paper routes, and school work, they reluctantly agree to prepare some suppers, learn to use the washer and dryer, and help clean the house on Saturday mornings before they are all off to their weekend activities.

January, 1977

"Some of you have your mind pretty well made up by this time about some things," Dr. Hayes says as he hands out a syllabus for the "Intro to Religion Class." "I'll answer questions about the requirements when you've had a chance to look this over."

I was lucky to get into this course, popular because of Dr. Hayes.

Except for his southern accent and funny sayings ("My momma said I was born when two buzzards bumped their butts together."), he is the epitome of the clichéd tall, dark, and handsome man. He wears a navy blue suit, white dress shirt, open at the neck, and wants us to call him Rick.

"Any questions?" Professor Hayes asks.

"Yeah," a male voice booms from the back of the room. "What's this thing about keeping a journal?"

I turn from my front row seat to see a scruffy young man holding the syllabus up and pointing to the bottom of the page.

"Well," Dr. Hayes answers, "in addition to class attendance and the reading material, I am requiring that each of you keep a journal and respond to each class period's topic and lecture. You'll notice that I want you to turn your journal in on those two dates listed."

"How many pages does it have to be?" another person asks.

"However many pages it takes for you to reflect on that particular day's topic."

"Every day?" a girl across the rooms whines.

"Every day that we have a class," the professor answers with a smile.

"You'll be reading what we write?" the same girl sighs.

"Yes. Be careful," Dr. Hayes warned and then grinned. "If you've robbed a bank, better not tell me."

Dr. Hayes' first lecture challenges the students to think about their faith. I am eager to write about my experience of the crashing light and my hospitalizations.

And I'm afraid.

I decide to risk it and discover I like putting my thoughts and feelings onto paper.

Journal: January 31, 1977

... For the last seven years I've experienced a lonely struggle to find someone who understood the powerful relationship between Christian symbols and mental illness. This has been largely a "wandering in the wilderness," and I have only found support in writings of theologians, Jungian psychology, and some personal accounts of great mystics ...

Journal: February 16, 1977

... I am afraid to talk about what happened to me. People would think I am a Jesus freak or that I'm psychotic ...

Journal: March 2, 1977

... These journal entries always end up sounding like sermons. Maybe I should be a preacher when I "grow up ..."

Journal: March 14, 1977

I am 37 today. Rick spoke about relationships in class. I feel more alone on my birthday than any other day of the year. There's an emptiness ... I have three piano students from 6:00-7:30 tonight. My husband and kids will be eating without me. My daughter has a victory party (undefeated basketball season). Another daughter has a babysitting job. My husband has a school meeting. My mother called yesterday to say she's decided to send me $10 rather than try to find a pair of earrings for my newly-pierced ears. And Stan's folks have informed me they'll bring me back something in April when they get back from spending the winter in Texas ...

Journal: April 27, 1977

Rick talked today about "poetic" religion. He said an artist doesn't rely on tradition, but *imagination* as the mediator between God and humans. The artist's ultimate value is individual authenticity, not conformity. He said the holy is revealed in art through the soul of the artist.

And then Rick wrote a Wallace Stevens quote on the blackboard that gave my 1970 "crazy" experience a home in my heart and mind: *"The final belief is to believe in a fiction which you know to be a fiction, there being nothing else. The exquisite truth is to know it is a fiction and that you believe in it willingly."*

For the first time I have heard someone say that all human attempts to define reality or God are ultimately stories we construct. Like I discovered in my 1970 "trip." I know the Jesus story better than any other one, so I might as well live out of it. Knowing it's a story frees me up to enter other stories. Of course, the Stevens quote and my belief in it are another story. Absurd. So be it.

Journal: May 4, 1977

… This will be my last journal entry. I find this technique (journal) to be a real benefit in my process of becoming. I have learned and grown from just talking *to myself about myself.*

October, 1977

A week after taking a career assessment inventory at the UW-O Counseling Center, I am back in the office of Scott Herschkowitz, who is beginning to explain the results of the hundreds of little circles I filled in.

"This assessment compares your interest and skills with people in the professions with the similar interests and skills, " Scott explains, pointing at several papers he has spread out on a table between us. "And you compare most highly with *Accountant* or *Insurance Actuary.*"

Scott sees my eyebrows squeeze into a perplexed squint.

"Well, you also compare with the interests of an artist ... and a priest, but those numbers aren't as high."

"Priest? That would be male, wouldn't it? And Catholic?"

"That's an interesting question ..."

"My major is Religion and Psychology," I remind him. "Accountant doesn't seem to fit."

I am reminded of my rationale for an independent major. I wrote that I was planning to go to seminary only so I could take the courses I wanted. The rationale worked, but I wasn't planning to go to seminary. Now what?

Scott sees my distress and suggests I make another appointment. A few weeks later, having heard me describe my psychiatric history and understanding that my career dilemma indicates other unresolved issues, he asks another therapist and colleague, Carolyn, to join the sessions.

January, 1978

"What classes are you taking?" Scott asks toward the end of another counseling hour.

"Two psych and one religion—toward my major," I answer. "I'm taking a drawing course. For fun."

"A full load then?" Carolyn asks.

"Yes. German and Orienteering to meet language and phy-ed requirements."

"Are you still undecided about your future plans?"

I nod. "I'm in Intro to Counseling this term. I like Dr. Lehman, and I think I'll like the course. He requires 20 hours of volunteering at a social service agency or institution. I can choose where I want to go from a suggested list he provided."

"Where did you choose?"

"I'd like to go to Winnebago."

"Why did you choose Winnebago?" Scott's eyes are opened wide in surprise at my decision to volunteer in a mental health facility.

"I want to see what it's like from the other side ... and this time I'll be free to come and go as I please." I lean over to pick up my fat bag of books at the side of my chair.

"You'll get some good experience there," Carolyn says and smiles.

"I'll let you know," I laugh, and, as I open the door to leave, I add, "Dr. Lehman requires students to keep a journal on their experience."

Journal: February 6, 1978

I'm waiting for Mr. Marsden, the volunteer coordinator, in the lobby of Sherman Hall at Winnebago Mental Health Institute. In front of me are locked doors. Childhood images of weeping tunnels at Rock County Insane Asylum and agonizing screams from behind the barred windows push at my memory. I'm nervous about this interview. I am afraid my psychiatric history will come up, and Mr. Marsden will reject my application to volunteer. What if he accepts me? How will it be for me on the *other* side of the bars?

My fears are put at ease somewhat when I see a tall, smiling, man come through the locked doors.

"Hi. I'm Jim Marsden." He reaches to shake my hand. "Are you Nancy?"

"Yes."

Mr. Marsden is about fifty years old, clean-shaven, and has a full head of dark-brown hair. He gestures toward a corridor to my right and says, "Come with me. We'll meet in a room down the hall, and call me Jim." He leads us past several closed doors and into a small, carpeted room with a couch, two comfortable chairs, a desk, and a round, Formica-topped, table. The only decoration in the room is an oil painting above the couch. I wonder if the lake in the picture is Lake Winnebago.

"Take a chair at the table," Jim says, standing several feet away at his desk. He picks up a pair of reading glasses, loosens his tie, and sits across from me, his arms resting on the papers.

"Tell me a little about yourself, Nancy, and why you want to volunteer here."

"You probably know about Dr. Lehman's requirement …" Jim nods his head and raises his eyebrows expecting me to continue. Though I've decided I like Mr. Marsden—he looks like James Mason, one of the movie stars whose pictures I collected as a 12-year-old—I still have some discomfort. I swallow and add, "I'm thinking of getting a Master's Degree in counseling. I thought this would be a good place to learn."

Jim prompts for more personal information. As I tell him about my family, my interests, and my major, I become more relaxed.

Then he asks, "Have you ever been in a hospital like this …, " I hold my breath until he adds, … "as a worker?"

"No," I answer honestly and breathe again.

Jim approves me as a volunteer in a locked forensic unit and gives me printed materials that cover details pertaining to my work. He reads patients' rights, lists rules I must follow, and answers questions I have regarding the simple mechanics of my work.

"Are the hours set for me?" No.

"When do I start?" This week if I want to.

"Who do I report to?" Mrs. Filpatrick.

"How do I contact her?" Same phone I used to contact Jim when I arrived for the interview.

I tell Jim I would like to start this Wednesday.

I do not tell anyone that I am very frightened—not of the patients—but seeing myself in them. I've decided not to ask anyone if they are "patient" or "help." I will wait for the information to be given to me in some way. My goal for Wednesday night is to learn some people's names and try to be aware of my internal reactions especially when the messages are: *You, Nancy, were a patient in a psych ward. You looked just this depressed. You had to be taken care of. You are a failure.*

I want to use this volunteer work to try and determine if counseling is something I really want to do and can be effective at, or if a counseling career is more an identity search to help myself rather than a desire to help others.

Journal: February 8, 1978

Mrs. Filpatrick, answers my phone code immediately and lets me in the locked unit. She takes me to her desk, which is behind another door, and gives me my Volunteer Activity Report to fill out.

"Do you have any questions?" she asks, rubbing her cheek and grimacing as if she has a toothache.

"No, not now, but I probably will later on."

She reaches toward a file box on her desk. "Some of the patients' records are in here and you can look at them … if you want to."

"I'd rather just observe for awhile," I say. "I want to get acquainted first."

"Well, let's go into the unit." I can tell by her abrupt manner that Mrs. Filpatrick is in pain and has other work to do.

She takes me into a large room with a television in one corner. She introduces me to a nurse, two student nurses, and one patient who are all in the middle of a card game. While I'm standing at the edge of the card table and having an anxious *what do I do now* flash, a young man in a short-sleeved shirt approaches me.

"Who are *you*?" he asks, fiddling with the buttons on his beige shirt—a cotton print splashed with ducks and cattails. And blobs of ketchup.

"I'm Nancy. Who are you?"

"I'm Steve. Why are you here?"

"I'm a student at UW-O."

"Oh." Steve, who has been looking around the room, turns his head toward me. His interest is piqued. "Do you know my sister?"

"What's her name?"

"Jill Metcalf."

"No, I don't know her."

Steve sighs and then offers to show me around the room. He explains the wall charts, tells me people's names, and says he doesn't know where Laura is. He points at a rocking chair near the television and says, "Laura usually sits there."

We sit in folding chairs shoved up against a wall, and Steve says, "I used to fight with my sisters, but I'll never fight when them again. Not after what I've done…" His voice trails off and his chin falls into his chest.

Hmm…Maybe the stuff on his shirt isn't ketchup. Though I'm curious, I don't prod Steve further. I tell myself I'm more interested in psychological dynamics, diagnoses, and treatments than what crimes the people have committed.

Journal: February 13, 1978

Tonight I arrive just as the nurse and orderlies are deciding how to handle a hostile new admittance. They decide on cuffs and an injection. I get out of the way. The whole unit is tense. All the patients seem glued to the room's various chairs. None of them are in their usual slow, amble around the room.

Another patient, Fred, afraid he would be next to be restrained, suddenly gets up from his chair, shaking and hollering, "I didn't do anything! I didn't do anything!" He is wearing a hospital gown and heavy work boots and he starts stumbling around the room.

When he flops back into a chair, I move to the chair next to him and sit quietly as he rocks and cries. After several minutes he asks me, "Do you hear that song playing on the radio?"

"Yes."

"There is a UFO plot in it. Listen. Do you hear the take-over plot?"

"No, I don't." *Was I like this? What about the demons? How did I ever get rid of them?*

Fred gets up, walks and cries himself through the door to his room.

I have a headache, but when Bob asks me to play cards with him, I agree.

He has nine cards. He gives me four and holds his five with dirty hands. His hair, the color of dry cornhusks, is greasy and knotted, his fingernails ragged and grimy. He hunkers into a green plaid flannel shirt that covers a ripped T-shirt. He makes up words and mumbles into silence in the middle of a sentence. He makes no sense at all. I suddenly become face to face with me in my schizophrenic state in 1970. I remember how sure I was that *my world* was the true answer—that I'd finally found the prescription for life. I couldn't understand why Dr. Nagler wouldn't respond *correctly.*

Patients begin to touch me. One week Laura brushes back my hair in a gentle gesture. Another night Ralph takes my hand and turns it over to see my cameo ring. Harold lays his hand on my arm while he prints my name. I could cry. They're giving me a beautiful gift. Having not been touched as a child except to get hit, I do not know how to touch. Their touch awakens and soothes a deep hunger.

Journal: February 27, 1978

"Marie told me she sliced up some man in an armed robbery," I tell Mrs. Filpatrick. "Is that true?"

"No, she didn't."

"Well, someone has sliced up *her* arms. She's got all those scars. Some are so new the stitches still show."

"I know. I've seen them."

"Who did it?"

"We don't know for sure, but Marie is a cutter."

Marie is braver than I am. I could draw blood, but I didn't cut anything deep enough to require stitches. Why do I wish I could have cut myself more severely? Did I want someone to take care of me when I hurt?

Journal: March 1, 1978

For the first time since I began volunteering, I don't want to be here. I had two exams today and two more to go before the end of the quarter. The mood of the unit is "up," however, because the student nurses are planning a dance party with records and refreshments.

I decide to stay for the dance, and I am sitting in one of the lounges with a couple of patients when John appears. He is just out of seclusion, still in his hospital gown and robe, with the cuffs hanging from his waist. He has on heavy hiking shoes that are too big for his feet. He starts nervously clomping back and forth and hollering non-stop about his money being stolen. One of the new patients eggs him on. Tempers and tensions rise until John walks out of the room.

He comes back later still in his hospital gown, robe and cuffs and walks stiffly over to me and asks me to dance. With no hesitation, I join him. It is a strangely pleasant feeling to dance with him, his sweaty palms and the cuffs bouncing at his waist with every hop. He kept turning around to keep commenting to no one in particular about his money. I had to keep my feet out of the range of his stomping. He kept sneaking looks at me, and my smiles were real. When we finished, I said, "Thank you, John."

He blushed and stammered as he mumbled, "You're welcome."

I felt as if I gave something with no strings attached to someone who needed me for just that moment. If I could only learn how to do this with Stan and the kids.

Journal: March 6, 1978

I still do not have a clue as to whether counseling is a good option for me. I am very depressed. In the last few months, I have been so closely in tune with my inner self that I can almost immediately report feelings-level reactions. I know that school in general is now a negative demand. I am tired of the hoops, the striving for approval, and my own impossible standards. I am disturbed at home with undone housework, a "perfect" husband and fighting kids. I am suppressing my anger at church where I was once involved and excited.

In all those arenas, the feeling-messages are anxiety, guilt, and depression. But in the forensic unit, my feeling is one of belonging.

I fit there.

Friday, March 10, 1978

Stan, Joan, Steve, and Jerry drive down from Appleton in a separate car to join me in a counseling session at UW-Oshkosh. Five of us sit with Scott and Carolyn in Scott's office in the Counseling Center. Everyone in the family except Julie, who chooses not to join the sessions, is participating in the appointments recommended earlier in the year by my counselors.

Jerry, almost 15, cries throughout this session with Scott and Carolyn. Several times Scott, sitting at Jerry's right, turns and asks him why he is crying, but Jerry won't explain. He just sits bent over with his arms resting on his thighs and stares at the floor, moving only to clasp and unclasp his hands. For almost an hour tears trickle slowly down his cheeks. I am surprised at Jerry's reaction. I have no idea why he is crying and want him to talk.

Toward the end of the hour Scott brings up the possibility of including members of our families of origin in an appointment. Scott looks around the silent room for reactions.

"Nancy, you look skeptical."

I nod. "I'm afraid."

"Of what?"

"I don't know. Something about my mother. Probably I don't feel protected emotionally from her intrusiveness. I don't tell her anything that would make me vulnerable."

Scott and Carolyn nod.

"Why are you suggesting our families be involved?" I ask.

"Patterns in families of origin help us help you," Scott says. "They can provide important information."

"Who would be included?" I ask.

"Just your family members as you were growing up."

"There's just my mother, brother, and sister," I say. "I've already told you my father is dead."

They nod.

"No spouses?"

"No." They both say in unison. "A meeting with your birth family will be helpful to Stan and your children, as well," Carolyn says.

I have wanted to help Stan and the kids since my first hospitalization. Convinced, I take a deep breath and reluctantly agree to participate. Scott and Carolyn both consult their appointment book and propose an appointment in two weeks. March 24 at 8:30 a.m.

"That's Good Friday," I say. Both counselors nod their awareness of that day's religious significance and assure me that the date is okay with them. I promise to contact my family members and call Scott to confirm the appointment. Appropriate, I think as I swallow my fear. Good Friday. I'll probably die.

"What about you, Stan?" Scott asks. "Will you meet with your family?"

My husband, who has been silent through most of the hour, shakes his head. "We're just here to help Nancy get well," he explains, sweeping his arm to indicate our three children in the room.

Anger I don't understand crackles inside my eggshell skull as we leave the counselors' office and head for the cars. Stan, Joan, and Steve get into the Gremlin. Jerry rides with me.

Furious, I grip the steering wheel, clench my teeth and press down hard on the accelerator. I run stop signs and pass cars already going over the speed limit. Jerry, in the passenger's seat, stares straight ahead, the blood drained from his face.

Though driving while enraged, I get myself and Jerry home safely. He goes downstairs to the family room. I go straight to the refrigerator and am half-way through the second glass of Gallo Red Rose when Stan, Joan, and Steve come in the back door.

No one talks. I gulp down the last inch of wine, break into sobs, and begin to choke. I run up the blue plush carpeted steps and make it into the bathroom before I vomit. Still crying, I wipe my mouth with the washrag hugging the edge of the tub.

I stumble down the hall to the bedroom. I throw myself on the Victorian bed and begin to sob. My sobs turn into screams. Then icy rage. I pound my fists into the pillows.

In between gasps of breath, through the open bedroom door, I hear Stan's steady plod up the stairs. "I called the doctor," he says as approaches the side of the bed. He heard you in the background and thinks I better bring you in."

This time they put me in 216, bed 2.

Chapter 13
Strike Three

Reality is the leading cause of stress among those in touch with it.
— Lily Tomlin

ADMISSION FORM
St. Elizabeth's Hospital: March 10, 1978
Patient: Ore, Mrs. Nancy L. (Bauer)
Birth Date: 3/14/40
Occupation: Student
Nearest Relative or person to be notified-relationship: Stanley H. Ore, Jr., husband
Religion: Methodist
Admission Time: 10:10 p.m.
Attending Physician: Dr. R.H. Wahlbruhn

March 11, 1978
HISTORY OF PRESENT ILLNESS
Dr. R.H. Wahlbruhn
Third psychiatric hospitalization for this 37 year-old white female, mother of four, admitted now with increasingly severe depression... First St. E's hospitalization in 1970 for apparent psychotic depression. ...She was hospitalized again in 1976 for depression, apparently not psychotic at that time. She currently comes with a great deal of uncertainty with careers...

...Nancy is presently a senior at Oshkosh majoring in psychology and religion. The career uncertainty apparently led to a counseling situation, which has been quite upsetting to her and has involved having her family in on the counseling session. She also is receiving individual psychotherapy at Oshkosh.

Yesterday she took several Ativan which were prescribed by Dr. Nagler and then in the evening several glasses of wine and became sick to her stomach, vomited several times and became extremely agitated and tearful. She decided it was a good idea to come into the hospital for several days rest and recuperation.

ASSESSMENT: Unipolar depression

PLAN: Dr. Janssen agreed to consult on this case.

R. H. Wahlbruhn, MD

Saturday, March 11, 1978

I am sitting on the edge of the hospital bed working on German declensions when Dr. Janssen comes in. I have my homework spread out on the table with wheels that wraps itself over the top of my hospital bed and holds my glass of water, box of tissue, and breakfast.

Dr. Janssen is wearing a brown plaid sports jacket, white shirt, tie, and a scowl. Maybe's he's miffed about covering for Dr. Nagler on a Saturday. He says hello, acknowledges he knows me, asks a couple of questions and makes a brief reference to the high school friendship between his son and my daughter. As he turns on his heels to leave, he says "Monday … Monday, we'll see how you are sabotaging your family."

Sabotage? He pulls the pin, lobs the word into my belly like a grenade and leaves me in 216-S to do triage alone. I look at the wounds. I already know I am a bad wife and mother, but *sabotage*?

Sabotage? I see me in the living room squeezing sticks of dynamite between the cushions of the love seats. I see me stringing piano wire over the railing in the vestibule, slipping poison canisters under beds. I see me in a trench coat and locked up locked up locked up. Locked up again and forever because someone residing in me continues to commit horrible crimes against those people someone else within me loves. Stan. Joan. Steve. Julie. Jerry.

He leaves me with the enemy. Me. I am the saboteur. And, he says he will see me on Monday. Today is Saturday. I will have to wait until *Monday?*

"We'll see …" he said. We'll. We will. *We*? Does he mean both of us? "We will see how you are …" No. I know how this works. He means some other people will decide how I am.

Sabotaging. Sabotage. He leaves me alone with myself. And, I will have to wait until Monday? I will have to fend off the enemy inside me for three whole days?

I remember my promises to myself. I have promised myself to face my fear and anger. I have promised myself not to bend, fold, staple, burn or mutilate my body in any way. Instead of boiling water, carving on my stomach or banging my head, I have promised I will write. I have promised to record the arsenal of thoughts I fire against me.

I grab my pen and notebook with its careful columns of German verbs and quickly write:

"See how you sabotage the family." Felt as an attack. Couldn't stand the attack. Wanted to shut it out. Have trouble really accepting my faults – have to be perfect at one level, but constantly dwell on how miserable I am inside. Something drives me to feel internally bad. The I—the other side—comes back and defends with "You have worked, trusted, risked." And, then the Janssen condemnation beats me. I must ask "What is my manipulation for? Where did it come from and why?"

Rusty's words from my previous hospitalization push through the din. "It's okay to want something, Nancy. What do you want? Nancy, what do you *want*?"

I quickly realize that I *know what I want!* I *want* to know how I'm hurting my family. I *want* to talk to Dr. Janssen. I *want* to ask him to help me discover how I am sabotaging my family. If I am doing something that destroys my family, I *want* to change it. Now. I *want* to change it NOW. I don't *want* to wait until Monday.

Confident I know what I want, I put down my pen and hurry out of Room 216 to find Dr. Janssen.

Patients and staff are standing at the counter of the nurses' station. They stare at me as I approach. Then, glancing past them, I see Dr. Janssen. He is sitting behind the desk just a couple of feet from the counter. He has a chart on his lap and is writing in the chart. I want to ask him to help me.

I think I can swallow the horror of who I am if it will help my family. If I know what I'm doing wrong, I can work hard and reach out and save my family. Those I love. I want to try.

I want to try so badly I break a rule and step one foot behind the counter into the nurses' area. I quickly drop to my knees in front of Dr. Janssen.

"I want to help my family," I whisper.

He looks down on me over the chart with narrowed eyes squeezed thin under a menacing scowl. He raises his right arm at me and swings a back-handed threat.

"Get out of here!" he snarls. "I told you I would see you on Monday!"

I run back to my room. I run past startled nurses, nurses' aides and patients in the hall. I can't breathe. I go into the bathroom of Room 216 and begin whacking mein kopf against the bathroom tiles.

PROGRESS RECORD

Onset of p.r. seems related to patient being in family therapy. Last session Friday resulted in patient banging her head struggling with wishes to injure herself. Had been taking Lorazapam, prescribed by Dr. Nagler. Patient wants to continue her college courses and make hosp. stay brief—However became upset with even gental (sic) suggestion that her behavior may be an effort to disrupt family therapy. M. Janssen

Sunday, March 12, 1978
PROGRESS RECORD
Settled today after hypomanic response to meeting with me yesterday. Wants discharge. Janssen
PROGRESS RECORD
7—3 LPN Back and forth on unit. Pleasant mood. Dramatic appearance.
12:30 Discharged with husband. No meds. Ambulatory to lobby. M. Scoville

Stan picks me up after he and the children get home from St. James. I do not ask him how he explained my absence to my church friends. He does not ask me about my weekend.

Journal: March 13, 1978
I remember that I chose to do my volunteer requirement at Winnebago because I wanted to face my fears by seeing what happened in a psych unit from the "other side."
Tonight, my other side perspective is 24 hours fresh.
I'm worn out. I decide to stay here for an hour and try to forget about sabotaging my family and focus on the patients.
John finds me sitting in the rocking chair. He is in his hospital gown and robe. The cuffs dangling from his waist let me know he has been in seclusion again.

"Wanna play cards?" John says.

I 'wanna' say no to John. I don't even 'wanna' be here tonight. I haven't told the staff that I'm tired and depressed. And that I spent the weekend in another psych unit. As a patient.

Tuesday, March 14, 1978

I am 38 today. Stan hands me a broom for my birthday gift. I try to act pleased, but I want to say, "How about a black hat and cat, too? I'll just fly away."

But the broom is the kind I like. Straw, with four rows of red cord stitched in between the long, thin, bristles to hold the broom together. Later when I sweep, the straws will spread out and the dust will stick to the rough fringe at the end of each dried stalk. The well-controlled dirt will pile up nicely as I sweep. Not like the yellow plastic O-Cedar brooms that flip and fling toast crumbs half-way across the linoleum.

I like the broom, and Stan tied a red ribbon around the red handle. So, I don't hit him with wicked witch words.

I say thank you.

Journal: March 22, 1978

Tonight, Phyllis, an aide, is assigned constant surveillance of Mary. A week ago Mary was strapped into a wheelchair and banging on her tray. Her head slumped onto a stained beige knit sweater, and her gray hair looked like it hadn't been washed or combed for weeks. But now Mary is untied, dressed nicely, and walking around with Phyllis close behind like a shadow.

Later in the evening, Mary is in the rocking chair in the lounge. She calls me from across the room and gestures with her hands. "Hey you! Hey you! Come 'ere." At first, I panic, but I go over, pull up a chair, and spend a half hour with her. She holds my hand. She cries. She cups my head in her hands. She calls me sweet. She sobs and says, "Something horrible happened in my family." She doesn't elucidate.

I tell Phyllis I'll be with Mary until 8:00. We walk. We rock. At one point, she looks straight at me and says in a sniffling whine, "Do you like me?" I surprise myself by answering, "Yes, I like you, Mary." And it is mostly true. My reaction last week was a mixture of revulsion and confusion, but somehow I respond to the total of who Mary is rather than her contorted, sniveling, countenance. I do like her in the sense of wanting her to recover her whole self or to actualize or whatever the hell the term is that whoever the hell put on that process of healing.

March 24, 1978

A gray and drizzly Good Friday. Today my mother, brother, and sister are joining my counseling appointment. Today I'm afraid I will be crucified on the family cross. Like Jesus. I haven't eaten breakfast. My mouth is dry. My stomach tight. I drive alone to the Oshkosh campus. Because of the Easter holiday, the parking lots are empty, and I park close to the door of Clow, the red brick building in which I have several classes. I don't recognize any of the cars in the lot and wonder if my other family members have arrived.

The closest path to Scott and Carolyn's office is through the basement of Clow. I wind my way through tiled hallways like a Via Dolorosa, Jesus' route from Pilate's judgment to Golgatha. I round a corner and see a black and white glossy advertisement tacked to a bulletin board. A group of smiling people, looking directly at me, proclaim with happy conviction, "You are in the picture!" I don't know what the posing pilgrims are selling, but I buy their words as a personal sign to me from a soon-to-be-dead savior that I *belong* somewhere. I continue trodding the path toward my cross with new confidence. I belong in this world, and I probably will not die during the counseling session.

The first floor of the Counseling Center, usually filled with people and humming with conversation, is empty. Half-way up the stairway to the second floor, I hear my mother's voice. The counselors are already greeting my mother, brother, and sister when I arrive in the waiting room. My family drove the two-hour trip together. Scott and Carolyn usher us into their consultation room. Mother and Margaret sit next to each other on a couch and Phil in a chair next to Margaret. I am on a chair between Scott and Carolyn. Shortly after we sit down, the focus of the meeting is on me.

Mother looks at Scott and tries to explain my precarious mental condition.

"She got married at 18 and then immediately began having babies… bing, bing, bing…"

"BING!" my brother, sister and I say in unison, ringing another bell for my fourth child, Jerry. Everyone laughs. Except my mother, who sits during the remainder of the hour looking down at her hands, folded on her lap. She comments only to disagree when one of us describes a behavior of our father that influenced us negatively.

"He hid the mail."

"Oh, that was just a joke." *It was mean.*

"He wouldn't let me take an art class."

"You needed math classes." *For what?*

"He *never* complimented me."

"He didn't want you to get a big head." *Well, he got what he wanted.*

After our meeting, worn out from my mother's continued inability to hear my anger, but relieved that I am still alive, I suggest we have lunch at Down to Earth, a favorite restaurant. Between spoonfuls of home-made corn chowder, Mother reveals that when she got married she didn't know anything about sex. My siblings and I share a brief locked look of disbelief. How could someone raised on a farm not know about sex? Mother's comment cracks open the perception of her I've had for years.

At home, I report my experience to Stan. I tell him the bing, bing, bing,…BING! story. He laughs. Then I say, "We went to Down to Earth for lunch, and Mother said she didn't know anything about sex before she got married."

"Huh …"

"And, for the first time, I was comfortable while we talked. I wasn't frightened of her. I think my mother was the one who became vulnerable."

"Huh …"

"It was a good experience," I add. "Have you changed your mind about meeting with your family?"

"No. I do not want to put my mother through that," he says.

Journal: April 3, 1978

Back at school and Winnebago after Easter break. Lots of new faces in the unit. I look for Mary. Dressed nicely and functioning by herself, I don't recognize her at first. She sits with me several times during the evening and tells me stories about zebras, gardens, her brain operation, and her childhood in Panama City. I interact as if I believe it all. Then she says, "I know you are Methodist."

"How do you know?" I am surprised.

"You told me," she says with a smile.

I don't remember telling her. Did I mention it in the conversations we had two weeks ago? She seemed so out of it then. Other patients on the ward had forgotten me completely and thought I was a new patient.

Mary must remember our conversation. Maybe she grew up Methodist or had a Methodist friend or lived near a Methodist church. Who knows what is deposited in our memory banks? Or why?

I can remember quite a bit from my own break *down*. Break *through*? I remember when I was being discharged and showed Rusty the pimple on my nose, she said, "Nancy's breaking out!"

Journal: April 17, 1978

My last night at Winnebago. I rock and talk with Laura and spend about ten minutes with Bob. I watch a substitute aide keep a lid on a conflict between two new patients. The desk area is quiet and things seem under control, so I spend most of the evening reading the flipping folder of cards, one on each patient. I read the cards of about twenty people that I've interacted with on the unit.

Earlier I didn't want to know diagnoses. Now I do. I am surprised to read Tom, diagnosed as a sociopath, is believed to set fires. John has a low IQ. Many of the patients are diagnosed undifferentiated schizophrenics. A nice catch-all. Some aren't diagnosed at all. Goals and suggestions are sometimes included for the staff in their treatment of the patient: what to push, what to avoid. After I read several, they all begin to blend. I don't remember much of what I read and I don't reflect on my interactions with the people. I just wonder what the St. Elizabeth staff has written about me during my "little spells" (as my mother calls them) in the psych unit.

I say goodbye to the nurses and aides and thank them for their help, but I don't say any goodbyes to the patients. I'm glad I did this volunteering. My goal, to face my fear, has been met and all I really did was observe, interact, and reflect.

May, 1978

In the fall, one more required science class and two psychology classes will complete my independent major. I sign up for a watercolor class for fun.

At home, I fall into the pit of housewifery. Floors to sweep, four bathrooms to scrub, and the damn Victorian bed to dust, oil, and keep in good running order. I line up tater tots in military phalanxes to convince myself I have some control over my life. I still don't know which career path to take, and my image of a graduate degree washes away with weekly piles of laundry.

One spring day, while sifting through a stack of old Ecumenical Institute papers, I find and reread *Schizophrenia—the Inward Journey*. I decide to write to Mr. Campbell.

May 30, 1978

Dear Mr. Campbell,

I'm sitting at my kitchen table and asking myself why I'm writing to you. I guess it's because I hope there is a chance you may be of some help. I feel as if I've come to a place in my life where all other doors seem closed.

A brief explanation: On February 14, 1970, I experienced a radical "conversion." (Christian) I was immediately catapulted into another world and spent the next four weeks encountering almost every "reality" on which I base my present existence. March 16, 1970, the rescue squad hauled me away to St. Elizabeth's psych ward where I was diagnosed psychotic. A couple years later I was given your article *Schizophrenia—the Inward Journey*. The article was then and continues to be the most comprehensive description of what has happened to me, most particularly the mention in some myths of that wonderful, crashing, overpowering, *mysterious*, light.

All of this is to say that I have spent eight years reading a wide variety of writings (by psychologists and theologians), meditating, and questioning, to 1. Try and explain what happened to me, and, 2. Try and find someplace in the world to use what I have learned and experienced in order to help others…

...I am now 38 years old and six credits away from a BA in Psychology and Religion. I am impatient in trying to find a place to "plug in" in a professional way.

Do you have any specific suggestions as to what professions you feel are especially needed now? Or, do you foresee a particular need in the near future? Any suggestions you have would be appreciated...

...Even if you do not know how to answer this letter, or do not care to reply, I would like you to know that until I read *Schizophrenia—the Inward Journey,* I believed the story the rest of society was telling me—namely that I, Nancy Ore, was crazy. Because of your paper I have seen my psychoses as a privilege—an invitation to participate in a life-giving event.

Today, though still neurotic, I have become confident enough in the strength I touched to continue to grow. Thank you for that affirmation.

Sincerely,
Nancy Ore

July 16, 1978
Letter from Joseph Campbell
Dear Miss Ore –
Thank you for your very kind letter of some weeks ago. I am sorry that I do not know how to suggest an area of action to you, but in general, I think that work in some field of education should be rewarding ... either academic or maverick (such as in connection with one or more of the various "growth centers" that are now coming into their own; for example The Esalen Institute at Big Sur, California, 93920 or Oasis center [7463 North Sheridan Rd., Chicago 60626]). There might be something for you closer to home, in connection with your church, for instance. But helping, one way or another, people who have experienced or are close to experiencing something like the "trip" that you yourself experienced

seems to me the likely answer to your question. The academic world is difficult to break into without a degree, but even there, there are non-academic posts to be filled. My guess is that you would find work with people in middle life more rewarding than with younger folk. There are many in middle life who have run off the standard track and do not know how to profit from their unexplained experiences.

I greatly appreciated your letter, and thank you for it. All good wishes to you.

Cordially,

Joseph Campbell

December 15, 1978

The Mid-Year Commencement program lists Nancy Bauer Ore graduating Magna Cum Laude with a Bachelor of Arts from the College of Letters and Science. I do not participate in the ceremony. I don't want to sit while hundreds of people I don't know go through the interminable ceremony. And, I don't want spend the money on a cap and gown that I'll use for a couple hours.

After the holidays, I begin looking in the Appleton Post Crescent's want ads for a job. No one seems to want a 38 year-old woman with an independent degree in Religion and Psychology. I am sitting in the kitchen at the counter sipping breakfast coffee and staring out the window when Stan comes up behind me. He is dressed in his school administrator uniform—suit, dress shirt, and tie—and is ready to go to work.

"What are you going to be doing today?" he asks.

"I don't know," I say. "Maybe clean the family room."

"What about looking for a job?" he asks.

"I don't know," I shrug. "I haven't had much luck."

My husband doesn't like my answers. "You aren't trying very hard either," he says through tight lips. As he opens the back door ready to leave, he growls, "I want a return on my investment!"

Tears begin as he slams the door and leaves. I sit at the table and sob. I'm not working. Nothing works. Nothing.

A few days later I see an ad for a part-time receptionist at a veterinary clinic on the north side of Appleton. I am interviewed and hired. I learn the job quickly, but the work is neither challenging, nor profitable. Stan puts my paltry paycheck into our joint account.

Still trying to stay sane, I dabble in fad projects that come along: bread dough dolls, piggy banks carved from bleach bottles, wall hangings out of 78 records—baked at 350 degrees until pliable, scalloped on the edges, weeds glued on, and the whole mess sprayed gold. I sign up for a course in sewing knit fabrics. I buy yards and yards of tricot and elastic, but make only one pair of underpants that Stan dubs "Ore's Drawers." I sculpt "Tortoise and the Hare" out of papier mache and arrange my creation in their eternal race on the dining room table—a table that my friend, Dorothy, and I previously antiqued along with six matching chairs. I reupholster an old chair that my mother discarded. I sew and stuff red-checked gingham Christmas trees, make a quilt, decoupage a hinged box, fashion candle holders out of stacked glass jelly jars, and make Christmas cards with stamps from cut potatoes.

My Grandmother Bauer hangs the weedy, baked and sprayed gold '78 record on her dining room wall, but nothing works to satisfy an aching discontent.

No thing.

Chapter 14
Breaks Through

The future enters into us long before it happens.
                                             -Rainer Maria Rilke

November, 1980

Dream

I am coming home from grade school and walking in the front door of 707 Blaine. From the dining room I can see my mother standing between her ironing board and the wood stove. She is ironing one of my dresses. And there, in front of the ironing board, on the kitchen table, wrapped in pure white tissue paper and tied with a shiny red ribbon is a shoebox-sized package.

I am excited.

"Is that package for me?" I ask and reach for the gift.

My mother nods her head and I quickly slip off the ribbon, tear off the tissue, and lift the cover. Lying in the box is a beating and bleeding heart. A scream sticks in my throat. I look up and see a knife sticking out between my mother's breasts. Her head slumps, her body begins to deflate like a punctured balloon. As she sinks to the kitchen floor she groans out her last words to me.

"I cut my heart out for you!"

"It's a nightmare," I tell Father Townes, a Jesuit priest, whom I contacted to be my spiritual guide as I explored my dilemma about a career choice. A slight man about my height and age, Father Townes says I am the first Protestant woman he has ever guided. Now, sitting across from me, in his study, he raises his eyebrows in expectation.

Father Townes is quiet for a few moments before breaking the silence. "This dream was a few years ago?"

"Yes, while I was on a week-end pass at home from the psych ward. Stan woke me up out of it. He said I was whimpering."

"Did you tell him the dream?"

"No. I've never told anyone. The dream freaked me out … still does."

"What do you think the dream is trying to tell you?"

"Obviously, how my mother sacrificed for me."

"Did she?"

"Well, you know, the kind of sacrifice…'Oh, *I'll* eat the chicken gizzard…you can have the nice white meat…' She was good at that kind of sacrifice."

Father Townes smiles and waits for me to continue.

"Naturally, there are the years of her washing, cooking, ironing…she was ironing the night I wanted the hot water bottle, but I've already told you the story about me pouring the boiling water down my stomach. And, she *didn't* sacrifice for me *that* night.

"More often she sacrificed *me*…and tied my sacrifice to being a good Christian."

"What?"

"She made me walk to school with a crippled girl. She made me play with a kid with a deformed ear who pushed my friend off the bridge onto an ice block on Saunders Creek. She made me invite Jane Klaus to my tenth birthday party. Jane brought a Kotex belt and snapped everyone with it. The rest of us didn't know what the thing was. The worst sacrifice of my whole body was the worms."

January, 1946

Mother hangs up the telephone, looks at me, and announces, "Mrs. Englander is coming over. She wants to see your worms. She's worried that Teddy and Jimmy might get worms, too."

I am standing next to the kitchen table and itching my butt through my brown corduroy overalls. I shake my head no.

"Take your hands away from there," my father scolds between bites of his supper, "and quit biting your fingernails. You got worms from biting your fingernails."

I don't like Teddy and Jimmy. They bite and kick sand when I'm playing. And I don't want to take my pants down in front of their mother.

"Mrs. Englander has never seen worms," my mother explains. "What if Teddy and Jimmy get worms, too? You have to help Mrs. Englander."

"No," I whine. I don't want her to see my butt.

Mother scolds. "You don't want Teddy and Jimmy to get worms. You have to be a *good* girl and let Mrs. Englander see your worms. She needs to know what to look for."

I don't know what my worms look like either, and I don't care if Teddy and Jimmy get worms.

When Mrs. Englander walks across the neighbors' back yards and into the kitchen, Mother takes me by the arm and pulls me into the downstairs bathroom. Mrs. Englander, who is even bigger than my mother, follows. Mother stands me on the blue flowered chenille bath mat, slides the straps of my overalls over my shoulders and presses her hands into my shoulders.

"Now turn around, Nancy, and lean over the tub," she orders and turns me toward the claw-foot bathtub. I press my chest into the hard white enamel. I am looking across the tub at the pink and blue and yellow soap bubbles on the bathroom wallpaper as Mother, in one quick sweep, pulls down my overalls and underpants.

"Nancy Lu! Mrs. Englander can't see. Lean over *further!*"

Mother is angry. I stretch my five-year-old arms down into the tub. Then, as Mother pulls apart my cheeks, I squeeze my eyes shut and push. And with a blinding flash, I pop like a tiny pink bubble and float away into a dark velvet pocket.

Father Townes hands me a box of tissue from a table beside his chair, shakes his head as if in disbelief and says, "So, you survived by completely popping away in your mind…like a bubble."

Whoa! Father Townes' comment blows new bubbles into my consciousness. I wonder if there is a connection between the bubble bursting my mind away from my body at the age of five and a lightning bolt sizzling through the dark velvet pocket twenty-five years later. Did that bone-jarring strike pop my mind *back into my body?*

"So, did you make some kind of sense about your gruesome dream?" Father Townes asks.

I hesitate to answer because I am remembering that my mother's red ribbon package looks like the gift the red rubber demon gave me while I was sitting on the floor of my hospital room with Rusty in St. Elizabeth's. I didn't unwrap the gift then and didn't see it again until now. Too many connections are happening all at once. I don't know how to answer.

"So, what are you feeling about the dream now?" Father Townes prompts.

"Like I told you, at first I was terrorized…"

"And, now?"

"Now I am pissed!" I'm surprised at my response and realize my raised voice and crude language may upset this priest, but he nods as if I uncovered an important piece of information.

"I didn't ask for her to sacrifice for me," I continue. "And, I didn't *want* her sacrifice—or, her bleeding heart!"

Father Townes nods again. "Kind of like what we've been taught about Jesus for centuries."

"You mean the 'Jesus died for me' stuff? Like I didn't ask Jesus to sacrifice for me either…or be forced to take his ribbon wrapped cross gift and string me up tight with it for the rest of my life?"

Father Townes is smiling. "That's one interpretation," he says.

"But I've been baptized. One of the teachers at the Ecumenical Institute said, 'We've been branded just like cattle.' And, he said we can't ever be *unbaptized*."

"Do you want to be unbaptized?"

"I don't think so. I think there is value within it somewhere."

December 15, 1980

Dream

No one is in the church when I arrive. A plain wooden table is in the center of the room. I feel a need to straighten a throw rug and toss some pillows to the back of a couch. Now I hear people arriving, chattering and laughing together. I freeze separate, when I see a strange man is approaching me. He is dark-haired, about an inch taller than I am. I notice his chest is crooked as if twisted by a brace. He pulls me into his arms and holds me close.

"We need each other," he whispers. And, is kissing me…we are still kissing. I am in a deep, soft, black pocket…we are still kissing…I am completely whole and just floating…in the moment…kissing.

As we part, I notice the others gathered into a circle. The stranger with the broken chest says to me, "Now, you'll kiss like that all around the circle!" I am scared! I say, "Oh no! Oh no! I can't. That would be too much joy for me! I couldn't stand it. I might burst."

People begin to leave the circle and wander around. Some sit down. A group to my right is discussing how important the kissing is to them. A woman's name is mentioned. The voice continues, "She's a neat lady, but she will not let herself be kissed." Now I am beginning to feel familiar discomfort with the group. I feel sorrow at being invited to ecstasy and turning it down. I think, "I've missed something wonderful!" Familiar little hammers beat on me, pounding out thoughts: "What's wrong with me anyhow?"

March, 1981

While shopping at Conkey's Bookstore in downtown Appleton, I'm surprised to see Rusty in the recent fiction section. After we greet each other, she asks, "How are you?"

"Oh, I'm okay," I answer, wondering if Rusty—out of her art therapy setting—is asking more than a polite surface question.

"Really?" Her eyebrows slip into a sceptic scrunch.

"Well, I'm working part-time at a church."

"Oh?"

"Yes. My pastor created a job for me—Ministries Coordinator. I work with education, programming… "

"Do you like what you're doing?"

"Mostly, but it's Lent and March is a bad time for me. I get depressed …all my hospitalizations were at this time."

"*All* of them?"

Heat flushes into my cheeks. I check the aisles for other shoppers before I blurt out, "I was hospitalized again in March three years ago. Just for the weekend. Nagler was off. I got Janssen." I wrinkle my nose. "He was terrible."

Rusty is quiet, waiting for me to say more.

I briefly describe Nagler's grenade word "sabotage" and my explosion, a courageous, but humiliating attempt to work it through.

"I'm sorry," Rusty says. "What are you working at now?"

"You mean at the church?"

"No. I mean your own growing."

I'm surprised to hear myself say, "I'd love to know what Nagler wrote about me."

"You can see your records, Nancy."

"Really? How?"

"I'm not sure. Ask Dr. Nagler. Tell him what you want. He'll tell you what you have to do to see them."

Dr. Nagler agrees to see me at his St. Elizabeth's office. Nothing has changed in the first floor hallway of the hospital. As I walk toward the elevator, I walk past the same information desk, same bank of telephones, same statue of the suffering Jesus, his bleeding heart dripping down his chest and eyes rolled up into his head in eternal agony. My finger shakes as I push the elevator buttons.

Dr. Nagler's door is open. He invites me into his sea-green office. The office I have flooded with waves of tears. The office in which he leaned back in his tan leather chair on rollers and said, "No, you can't go home yet...No, not yet...No. No."

He sinks down into his comfortable chair. I sit on one of the two straight chairs. I have rehearsed my opening line. I deliver it well.

"I want to see my records."

"Hmmm. They're downstairs in the library."

Okay, Nancy. We're doing fine here. What's your next line?

"How do I see them?"

Good girl, Nancy. You're behaving appropriately. You didn't say, "Which hoops do I have to jump through?" You simply said, "How do I see them? Atta girl!"

"You may visit them during the hours the library is open. Just tell the librarian—the clerk behind the counter—you want to see them."

Visit? Did he say VISIT? I can VISIT myself? What a privilege! A missing chapter of my life is lying on a library shelf like a sick patient and I can visit? Maybe I can take myself out on loan? Or, parole? Careful! Be careful Nancy!

"When is the library open?" I ask politely.

Dr. Nagler looks at his watch. "It should be open now," he answers.

Anxious to see my records, I stand up ready to go downstairs. I am relieved because getting what I want has been easier than I thought. I'm confident. Strong ... until I open Dr. Nagler's office door to leave and hear his cautionary words.

"Sometimes people see their records and have questions. If you do, you can call me."

What? What am I going to see that will raise questions? What does he know about me that I don't know about me? What terrible demons are lying there just waiting to be let loose?

"Thank you," I manage to say and pull his door shut behind me.

Now frightened, but still determined to see my records, I follow the doctor's orders and take the elevator to the ground floor. Library hours are posted on the door. It will close today in one hour. I can visit myself for sixty minutes before part of me will be locked up again.

A middle-aged woman in a green smock, dark hair, and washed-out face is standing behind the counter. She looks at her watch and scowls at me as I approach.

I can barely squeak out my name and my request past pinched vocal cords. She sighs, walks back between rows of metal shelving, and returns with an inch thick folder.

"There is a table over there," she says pushing the folder toward me and pointing to the end of the room. "You can stay and read until we close."

As I pick up the folder, she adds, "And those records *must not* leave this room."

"Okay," I say, nodding my head and clutching the folder to my breasts. I do not add the cynical questions that accompany me to the table.

No strolling me down the hall to see the babies?
No release for temporary sanity?
No daring escape over the wall via helicopter?

Still trembling, I sit at the table and open the folder. My three hospitalization records are arranged in chronological order. The first page is an admission form dated 3/16/70. I barely see my name, age, gender, and religious affiliation because Dr. Nagler's diagnosis, scrawled in thick, black, ink, is the most prominent writing on the page: **Acute psychotic reaction, other.**

The psychotic reaction wasn't so "*cute*," I think, trying to ignore the stab in my belly from the diagnosis. And, what the hell is *other*?

I flip to page two. Dr. Nagler lists follow-up plans and medications in one short paragraph. Page three—Stan's signature on a consent form authorizes medical care and treatment. Dr. Stein and Dr. Nagler fill the next four pages with physical examinations and consultations: *This is a 30 year old mother of four who presents with the chief complaint of 'I think the world is coming to an end.' Patient has an extensive past psychiatric history of perfectionistic, rigid personality patterns, the need to receive straight A's all through high school ...*

I notice mistakes in details of my father's death (in 1970 he is still alive) and mistakes in spelling, ("her husband is a *principle*"), but I keep my perfectionistic personality bridled and don't correct anything.

And then I read the next to last paragraph in Dr. Nagler's summary: *Treatment they (MMPI) predicted would be slow and prognosis for psychotherapy quite poor. It was felt that her pattern was consistent with a psychotic individual.*

Psychotic? *Psychotic?* An *incurable psychotic?* I can't swallow. I am worse than worthless.

I am bad. Evil.

Forever.

Tears blur the words of Dr. Nagler's last paragraph:

Diagnostically, I would see her as going through an acute hypomanic reaction shortly following an intense emotional experience at the Ecumenical Institute. Her chances for recovery from this acute condition are favorable, but the underlying chronic depressive disorder would require much more intensive psychotherapy.

Dr. Nagler's *last* sentence sounds like a *life* sentence.

I wipe my eyes and look at a clock on the wall above the library door. Twenty minutes until closing time. I turn past my condemned future to several pages of nurses' records: medications, blood pressure, temperature, weight, and bowel movements.

Then, immediately following a page on blood work, I find what I've been looking for—The Progress Record. I begin to read Dr. Stein's first entry.

…*Psychotic depressive reaction in last 48 hours with overt suicidal gestures, garbled speech, memory regression, and marked feelings of inferiority.*

I begin to read Doctor Stein's orders:

1. General Diet
2. Restrain only if violent
3. Watch carefully
4. Tuinal gr iii per mouth – repeat to keep resting…

and then, my attention is snagged with a verbal order recorded by R. Tillitson RN—"*If won't take oral med give Nembutal gr ii IM.*" Does that mean if I hadn't swallowed that little red pill bomb they would have held me down and forced an injection? An intrusion like a rape? Rage at my powerlessness begins to bubble in my gut like a cauldron. Stomach muscles begin to spasm just as the irritable clerk interrupts to tell me the library will close in five minutes.

Before I leave, I want to know what Dr. Janssen wrote about my nefarious plans to sabotage the Ore family. I quickly pick up records from my third hospitalization and on page seven find what I'm looking for:

3/11/78

Pt. wants to continue college course and make hosp. stay brief. However, became upset with even gental (sic) suggestion that her behavior may be an effort to disrupt family Rx.

Gental? *gentle?* Can't he spell? "*Let's see how you're sabotaging your family*" didn't sound either gentle or gental to me.

I count the pages before I turn in the records. 162. I will need to come back.

March 14, 1981

On my forty-first birthday I visit myself again at St. Elizabeth's Medical Record Library. I think about taking flowers, a candle, and a birthday card, but instead I take tissue, a notebook and a plan to ask the library clerk for a copy of my records.

I want to take me home.

During this visit, I have enough time to read the entire three reports all dictated or written by doctors, nurses, aides, and social workers. Some written in another language. Some simply illegible. I have time to make some notes before the library hours are over.

"I would like a copy of these records," I tell the clerk as I put the folder on the counter.

"I can make a copy for you," she says. "There is a flat fee for the first few pages and then an additional charge for each page after."

"How much for the whole folder?" I ask.

"Well, I'd have to count the pages," she sighs.

"I counted them," I say, and hoping to save her some time and relieve some of her obvious frustration, I add, "There are 162 pages."

"Oh. Well, by the looks of it, I think it would cost you about $80."

$80? That much?"

"Yes," she says, and scolds, "I *told* you that there would be additional charges after the first few pages!" She realizes that I am not ready to ransom myself and she reaches for my records.

As I step out of the library I notice a copy machine hugging a corner in the hallway. The copier wears a hand-printed sign: $.05 a copy. I calculate again. .05 X 162 = $8.10. I can get me back at a sale price!

The clerk steps around the stack of metal shelving and is irritated to see me back.

"I would like to make my own copy," I say. "On the Xerox in the hallway."

"You can't *do* that!"

"Why not?"

"I *told* you. Those records cannot leave this room!"

Even though I can see she is peeved, I push it with the same kind of behavior that got me into trouble in the unit two floors above.

"How about if I keep one foot *inside* the door and stretch around the corner? I think I can reach the nickel slot."

She glares at me but does not relent. I leave quickly—push through unlocked doors. Am I crazy? Am I crazy "in" this place or crazy "out" of this place? Angry tears flow as I leave, but at least I'm free.

Though Dr. Nagler told me to call if I have questions, I call Rusty instead. After describing my experience—including my perverse behavior—she suggests I call Dr. Wahlbruhn, the doctor who attended my third hospitalization.

Dr. Wahlbruhn agrees to order a copy of my records that should be ready in a few days. He informs me that I will not be charged.

April 3, 1981

I have them! I have them! I cradle this imprisoned part of me on my lap all the way home like a new baby swaddled in a plain brown wrapper. I laugh. I cry. I croon. Baby. Nancy. Baby…I don't brake driving down Lawe Street hill. The tires hum as I cross the waffled steel drawbridge over the Fox River and belt out the last stanza of *Love Divine, All Loves Excelling*: *"Finish then, thy new creation; pure and spotless let us be…"*

April 16, 1981

Rusty agrees to meet me for lunch at the new restaurant on the corner of College and Oneida.

"I'm buying," I say when she arrives.

"What's the occasion?" she asks, sits down, and picks up the menu.

"I got a copy of my records, and I want to thank you for your help."

"Oh. How did you get them?" Rusty asks. "Did Ted Nagler help?"

"Not really. I got them by calling Dr. Wahlbruhn." I quit talking when the waitress arrives to take our orders. "Dr. Nagler," I continue, "said I could call him if I wanted to talk with him about what I read."

"Did you?"

"No. I don't trust him. Nor Janssen. I'm seeing Father Townes."

"Who's he?"

"He's a spiritual director at the Jesuit Retreat Center in Oshkosh."

"*Why?*" Rusty, who calls herself a born-again pagan, narrows her eyes at me. "Dr. Nagler wouldn't let me talk about God," I answer in a defensive whine.

"Is that important?"

"Well, my image of God—at least as 'father'—blew up in 1970, but Father Townes helped me with my guilt about trying to kill myself. None of the psychiatrists ever mentioned my suicide attempt. And, I'm upset with some of the things I read in my records. Dr.Nagler's summary report made it sound like I'm a psychotic with no hope of recovery. I get panicky. I cry a lot."

The waitress appears with our salads. We thank her and begin eating. After a few bites, Rusty breaks the silence.

"What about Stan?"

"What about him?"

"Do you talk with him? About your fears ... the records?"

"No! We never really talk, and we're not in a very good place right now. We hardly ever see each other. When we do, we argue."

"What about?"

"Everything. He bulls ahead with plans and makes decisions without telling me. I get pissed. He gets silent. The other night I screamed that I felt ignored. He said that I was just trying to be in control and told me to 'just go ahead.' So, he even wants to be in control of my being in control."

"How did you answer?"

"I said I didn't want to be in control. I just wanted to be part of the decision making process going on. He picked up the latest Newsweek and headed for his crappy green chair. I started crying and climbed up into the loft. When I start crying, it's like I've opened a scrapbook of old tragedies. Cry over every picture I see in my head. I'm afraid I will end up back in the crazy camp."

"When was the last time you were hospitalized?"

"March, 1978. Just for that weekend I told you about."

"Who admitted you?"

"Dr. Wahlbruhn. He wrote in his report that I thought I just needed some R and R."

"Is that true?"

"I don't remember."

"Did you get R and R?"

"No. Janssen was on call for Nagler."

"Oh. Now I remember Janssen's *sabotage* comment to you."

"I'm still hurt by the way he back-handed me when I pleaded with him to help me. *I really* wanted to understand what I was doing that was sabotaging my family. It was terrible. The mental health folks might as well say, 'You'll get healthy if you learn to ask *appropriately* for what you want, but if what you want doesn't suit us or doesn't fit our rules, we have the power to deny your request. Oh, yes. And, while we're at it, we'll humiliate you, too.'"

"I'm so sorry," Rusty says and reaches out to place her hand over mine. "Nancy," she says, looking calmly into my eyes, "if you need a break, why don't you go to the Holiday Inn?"

I laugh, but Rusty's words drop like sweet, new rain into cracks of my parched brain.

July 25, 1981

Dream

I am on a dark street in a foreign country and to escape a rainstorm I run into a building that turns out to be a men's club. I see a man wearing glasses and dressed in dark clothing coming toward me. I notice the right side of his head is all shaved and bandaged as if he had either surgery or a bad accident. The bandages are flesh-colored and lumpy. I wonder if he is okay, but I don't say anything until he is passing me. As we say "Hello," the man begins to slump and his coat falls open. I see he's wearing a collar and is an Episcopal priest. I feel strong rescuing buttons being pushed – great concern about his well-being. I go to him quickly and ask, "Are you all right?"

He says, "No," and slumps down further. I reach out. He hangs onto me and I cradle him. Now we are standing. He is only a little taller than I am and he has his head resting on my left shoulder. The embrace feels very good. Earlier I had thought he was rather ugly. Now I am aware he's a nice-looking man. I say, "Can I do anything for you?" He looks me straight in the eye and says, "Yes, you can go to bed with me." I am torn. He puts his head back on my shoulder. I put my tongue in the upper fold of his ear. I kiss his ear. I say, "I am married." He says, "I thought you would be." Now, he breaks away and begins to quickly run down the street. I begin to run after him, but am unable to catch him.

July 28, 1981

Rusty and I meet for lunch at the Chinese restaurant near St. Elizabeth's. Between spoonfuls of egg drop soup, we catch up on family news, and, as we're finishing our meal, I describe my latest unfulfilled sexual priest dream.

"You're meeting your shadow," Rusty says.

"But my shadow men keep running away or refusing to go to bed with me," I say and picture the caped silhouette logo on the spines of the crime books at the library. I swallow more soup while silently stirring memories of recurring dreams.

"Maybe you are doing the running," Rusty says, interrupting my mental scan. "What's happening with you and Stan?"

"What does he have to do with the dreams?" I scrunch my eyebrows in confusion.

"Well, maybe the dreams are giving you clues about how you make decisions with him."

"You mean sex?"

Rusty shrugs and brushes back a wisp of auburn hair that has slipped onto her cheek. Several times she has heard me describe my difficulty saying no.

"I feel paralyzed now when he wants sex," I say breaking a silence. "I'm aware I want to say no, but I always submit."

"Do you see any connection with your dreams?"

I shake my head and look down. All I can see is an empty soup bowl.

"When are you going to go to bed with an Episcopalian priest?" Rusty asks, nonchalantly, as if unaware her words have landed like a lit fuse in my gut.

"They're your dreams," Rusty adds, "but you can't really say 'no' until you can say 'yes.'"

Journal: December 21, 1981

Several days ago, I had coffee at the Casbah with Reverend Somers. He told me he would be requesting a new appointment in June. Reverend Somers had created a paid part-time position for me as a Ministries Coordinator and I've enjoyed my job.

After I expressed my disappointment that Reverend Somers would be leaving, I told him that once-upon-a-time I had considered ministry and asked him about steps toward entering seminary. As soon as we returned to the church office, he gave me a book *The Christian as Minister*. I read the complete manual before leaving the office.

At supper, I show Stan the book.

"Are you planning to go to seminary?" he asks, his eyes narrowed.

"No ..." My answer is tentative. I put the book next to my plate and continue. "But when I had to write a rationale for my independent major, I included my intention of pursuing ordained ministry. So, I guess I was thinking about it then."

The only sound from my husband is the scrape of the knife as he cuts another piece of his pork chop. I keep talking.

"This book describes several options for ministry that I wasn't even aware of. Not all of them require seminary."

"Like what?"

"I could work with church music, or Christian Ed. I'd probably need some more education, but ... this house is finished ... the kids are gone ..."

Stan's shrug reminds me that I'm not convinced myself of future career options. No longer hungry, I push mashed potatoes around my plate, while Stan describes an issue he's facing at East. Later, I tuck *The Christian as Minister* in the bookcase between my 1952 RSV Bible and Stan's copy of Michener's *The Source*.

December 22, 1981

Dream

I am at a grayish-white door of an elevator, trying to decide whether to get on or not. I somehow know that if I do I will die. I decide to leave everything behind me and get on the elevator. I am afraid. I look up. About 5-6 flights up is a hole. I am in a chute. It is all white and very smooth. At the top a dark haired nurse with glasses is waving. I feel safe now to make the trip. I get out at the top. As the dream unfolds I realize I am not dead really – but I will be sent back to earth to help someone learn to accept his/her dying of cancer.

June, 1982

"Prayer is not a method. It's how much love of God you receive," Father Rossi smiles as he introduces prayer as the topic for the third day of this eight-day Sadhana Retreat. Father Rossi, a contemplative East Indian with an English accent, blends eastern and western mysticism into his leadership. Each day, wearing informal street clothes instead of a collar, he repeats his definition of the Gospel: *My Father is madly in love with you sinners. Receive the love.*

In love? Madly? After a decade of therapy, I believe I'm *okay*, but *loved*?

In April, when Father Townes encouraged me to attend the retreat, he assured me my presence as a laywoman among three dozen nuns would be fine. I am grateful that the retreat is a silent one and that the only conversation is to reflect with others after we experience one of this guest priest's spiritual exercises.

Yesterday, Father Rossi led the participants in an exercise that included a dialog with one other person. A nun sitting to my right and I followed the directions to look at each other as if we were Jesus and, after we shared what we saw, we were to report what we thought the other person's Jesus was like. Loving, kind, and open, were the words my partner and I used to describe what we saw and heard.

This morning, I am sitting in the back row next to the same nun I talked with yesterday. Again, she is encased in her black and white habit. Again, straight gray hair peeks out from underneath a tight band across her forehead. Again, her smile ripples soft wrinkles across her cheeks.

"Why do we pray?" Father Rossi asks. "We pray to remove internal blocks," he answers his question, and adds, "God is already within."

Veiled heads blot out my view of his slight frame as he walks across the front of the room. "So prayer is making love to God," he continues. "There are only two things that can prevent your experience of receiving God's love. You have the wrong idea of God or you have not experienced human love."

As he finishes his description of prayer, he invites us to close our eyes and be in touch with our breathing. Wrapped in my black, velvet cloud safe space, I open my consciousness to the warm words of this man of God.

"Look at Jesus who is looking at you. He is looking at you lovingly and humbly. When love is very deep it is humble…and you surrender. Jesus feels privileged to love you. Allow yourself to be loved by Christ…"

Stunned with what happens in my meditative silence that follows, I am relieved that Father Rossi doesn't ask us to share our experience. Although I have heard that nuns become brides of Christ, I have never heard a nun describe her wedding night with their Lord. During this love tryst with Jesus, did any of these other women crumple a cap? Snap a cincture? Tear a tunic?

No wonder silence is the preferred milieu. I'm way too embarrassed at my x-rated response to an image. A gentle man, but still an *image*. I don't *ever* want to describe my encounter with Jesus. To anyone.

Anyone includes Father Townes a few days later.

"Did you like the retreat?" he asks, sitting behind his desk. His usual spot.

"At first I was uncomfortable with all the nuns, but I liked Father Rossi a lot and learned a lot."

"So, what's happening with you, now?"

"Well, I took pages and pages of notes. Father Rossi had completely different takes on the Bible stories than I learned as a kid."

"And?" Father Townes leans forward.

"I want to know more."

"You've talked several times about going to seminary. Have you given any more recent thought to it?" Father Townes raises his eyebrows inviting my reaction.

"I think about going," I sigh.

I don't share my list of hindrances: money, fear of failure, leaving home, family and friends. Father Townes has heard my hesitations ad nauseum. Still waiting for me to answer he spreads his hands out toward me, prompting my response.

"Not now … " I say.

"Well," he says and smiles, "if you don't go now, when *will* you go?"

IV
From School to Seminary
1982-1985

Chapter 15
Back to the Future

The longest, most arduous trip in the world is often the journey from the head to the heart. Until that round trip is completed, we remain at war with ourselves. And, of course, those at war with themselves are apt to make casualties of others.
                                                -William Sloane Coffin

Garrett-Evangelical Theological Seminary
Journal: September 7, 1982
    9:30 p.m.

    I'm here—at present sitting on a bed in a double room—the other side of which will not be occupied this term. I have a view of Lake Michigan. The room is pleasant and has just enough space in the form of wardrobes, desks, and drawers to hold the paraphernalia I brought. I have gone through two days of unpacking, orientation, and trying to remember names of new strangers—people with whom I'm supposed to build a community. I'm called a Level I – first year seminarian. I have not met anyone in my situation. Most are younger than me and I can see young women—many right out of college—inspecting me. They look me up and down. I look in the mirror and see weepy, schizophrenic, eyes looking back at me.

    Yesterday, holding back tears, I left home and Stan. He seemed choked up, too. As I drove I felt something die, but I don't know what it was. The sky was gray and sweating a fine mist. I cried all the way to Fond du Lac, periodically asking myself "What *am* I doing?" I don't have an answer. I had such an urge to call it all off and rush home. But something else kept me coming—and made me promise to try it for at least three weeks.

The 200-mile trip took four hours with a coffee stop at Hwy Q north of Milwaukee. Several other Level I's asked if I'll be commuting. Even though I'm here all week, I'm considered a commuter because I plan to drive home on weekends.

Now I'm preparing my "home" here for a while. I took out a checking account, bought a parking sticker, went to the post office to provide my address, and registered without a major foul up. All these feed my sense of competency.

Perhaps a new birth has already occurred.

Tonight, as I walked into Howes Chapel for vespers, I was hit with the musty smell of old church buildings. The smell was *identical* to the buildings at Camp Byron—Ingraham Hall Dorm and the Tabernacle—and I was back in my teen years. I could feel the idealistic commitment—high religious stuff—that I felt then.

Summer 1953

I sit with other junior high campers on the lawn in front of Ingraham Hall for the Thursday night Consecration Service. Reverend Herschberg stands by a blazing campfire in front of a rough-hewn cross. The flames cast an aura around his towering frame as he preaches to a hundred boys and girls about following Jesus. His voice is smooth, like honey. His hands, with long, tapering fingers, are spread out in huge, soothing fans. I am mesmerized.

As he finishes his sermon, he invites us to commit our lives to Jesus.

"Some of you may want to stand to indicate your allegiance to Jesus," he says with a slight lisp that twists the word allegiance into a rolling sigh. "Or if you plan to serve Jesus in your local congregation, you may decide to come part way forward. But if you want to give your *whole* life to Jesus, I invite you to come all the way up to the cross. Now is the time for you to decide."

Hesitant to go "all the way" with Jesus, but entranced by Reverend Herschberg's luring words, I get up and walk part way to the cross. I stand with several other campers in a warm glow while Reverend Herschberg prays. He thanks the heavenly Father for dedicated boys and girls and then sends us back to sit on the grass for a song that we sing softly, slowly, and unaccompanied.

In'a my heart. In'a my heart. Come into my heart, Lord Jesus.
Come in today. Come in to stay. Come into my heart, Lord Jesus.

Tingling with holy fervor, from my place in the back row, I hear Reverend Herschberg give a prayer of blessing and then address those who stepped forward toward the cross.

"Boys and girls," he says in melodious tones, "you may wonder what you can do if you've given your life to Jesus. Boys," he continues, "you might become ministers. Girls, you may become minister's wives."

While walking back from Howes Chapel to my dorm room, I remember picturing myself then as a minister's wife, wearing a dark-blue paisley dress, hair pulled back into a bun, and married to some gray-haired man with wire-rimmed glasses.

What is that about? Those feelings plus my experiences for 30 years are complex and there must be important information in there somewhere for me. I want to sort it out, but how?

I wonder if my years between 13 and 42 were years of wilderness—29 years in which I wandered around, carrying some golden calf or other and looking for the Promised Land. And why *now*? At 42? Am I where

I'm supposed to be now? Or am I here to exorcise that musty smell of dead saints and dead commitments?

Earlier, during vespers, I let myself "feel" the smell and emotions surrounding it. I felt loneliness—and the old *longing* to feel loved—the hope that God/Christ/*Something* does love me, although I certainly can't feel it. Briefly I felt trapped, as if I were one of the cement statues carved into the altar and adornments. Still imprisoned by my 1953 commitment to Christ. While those camp years were bitter sweet years experienced in my adolescence, I wonder what impact they've had on my life journey. I plan to sit in Howes Chapel again. Perhaps I'll get some clues that reveal the very thing I'm looking for here—*and* the *only* thing.

Old Methodist buildings smell musty as if saints left their clothes in the walls. I still sit in hand-me-down clothes and stale traditions… dressed in a campfire promise made thirty years ago.

September 7, 1982

Dream

I am in a group of people at an outdoor party. I see Stan with his arms around a woman I don't know. I realize he is not my husband any longer. Now he is talking and touching someone else. He is popular and being sought out as a lover by several young women. I know I have no claim on him. I realize that our separation was my idea. I was the one who wanted time and space to explore. He is walking past me now with his arm around a young woman with long, blond, hair. She knows who I am and scowls at me. Now he is alone. I go to him and say, "I love you. I know I have no claim on you, but I hope you will want to get married again." He just listens, says, "Perhaps," and leaves.

September 9, 1982

Three other students and I are sitting at one end of Loder Lounge ready for the first meeting of our Intro to Ministry Group. The professor who will lead our group arrives and asks us to arrange our chairs into a small circle. He introduces himself, "Please call me Rand," he says and adds, "I'm new here, too. This is my first quarter at G-ETS. I was raised in Montana, taught various places, most recently in Boston. I apologize for having us meet right next to the cafeteria," he says, referring to the noisy group of people exiting the seminary lunchroom. "Next week we'll be meeting in a quiet setting. I'll contact you to let you know which room."

No one in this group is my age except Rand. He has a square, tanned face framed with salt and pepper hair, a neatly trimmed beard and piercing, dark brown eyes. "Let's begin by introducing ourselves," he says. "Give your name, then tell a little bit about yourself and why you have come to Garrett."

I listen as the other Level I students give their names and reasons for entering seminary. Each of them is clear that God has called them to some form of ministry: local pastor, missionary, chaplain.

When the others have finished commenting, Rand looks expectantly at me.

"I'm Nancy Ore," I say. "I live in Appleton, Wisconsin. I'm a commuter student...plan to go home most weekends. My husband and I live in a passive solar home." But my reasons for being here? I look around at the others whose entries to seminary sound as if God sent them a personally signed letter in calligraphy. I can't tell these holy people that I'm here because I want to interpret the Jesus stories for *myself*. Instead, I say, "I really don't know *why* I'm here. I think I just wanted to get out of Appleton."

No one laughs.

As the noisy chatter of students and clink of tableware dies and the late lunch crowd disperses, Rand begins outlining the course's expectations.

"We'll meet once a week during the year. We'll discuss various issues around ministry. You'll have time for questions and problems you may experience. All our conversations are to be kept confidential." Rand looks directly at each of us. "This is meant to be a place of support for you."

He then spends 20 minutes talking about a Ministry Project, a paper that will be due at the end of the second quarter. "This paper is required and it's content will determine whether or not you will advance to Level II. The paper must address your view of ministry and understanding of your call. We'll be talking more about this during our weekly meetings."

Call. Great. Maybe God's call to me is a wrong number.

Curt, the man who said God is calling him to be a pastor, groans, and asks, "How many pages?"

"At least ten," Rand answers.

Like me, Curt must feel overwhelmed with the other class syllabi and professors' expectations for Level I students. Unlike Curt, I welcome the challenge of this paper. I can always come up with bullshit that sounds good, but I want the search to be real. Whatever *that* is.

"Your paper will be read by two professors," Rand adds. "I'll be in touch with you." As we're dismissed, Curt asks to see Rand.

I walk out of Loder and through the main building back to Howes Chapel, where I smelled thirty-year-old memories. No one is here. I put my book bag on the back pew and sit next to it. This time the musty odor is barely detectable. Maybe the worship space needs night and people.

How am I ever going to figure out God's *call* to me? I want God's idea for me to be revealed in neon lights or a personal ad in the classifieds. I thought the 1970 weekend at the Ecumenical Institute was God calling. And then I thought God was demanding I kill myself to prove my love for him. Always a *him*. Kill myself for some man. And then I got locked up. Shame and isolation don't fit my picture of the deep joy that supposedly comes from answering God's call.

Is there something wrong with me because I don't have a clear message from God-whatever-whoever-that is about what I'm doing here?

Journal: September 16, 1982

Garrett's buildings used to be right next to Lake Michigan's shore, but years of land-fill and a sprawling Northwestern University pushed the lake several hundred yards from my dorm room. I like to walk over to the lake and sit on the huge rocks to meditate. The rip-rap keeps the waves from washing both campuses away.

Today on my way over, I picked up a two-foot long weathered board I found lying under a weeping willow. As I held the wood, I felt old and used. Stiff, with slivers and knots. I couldn't decide which end was the head and which end the toe and began to cry.

A few days ago, while driving down here, I felt something had died and I didn't know what it was. Maybe the "old" Nancy is dead. I think my relationship with Stan—at least the old marriage—is dead, too.

This morning at breakfast someone asked a woman sitting across from me why she was here. She answered with a quote from a newspaper article about a Native American woman who had trekked from Washington State to Door County. "This is my soul's journey," the woman answered when asked why she had walked such a long way.

I wish I had heard that quote before my Intro to Ministry Group. Instead of saying something stupid like wanting to get out of Appleton, I could have said that being here feels like I'm taking a step into my soul's journey. I drag along my soul's needs like I lug my body, mind, and books from class to class. I'm not clear whether ordained ministry is a part of my future, but I am clear that the need for me to exist and survive alone for awhile *is* part of my growing.

Curt told me I could get coffee at Norris Student Center, only a block from the rip-rap. This morning as I went to a cup of coffee, I put the old board back where I found it.

The willow tree can do the weeping.

Journal: September 19, 1982

When I spotted Stan coming down the concourse at O'Hare, I was startled to see my father's face replace my husband's in a quick flash, then disappear. Stan was on his way home from a week-end meeting in Kansas. I was glad to see him. We planned to visit a couple hours before he caught Air Wisconsin back to Appleton.

He stopped on the concourse and said he could stay and take a morning flight. Lots of people were hurrying around us so I don't know if he saw my reaction. At least he couldn't see my sinking stomach. When I asked him *why,* he said he thought he would surprise me, that we could get a motel and I could bring him back to O'Hare in the morning.

I didn't like his surprise. I asked him if he didn't have to be back at East early tomorrow? He said he told his secretary he would be back in the afternoon. So he had already planned it. He said I could show him Evanston. Though I felt strange being in charge, I enjoyed showing him the campus. I drove. I knew the roads.

We ended up at a Holiday Inn in Skokie. I tried to tell him what I was experiencing in my classes, but he was more interested in my body than my mind. I woke up in the night with a headache and nausea.

The heavy loneliness for Stan that I hauled around like a bag full of rocks is gone. Everything about our relationship has changed.

September 23, 1982

Evelyn Jacobs' office is a closet-sized room on the third floor of the main building with a desk, two chairs in addition to her office chair, and a small table near a window that looks down onto the seminary lawn. Shelves filled with dozens of psychology books line two walls. When I arrive—out of breath because there is no elevator—she is sitting behind her desk.

"Come on in." Evelyn grins a dimpled smile at me. She indicates a place for me to sit. I settle in the chair in front of her wooden desk and lean my gray canvas book bag against the chair legs. Her desk is piled with more books and cluttered with a stack of file folders.

"Thank you for seeing me," I say, and add, "I'm sorry to be interrupting your work."

"That's okay. How can I help you?"

I'm not sure how to explain why I want this 15-minute appointment.

This morning, in the Intro to Pastoral Counseling class, Evelyn showed the first part of "Everybody Rides the Carousel." Eight stages of psychosocial development a la Erik Erickson. During the birth scenes, I thought of my children and began spilling quiet tears about what a rotten mother I'd been. I was still weepy when I handed in my evaluation of the class that Evelyn requires of the students. I asked Evelyn for a 15-minute appointment.

But I don't want to talk about my mother guilt with Evelyn. I want to talk about Aaron, a man I noticed the first day of class. He always looks sleepy, and he never takes his coat off. He seems angry most of the time, and, when he speaks up in class, he stutters and blinks a lot and doesn't make much sense.

Evelyn is still waiting for my answer. "I'm worried about Aaron," I say. "I didn't want to write about him during my class evaluation."

"What are you worried about?"

"I think he might need help."

"What kind of help?"

"Well, during the brief discussion after the film this morning, he disagreed loudly with you and when you tried to understand what he was angry about, he ended up laughing. I've noticed he seems upset a lot, but when you try to understand, he gets even more defensive."

"I've noticed that, too." Evelyn nods and adds, "Is there anything else that you are worried about?"

"Well, after class I saw him in the hallway. I was carrying an empty pop can. To recycle. He grabbed it away from me. I hollered for him to give it back.

"He wouldn't. I tried to wrestle it away from him. Aaron was laughing that weird hawking laugh. Three other guys—I don't know their names—saw it. They began laughing, too.

"I was really angry. I managed to get to my room before I cried. Aaron still has the pop can and I am still angry. I think because he poked all my buttons of feeling powerless … with males."

"Yes …" Evelyn folds her hands, places them on an open file folder on her desk, and waits for me to continue.

"But I feel sorry for Aaron. Every time he opens his mouth, somewhere in the middle of his jumble of words, he includes an important piece of information. Like the death of his grandfather last month. Or his second wife coming from Minnesota to be with him."

"You said you felt sorry for Aaron. Do you know why?"

"I'm not sure. He always has that old black coat on. Unbuttoned. He's always dressed up—a shirt and tie and black dress shoes. But that coat … why doesn't he ever take off his coat?"

Evelyn looks at me with raised eyebrows as if she doesn't have an answer for Aaron's behavior either.

"He's clean," I say. "Neat. Shaved. Not one hair—of his thick black hair—is out of place." I can see Aaron's profile, from where he sits in class. Third seat back and two rows over from me. I add, "He's pretty thin and has a kind of a pasty complexion, like maybe he's not eating right."

Evelyn straightens the striped scarf around her neck and says, "Earlier you said you thought Aaron needed help," she says. "What kind of help do you think he needs?"

"Maybe counseling."

"Is there a reason you think that?"

"Well," I hesitate and then say, "I notice his eyes."

"What about them?"

"They're like eyes I saw in a psychiatric unit. You know, that steely stare. The pupils are the size of a pinhead and the rest of the eyes look like they're paralyzed. Stuck in concrete."

"You were in a psychiatric unit?"

I nod. Evelyn is silent, looking at me expectantly, as if waiting for me to add more information. I realize I am holding my breath and in a burst of air blurt out, "I was hospitalized three times. Locked up. Given pills. My eyes probably looked like Aaron's, too."

"Oh," Evelyn said gently. "That must have been a difficult time."

I nod and look away from my professor's penetrating gaze. She sees my lower lids fill with tears and hands me the box of tissue from the corner of her desk.

"How is class for you?" she asks. "Your evaluations let me know you are very aware of yourself. Your reactions."

"Class is fine," I answer. I remember that Evelyn is also my advisor as well as my professor and add, "But the conversations we have raise issues for me."

"What issues?"

"I don't feel as if I fit in here, and …" The tears spill over and trickle down my cheeks.

"And?" Evelyn prompts.

"I'm so lonely … and, things aren't right between my husband and me. I just need someone to talk with."

I reach for another tissue and look at my watch.

"I've already been here twenty minutes," I say. "I'm over my fifteen minutes." "That's okay," Evelyn says. "You have a lot to deal with. I've been thinking you might benefit from seeing a counselor. I don't take students as clients, but I do know a couple of people that might see you. If you decide you would like the contact numbers, let me know."

September 28, 1982

Dante is preaching. The flushing rush of terror is coursing through my body, and something is strangling my brain. I don't hear voices. I don't see shrouded figures. I'm panicked by an internal war between interrupting worship with screaming obscenities or clamping my teeth into silence. *Which behavior does God require of me?* The agony is excruciating.

And, then, Dante is done. The organist begins the last hymn. I have survived another attack.

The panic always hits when I'm in worship. I remember the other Nancy vomiting in Sunday School when we were little. Am I-Nancy trying to keep from "vomiting" angry words in church?

I don't feel comfortable here. The classroom hallways, the dorm, and the library are always bustling with people passing each other. I walk around with a half-frozen smile not knowing whether to greet people or to look down at my feet. I mostly keep my mouth shut.

Evelyn gave me the phone numbers of two counselors she recommends. I have an appointment on October 20 with Dr. Sheldon Pruitt.

I read somewhere that the worst thing about mental illness is to be called sick—or not normal.

October 20, 1982

Dr. Pruitt is at least 6' 3" and slightly overweight. His suit coat is on the back of his office chair. As he bends over to indicate the chair I should sit in, his tie swings out over his loafers. He invites me to sit in a chair like he has in his waiting area—a comfortable straight-backed chair with arms and gray upholstering.

"Tell me what brings you here," he says.

"I'm starting seminary and am having some trouble adjusting. Dr. Jacobs recommended you. She said you work with imagery. I've worked with imagery before and like it."

"What kind of trouble are you having?"

"Well, there is a man in my counseling class that ..." I don't know how to describe my distress.

"Tell me about the man," Dr. Pruitt prompts.

I talk about my interactions with Aaron and my meeting with Dr. Jacobs.

"I will lead you in a process," Dr. Pruitt says after I answer a few more questions. "Can you imagine a place where you are safe?'

I nod.

"When you are comfortable, shut your eyes, and imagine yourself in a place you are completely safe. When you are there, let me know by raising your right index finger."

I close my eyes and the black, velvet, cloud gently enfolds me. I raise my finger. As Dr. Pruitt leads me in a process, I let the images come and tell him what I see: Aaron; my mother forcing me over the bathtub; my father biting me...I go all the way back to Grandma Field. Through the soft curtain of safety I tell Dr. Pruitt that I see my grandmother standing over me. She says, "Be good to your mother, Nancy Lu. She's good to you."

Dr. Pruitt leads me gently back into the present. I open my eyes and listen to his summary of the various scenes I described.

"You were caught in a bind. Told to be responsible, but not how to do it."

I leave his office thinking about being responsible for everyone—including Aaron. I have another appointment November 3.

November 3, 1982

Dr. Pruitt leads me through another imagery process. I start with the pop can thing with Aaron and end with someone hurting me in the dining room of 707 Blaine. He summarizes, "You would rather have folks call you crazy than be angry—or have people angry at *you*."

I prefer being crazy rather than being angry? His words lurch around in my head like billiard balls until they fasten on my fear of being raped.

"I'm afraid of large males," I say and begin to cry. "My husband raped me when I was pregnant with our first child. After he raped me, I became submissive." I hesitate, then add, "And, I want to know what happened to me in the dining room."

"The dining room?"

"My childhood home. I think I was raped on the floor."

"Why do you think that?"

I reluctantly tell Dr. Pruitt about the red, rubber, demon trying to get into the dining room through the window.

He listens, is quiet for a few moments, and then says, "One of your issues is power. You give your power to other people. Do you want your own power?"

I nod. *Why wouldn't I? I think that's one of the reasons I left Appleton.*

"Okay. Close your eyes again and image your confrontation with Aaron. Let me know with your index finger when you are there."

When I indicate I am in the hallway with Aaron, Dr. Pruitt says, "Now, call on your creativity and think of three ways to express your anger without being overly angry, without people calling you crazy, and without people getting angry at *you*."

In the silence that follows, I think of tricking Aaron somehow, or playing the piano, or going to my room to write.

I don't have a clue about how to use my creativity with my husband.

November 8, 1982

"Thank you," I say to Evelyn when I catch up with her in the hallway after chapel.

Evelyn stops at the door to Room 205—the large room that seats our whole Level II class of 85 students. She smiles, puts a piece of paper in the pocket of her forest green skirt.

"Oh, you're welcome," she says and laughs. "What did I do?"

"You recommended Dr. Pruitt. I've seen him a couple times."

"How is it going?" Evelyn turns her head and waves at a man passing by.

"Fine. I am learning I don't have to save the world."

"Great!" Evelyn says.

"I think my sympathy for Aaron was partly my sympathy for my husband. I feel bad about what I put Stan through with all my hospitalizations."

"You are pretty hard on yourself," Evelyn says as we part.

December 1, 1982

"My creativity and energy are blocked," I tell Dr. Pruitt. "I was writing about my hospitalizations and for the last couple of weeks, I can't write. I'm stuck."

He leads me again with my eyes closed into the comforting black velvet cloud.

"Imagine yourself feeling creative," he says when I raise my index finger. "Where are you?"

"I'm in the back pew of the G-ETS chapel. I'm writing."

"When you feel safe and confident, bring in some people you like."

I bring Stan in and begin to feel uncomfortable. I tell Dr. Pruitt what is happening and I say, "I'm okay, though. Just floating. I want to wait and see what happens."

Immediately the scene changes. I see me collapsed by the fireplace in 1970. Stan is lying near me, waiting for the Rescue Squad to carry me off to St. E's.

I float away from that scene to the house at 707 Blaine Street. "I am standing at the front door of my childhood home," I say. "I'm ready to go into the house." When I see the linoleum through the window, I stop at the threshold.

"I want to go in and I'm scared," I tell Dr. Pruitt.

"Do you want to continue?"

"Yes." Though hesitant, I know if I go in the house I will learn something important. I open the front door and step into the dining room. I am lying on the brown and yellow flowered linoleum, when suddenly the red, rubber, demon jumps in front of me and rams his forked tail right up inside me. I'm getting ready to scream when Dr. Pruitt's loud voice breaks in. "What's happening?"

"Something ... someone was ... raping me ..." I stutter.

"Stop! Come out of there!" Dr. Pruitt orders, loudly, and pokes me—hard—on my right knee.

Startled and ripped from the filmy fabric of memory, I open my eyes and see a scowling therapist. I start to cry.

"You have to get over that rape," he scolds. "You'll never know who did it!

"And stop crying," he said, "Use your creativity to think of three other ways you can respond instead of crying."

I couldn't think of any. He stopped the session.

December 3, 1982

Journal

O'Hare was bustling tonight when I got to the concourse. Stan was flying home from Phoenix this time and not planning to stay overnight.

We had a couple hours to eat and as soon as we were settled at one of the restaurant tables, I told him that I saw Dr. Pruitt again.

Stan just said *oh* and started looking at the menu.

I told him I've been talking with Dr. Pruitt about being afraid of large males. I laughed and said that Dr. Pruitt was pretty big, too. Then I took a breath and said something like, "Anyway, since that time you raped me, I've been afraid of you, too."

Stan quickly picked up the menu and held it in front of his chest. I thought he might have been hurt by my comment. So while he studied the menu I decided that Dr. Pruitt was probably right. I needed to get on with my life. I cleared my throat, took a deep breath and said, "Stan, I want to forgive you for raping me."

He looked at me over the top of the menu and said, "Thank you."

That's all he said. Thank you was his only response. I didn't know what else to say. While we ate we talked about the meeting he attended, our kids, and Christmas plans. I don't feel like hugging him when he leaves for his flight, but I do.

Dr. Pruitt charges $140. I am concerned about how to pay him and I didn't like when he snatched me out of the process I was in. He suggested I wait until after Christmas break for another appointment. Maybe I'll quit seeing him.

Chapter 16
Rapped and Rapt

And we are put on earth a little space,
That we may learn to bear the beams of love.

-William Blake

January 26, 1983

Back at seminary after the winter break, the topic in the New Testament seminar is Luke 8.26-39. The Gerasene Demoniac. As I enter the classroom, I'm still trying to decide if I want to attend. What if the discussion gets too personal? Though I'm quite anxious, I'm also curious about a discussion of Jesus healing this man full of demons by sending the demons into pigs. I identify with the poor demoniac living near the burial caves outside of Gerasa, but I wasn't healed by having my demons transferred into pigs and the whole squealing mess sent into a lake.

The professor, Dr. John Hartford, arranges the tables in a U-shape. I sit at the bottom of the U between Jeffrey and Mark. I can smell cigarette smoke on Jeffrey's flannel plaid shirt. He says hi and so does Mark, who has a can of Coke sitting in front of him. If he leaves the empty can, I'm *not* picking it up and chance running into Aaron again.

I look around the tables. June and Margie are the only other women in this group of eleven. Jerry is pulling a comb through his rust-colored curls. Jerk. He dominates discussions with displays of his arrogance. He has three New Testament texts stacked under his notebook, which is already open and ready to show off. Tom and

Albert are here. I saw them pull in after their drive from Indiana early this morning when I was out walking.

Doctor Hartford opens his Bible and begins the discussion by asking us what we've learned about this story from our research. As usual, Jerry, the most verbal and obnoxious of the eleven students, is the first one to open his mouth. He looks at his notebook and says, "I consulted seven commentaries and learned some interesting things like pigs can actually swim…" Jerry waits for a class response, but he only gets a few fake grins.

"Anyway," he consults his notebook and continues, "I wondered why Jesus and his disciples go to Gerasa. There aren't many Jews in that area and he …"

"He'd just stopped a storm," Jeffrey mumbles, loud enough to interrupt Jerry. "Probably needed a rest."

"Well, when he hit the beach," Jerry says, glaring at Jeffrey, "he stepped right out into another storm."

Dr. Hartford quickly interjects. "Well put. The demoniac is a storm, and he caused a storm in the city. He kept breaking out of his chains, so people sent him away. When Jesus asks the man his name," Dr. Hartford continues, "the possessed man answers, 'My name is Legion.' At least that's what the New Revised Standard Version says. In the Good News, the demoniac's name from the Greek is translated 'Mob.' A large group of people. June, did you find any commentary that discussed this difference in translation?"

June answers Dr. Hartford's question and the conversation goes on for another fifteen minutes. We discuss the Roman legions in the area that could take anything they wanted by force, including the pigs. Unlike the Jews, they could eat pork. Jerry, of course, tries to impress us with his discovery that the 10th Roman Legion in the area had a symbol of a boar on its standard.

You should wear "bore" on your shirt, I think, but I don't enter the conversation until we talk about the townspeople being afraid of Jesus' power. "By healing the man, Jesus causes the people economic loss," I say. "And, people in the city lost their scapegoat. When the man was possessed, they could blame him for anything that went wrong."

Dr. Hartford nods and then asks, "This Gospel lesson is during year 'A' in the church's schedule of scripture—the lectionary. What would you preach?"

For a few moments there is no response. Even Jerry has loosened his tie and is chewing on his pencil. Then June says she'd preach about Jesus' power to heal. Tom agrees and others nod their heads. Jerry says, "I'd see what the *other* scriptures are assigned for that Sunday." This time Jerry's comment elicits some laughter. I laugh along with others who have expressed their discomfort with the story.

Then, Dr. Hartford says, "So, you are going to be pastors. How would *you* deal with the demoniac?"

During the brief silence following the professor's question, I consider whether or not to share my hospital experience with Rusty seven years ago. There are some similarities in the way Jesus healed and the way she helped me deal with the demons. But I would have to reveal my hospitalizations. Scenes of St. Elizabeth's begin to wash over me. I decide to wait and listen.

At first, the class comments are comparisons with the demoniac's ancient world and modern day mental illness: medicines, psychiatrists, and locked psych units. When the students begin to describe the demoniac's behavior, my body stiffens. I pull the shawl more tightly around my shoulders.

The judgments come quickly.

"He's uncontrollable," Tom says.

"Had to be chained inside the city," Albert adds. "Who knows what chaos he caused in the city?"

Speculations and jokes about the man's behavior rise, several people speaking at once. June breaks through the din. "He cuts himself with stones," she says. "I know a woman who cuts herself. She's a cutter. And so is he!"

"My mother does that," Margie says, softly. "She ends up in the psych unit every few months. She causes a lot of pain in our family."

I look down at my class notes. Press the fingers of my right hand across my forehead to hide my eyes.

"He needs to be shut-up in a mental institution," Jeffrey says.

"I couldn't be a pastor to anyone like him," someone else says.

And, as class time runs out, Jerry summarizes, "Anybody that sees demons needs to be locked up … for life!"

I hold my breath to keep from crying. I stay seated as people pick up their books and leave the room. As my breath comes back, so does my decision to share my experience, but not in class. I decide to make an appointment with Dr. Hartford.

February 2, 1983

"Come on in." Dr. Hartford says, sliding into his upholstered chair. He points toward a chair next to his desk. I ignore his offer to sit. I have followed him back to his office from class and plan to leave immediately after telling him my reaction to last week's discussion.

Dr. Hartford stretches his neck from side to side as he loosens his plain, light blue tie. "How can I help?" he asks.

I look to make sure Dr. Hartford's office door is securely closed, before I say, "I was upset in last week's seminar. The Gerasene Demoniac." I take another breath before I add, "I've had experience with demons."

"Oh?"

Dr. Hartford's thick eyebrows go up over the top of his black-framed glasses, but he appears interested, not frightened. I quickly tell him about my hospitalizations and my work with Rusty. I compare the process she used to the steps Jesus used in healing the demoniac.

"That's interesting." Dr. Hartford leans back in his chair. "What kind of sense did you make of your experience?"

"In conversation with Rusty and the pictures I drew, they took off their masks. I learned I had suppressed a lot of anger. You know, good Christians don't get angry ..."

"And, don't have sex," Dr. Hartford adds. We both laugh.

"They revealed both anger and sex to me. Now I think the hallucinations were gifts to me from the shadow side of my consciousness."

Dr. Hartford turns his head toward the papers on his desk.

"I'm glad you told me about this. The class experience must have been tough."

I nod.

"Well, I'm going to give you some advice. Don't say anything about the demons to anyone. Keep your experience quiet until you're ordained and then let your light shine."

I'm surprised with his advice. I nod again and am ready to leave, but Dr. Hartford begins to rant about rational liberals beating down evangelicals. I stand up ready to leave as he runs out of invective. I say thank you as I open the door and step into the hallway. I leave troubled because his advice raises a dishonesty issue for me. Not only should I keep quiet about demons, he has me tapped as an evangelical. I'm not *anything*! I'm searching. Now I'm caught. Labeled crazy *and* evangelical.

From Dr. Hartford's office I went to the Natatorium. The entire time I swim my 30 laps, I play the conversation over and over in my mind. In my distraction, I have forgotten my towel and have to dry off under the hand dryer.

The next day, I raise the issue of honesty in Intro to Ministry. This time, the four others don't say much. Rand deals with it and further confuses the issue. He tries to differentiate between *candor* (truth) and *telling it all* (transparency). Obviously, I am more on the transparent pole. I know what he's saying about the difference. I can tell the truth and not tell it all, but somewhere in the discussion I get the awful picture of selling out to some Christian "game" and I become depressed. I say "I know I am naïve. But being authentic is important to me. I want to learn to act honestly within institutions and keep my integrity …"

This feels just like St. Elizabeth's. I have to play a game to get out. Act normal, but when I act normal, I'm scolded. Sometimes to follow the rules is to sell out.

Another issue occurs to me: where can I work these kind of issues through if not here? And, at least I'm being told *not* to work my experience with demons out *here*. I realize my expectation of Garrett as a place where I can develop my ideas is kaput. Or, at least in the subject matter of demons. I wonder where all this will lead. I feel alone again. In a process.

March 7, 1983

Dream

I am in a restaurant. I meet a nice looking man. He propositions me. At first I decline. Now, I am lying next to him. We are both naked. I have a toothpick. I place a small sliver on my labia. Now, I take the sliver and put it on the man's lower lip. I see his erection. His penis is large and thick. I spread my legs. He says, "Hurry." I get on top of him. I am very aroused but think it is too soon for me to climax. He pushes until he is entirely inside me. I experience orgasm. So does he. I roll off him and we snuggle together. He says, "You know, you are very good. I knew you would be." I say, "Do you have herpes?" I am looking at his penis as if I expect to see germs. He says, "As a matter of fact," and after a long pause during which

I become frightened, he adds, *"I don't!" We both laugh and I am feeling glad we made love. I wake up.*

April 14, 1983

Tonight several of us gathered after dinner in the lounge. The conversation turned to the imbalance of academics and spirituality here. I was the only one who was angry about the lack of spiritual guidance for clergy. I said I wasn't sure if I was going to return in the fall.

Kenneth disagreed with me. He said something about immaturity. I took it personally. I chafed at his comments. By the end of the evening, I was steamed. I met Kenneth early last fall. We have had conversations over lunch, walking to classes, and over a cup of coffee at Norris Student Center. We discovered our theology and opinions on social issues are the same. We have become good friends and we have laughed a lot together. Until now.

After our argument I feel distanced from him. I have decided I'll try to see him tomorrow and be honest with him.

Journal: April 18, 1983

Today is our 25th Anniversary. Stan and I celebrated over the weekend with family and friends at a dinner party at The Paper Valley Hotel. Among the gifts was the silver plate squirrel nut dish from his parents, the same dish his mother taunted me with during holiday dinners at their house. I couldn't put the right pickles in the right section to suit her. I don't want the stupid dish now. I'm not sure about Stan, either. On our 23nd anniversary Marian said to me, "Well, Nancy, I had him for 22 years. You've had him longer now."

What is he, some kind of possession?

Last Friday I had to leave before I could work things out with Kenneth. I saw him in the cafeteria after lunch today and told him about my anger. We talked it through, and I feel okay now. His remark about immaturity wasn't specifically directed at me.

I'm looking forward to a week-long Healing Seminar in Detroit next week.

Journal: May 2, 1983

I returned to Evanston from the Healing Seminar on Friday. Stan came down and we spent the weekend seeing movies and plays. While the healing during the week was very subtle—an overall softening—I could feel a change taking place. But I was unprepared for a dramatic shift in consciousness that I noticed this morning right after Stan left. As I walked back into the dorm, I started skipping. I felt creative, excited, and tip-toe flighty. All at once, I was bombarded with thoughts and ideas like the days in 1970 after I returned from the Ecumenical Institute.

I had that stab of fear I would end up locked in a padded cell again, so I forced myself to get very purposeful and structured. I made a list and schedule for the day and I meditated, using the imagery process I learned at the seminar. The rest of the day played itself out beautifully.

Journal: May 3, 1983

Being alive and creative is still with me. Wonders of today included several touching conversations. Kenneth disclosed his feelings for me: his affirmations, his fears, his love. I listened carefully, but didn't feel anything more than a slight discomfort at the intimacy. Then I had a roller-coaster conversation with Evelyn in her office about the healing seminar and my fear of nutsville. As my advisor, she said I didn't need any more therapy, that I needed to be challenged to do my leadership, my authority, my decision-making, making mistakes, offending folks, etc.

The whole day I experienced the joys and terrors of these alive places. This afternoon I walked over to the lake and was captivated by the midnight blue of the lake, the insistent waves slapping the rocks, and the silver-streaks of the male mallard's feathers. I let pine needles caress my cheeks, watched cavorting rabbits, and stopped for a cup of coffee at Norris. Anthony was there. He has tear-drop shaped nostrils.

Dessert for supper was that insipid chocolate pudding, but I soothed the tasteless offering over my tongue and enjoyed each creamy swallow. Kenneth joined me at the table and I noticed the wrinkles at right angles in his neck. I found myself close to tears grieving my own death—not ever wanting to leave this incredible world.

I'm puzzled by my detachment during my earlier conversation with Kenneth. His comments of affection are nice. Yet, I don't *feel* them. I remember the line in one of William Blake's poems: *We are put on earth a little space, that we may learn to bear the beams of love.*

I grew up learning to bear the stabs of suffering and equating love with pain. Just before the one biting or occasional whack, my father said, "This is for your own good, Nancy Lu" or "This hurts me more than it does you."

I think when the lightning struck in 1970, it pierced the armor that I had worn for thirty years. I want to let good stuff in now, but that lightning and subsequent hospitalization was one hell of a beam.

And, Kenneth? I understand his need for companionship. He's thousands of miles from home and his wife. But, I deadened when he spoke of having romantic feelings for me. I don't feel the same way.

When I am open, creative, and alive, I'm afraid of being overwhelmed by an onrushing of the universe. Assaulted by sensations. Internal. External. It gets very intense. As I stood by the lake this afternoon, getting caught up in compassion about the exquisite beauty of the waves crashing over the rocks, I thought "It's okay to feel like this"—shattered, fractured, yet sensing.

Maybe it's the way I'm *supposed* to feel. Who knows?

May 4, 1983

At supper, Kenneth suggests that because the evening is warm we should find a park bench somewhere, and he wants to go to the Baha'i Temple. Though I don't remember seeing outside seating at the temple, I'm driving north on Sheridan past huge homes exploding with spring flowers and magnolias. "Look at those daffodils and tulips," Kenneth sighs from the passenger seat.

"This morning I saw the buds on a magnolia tree turn into pacifiers," I say.

"What? Pacifiers? Like nipples?" Kenneth turns away from the window toward me.

"I don't know how it happened," I explain, keeping both hands on the wheel, "but when I was walking back from Norris this morning, the blossoms on a magnolia changed before my eyes. I thought it was appropriate. You know, the early magnolia buds are comfort food for people who are starved for spring."

Kenneth nods.

I park at the south side of the Baha'i Temple and Kenneth and I walk around the back of the stunning edifice that looks like a pope's cap. We don't see a place to sit, so Kenneth walks up the steps toward the temple door.

"It's closed," he says, when he tries to get in the building. "But look at those flowers," he adds, referring to sculptured rows of tulips and daffodils in front of him. "A riot of color."

I join him. After standing together silently breathing in vivid reds, yellows, and purples, Kenneth sighs, and asks, "Will you bring me back tomorrow? I'd like to take pictures."

Journal: May 5, 1983

This noon Kenneth walked into the cafeteria dressed in his light blue v-neck sweater. When he saw me he grinned, waved, and pointed at me, indicating he would join me at the table. In addition to feeling my affection for him, I was surprised to feel a sexual stirring. I accept the feelings. They're nice *and* I have no intention of an affair that would include going to bed with him.

He is more reserved than I am. I more naturally touch him out of a comfortable, friendly style. He has more attachment, I think. As I write this, I wonder if I'm fooling myself. We'll see. Perhaps my feelings are deeper and I'm getting caught more than I think.

I wonder if it's possible to have a depth relationship with a man other than my husband without having sexual feelings.

Kenneth and I went back to the Baha'i Temple this afternoon. We went inside and looked up into the heavenly dome. He enjoyed it. Took pictures.

At this time, I feel *very* tired. The magical high I had after the Healing Seminar is gone.

Nothing else to say. I am *dead* in here now.

Journal: May 9, 1983

6:40 a.m.

Awake at 5:00. Again at 6:30.

Feel great peace.

Very relaxed.

Feel completely loved—my *whole* body.

Have never felt so completely and tenderly loved.

Guilt disappeared last night—shifted when I imaged the light around me.

I love Kenneth very much.

Nancy Bauer-King

It is as if he is my very *first* lover.
I feel I am more whole than I have ever been.

Chapter 17
Womb Before Word

Honesty: speaking the right truth
to the right person
at the right time
in the right way
for the right reason.

-Aristotle

June 29, 1983

When Stan leaves for work I climb the ladder into the loft and sit under the Guernica picture to meditate. Still grieving my separation from Kenneth, I close my eyes and try to count to my breathing. Inhale 1-2-3-4. Exhale 1-2-3-4. The scenes melt into one another as if they are a slide show.

I see Kenneth walk into the cafeteria dressed in his light blue v-neck sweater…his wide grin and my first sexual awakening for him.

I see me agitated in an ethics prof's office on that Friday afternoon.

"I am attracted to another man—not my husband," I say. "I don't know what to do."

"Let me recommend a book for you," he says. "The title is *Honest Sex.*"

The title of the book is enough.

Another scene. That same evening with Kenneth at the picnic table when I report my *honest* feelings to him.

"I've decided to stay at G-ETS this weekend," I say and look out at the waves spilling over the rocks. "I want to see what will happen between us."

"Oh my…" He reaches for my hand.

The two days are magic. We attend a Misha Dichter concert. We go shopping and I buy a pair of green and white striped slacks. We eat dinner at *Fritz That's It*. He asks me to waltz at a dance at Norris and he is just the right size.

And Sunday evening. We are sitting close to each other in the front seat of the car looking over the lake…and *his touch* pushes me back, back, back into an overcast November 1944 afternoon.

I'm four and a half. My baby brother is a couple months old. The rain has stopped. I take a baby bottle nipple, fill it with water in the bathroom sink, walk out to the front of the house, and stand next to the hickory nut tree.

As I place the make-shift penis between my corduroy pant legs at my crotch and point it toward the ragged tree bark, I anticipate a delicious feeling. I'm just ready to squeeze the nipple and spurt against the ragged tree bark when I hear my mother scream from the front door.

"Nancy Lu! Get in the house!"

I don't remember what Mother did when I went into the dining room. But I remember what happened that May evening.

As Kenneth began to touch me, my mother's figure filled the 707 Blaine Street front door and just as she opened her mouth to scream at me, she exploded like a Fourth of July sparkler into shards that fell and sank into the ground.

Afterward, Kenneth gets out of the car and picks violets. "Je' taime," he says, and hands them to me. "Je' taime beaucoup."

We don't see each other again until the day I am about to leave for summer break. Knowing that within days, he'll be flying back to his wife in England and I'll never see him again, I run up the stairs to his room. He meets me at the door. We hug. Without speaking I run my hands quickly from the top of his head to the tips of his shoes to say goodbye to him forever. I hurry down the steps to my car, choking on spasms to keep others from seeing my distress.

I can still see myself back in Appleton stumbling along the hills beneath our home, bent over and keening a lost love.

July 23, 1983

"I would like an hour with you sometime today," Stan says.

"Okay. What about?"

"Our sex life—or rather, lack of."

"Let's talk about it now."

"No. I have to get my motorcycle worked on."

He gets up from the table, puts his dishes in the sink, and leaves for the morning. I decide I won't bring the subject up. The issue belongs to him.

After supper, while drying dishes, Stan says, "So, I want to know why you don't want sex."

I move away from the sink and begin to wipe the counter before I answer. "I am in touch with lots of anger about my subservience. It's been a pattern for our whole marriage. Actually, it's the way I was raised. I'm supposed to do whatever is needed to make boys…men… happy. It's a sell-out of myself and my body. I think the tension between keeping you happy and denying myself made me bitchy, especially with sex."

"Early on you were real sexy. Then you quit."

Your rape of me, plus all the pregnancies, I think, but say, "I know I tried to forgive you, but you never said you were sorry. I couldn't trust you."

"I don't trust you, either," Stan says as he hangs up the dishtowel. "And I'm suspicious of all the time you are in Evanston."

I quickly laugh, shake my head no, and say, "I don't understand *myself* what is happening to me."

"Do you remember when you said you wanted an affair?" Stan asks.

"Yes." I sigh. "Do we have to replay that whole thing again? I told you at that time I thought we had promised we would tell each other if we wanted an affair."

"I don't remember making any agreement like that."

"To me marriage meant fidelity—no adultery. Anyway, you got angry, quit talking with me, and I didn't have an affair. I ended up in the hospital again, instead."

"Well, if you have an affair, it will be all over. I'd be through with you."

Stan walks past the trestle table toward his ugly, green recliner. Then seated, after a pause, he adds, "So, are you getting it somewhere else?"

"No," I manage to say and quickly walk past him. He doesn't comment on the hesitation before my denial, but as I leave the room, he says, "I believe you. You're so damned honest you *couldn't* lie to me."

I rationalize. I didn't exactly lie because I wasn't 'getting it' *at that moment*. And, I won't be 'getting it' anymore from a man with whom I could trust my *whole* self. But at 43 years old, I finally got it! Not just sex. I finally got *'It*! In one brief weekend, I learned that there was at least *one man* in the world whose love for me I could trust.

"I'm also still angry you didn't have your family come to a counseling session," I say to Stan, bringing up an old issue. "I thought we agreed we would each have one meeting with our parents and siblings. After I had mine, you said you wouldn't do it."

"I didn't know it was an agreement."

"It was! And your refusal effectively stopped our family counseling. You still refuse to take my side when your mother attacks."

"I don't want to hurt them," Stan says softly.

"You're afraid," I pronounce.

"No, I'm not," he argues more forcefully. "I don't want to hurt my dad. He has never shown emotion. He has stifled lots of stuff through his marriage. I don't want to be responsible for his falling apart."

"You can learn a lot about yourself," I say, and think about how much Stan is like his father. "Your refusal to learn how you've been affected by your family patterns keeps me from knowing you better, too."

"Are you talking about intimacy, now?"

"I guess so."

"I feel like I can never do anything right," Stan sighs, shakes his head, and adds, "But I am *not* going to talk with them."

"So you would choose them over me to protect them from hurt?" I ask, feeling like a spoiled child.

"Yes," he answers. "This issue of my parents could break up our marriage."

I can't respond. He is right. We quit talking with no resolutions.

September 9, 1983

Dream

Stan and I are driving on a state highway in a rural area somewhere in Wisconsin. Now, I see that he has stopped the car at the Fish Hatchery near Madison. I say, "Oh, I know where we are. This is the fish hatchery that I visited when I was a child. There was a huge snake that I almost stepped on."

Stan decides to park in the parking area. The parking area is in several inches of water with a raised area covering a huge pipe. Water is pouring over the pipe like water over a dam. Stan drives the front of the car—our old blue Ambassador wagon—up over the pipe. I warn him not to go too far or we'll drop into the deeper lake. It is too late! The car begins to slide nose first into the lake. I remain calm. I say, "Should I open the windows or keep them closed?" He doesn't answer. I make plans to escape. Now, the car seems to be settling into seaweed and muck. Evidently the water isn't as deep as I thought. I think, "I can get out of this. I will not drown."

Journal: October 23, 1983

Pastor Glen, my Field Ed Supervisor for this year of seminary, asked me to read the gospel lesson for this morning and I said yes before I knew what the scripture was. Matthew 15.10-20 is a red letter Jesus scold: "Listen and understand: it is not what goes into the mouth that defiles a person, but what comes out of the mouth..." Then, after the sandaled trouble-maker says that the defiling stuff comes out of the heart, he lists all the scarlet sins, including...of course...adultery.

I immediately thought about Kenneth. I couldn't read *that*! I'd lose it.

Even as Pastor Glen led the Call to Worship, I started mind-fucking myself into another paralyzing anxiety attack.

The congregation sat down as I walked across the chancel to the fat wooden lectern. The words of the last verse of the hymn still hung in the air.

"Now incline me to repent, let me now my sins lament."

Now my foul revolt deplore, weep, believe, and sin no more."

And, sure enough. As I opened the Bible my hands shook like Uncle Archie trying to hold onto the cigar with his Parkinson's fingers. There at the Word of the Lord, panic drained me white numb. I began to read convinced that when I got to the word *adultery* I would whimper.

But I didn't! I didn't even have to cough or clear my throat. Now, I'm pissed. Why do I go through so much shit?

There is such a push in me to be honest—to be *naked* to my sin. Or to my guilty skin. I know the struggle is with all the old indoctrination. With Kenneth, I felt completely honest, authentic, and growing—huge integrations. But now, a heavy saddle of guilt rides on my back.

November 8, 1983

"Can a male savior save women?" Dr. Ruether asks during a lecture on feminist theology.

What?! A male savior save women? NO! My ball-point stops racing across the note paper. I can hear Dr. Rosemary Radford Ruether (called R-cubed by students) still lecturing, but her words are muffled by a clanging inner argument.

No. I can't trust males. Bigger. Stronger. I remember the woman seated beside me in class a few days ago referring to power automatically vested in anyone with a penis. She dangled her index digit finger and whispered to me, "Him have extra finger."

Yet the name Jesus…just the word *Jesus* like an Open Sesame name…helped me open the door of a locked-up terror in St. Elizabeth's psychiatric ward.And, men, like Paul Tillich, whose words of Good News acceptance waved a magic wand of grace over my Sin Sick Soul. (S-cubed?)

And, my week-end love affair? Didn't Kenneth save me from my fear of giving myself completely away?

So. I guess it is possible for a male savior to save women.

But women have saved me, too.

Like Rusty, who wasn't afraid of the slick red rubber demon I saw and against my psychiatrist's orders, helped me talk with him until his mask melted off and my father's face appeared.

Or like Dr. Ruether, herself, who removed nine single-spaced typed pages of my final systematics paper, so that the second faculty reader—a male—would not see my explication of Process Theology through dreams. x-rated dreams that illustrated sexual and spiritual integration. What would have happened to me if Dr. Woodson had read those excised pages?

I'm tired of male saviors. I want a saving woman story. Not a virgin or a mother or a whore. Not an angel who announces, "Surprise! Here's an immaculate conception!" I want a story about the struggle that women and men have giving birth to one another.

And what is *"saved"* anyway? Snatched from the jaws of hell? I don't believe Lazarus lived again after the rags fells off of his three-day dead body. The Bible doesn't tell us how many days or years Lazarus lived after Jesus did his magic act. Lazarus might have tripped on the smelly rags and cracked his head open. Bled to death.

My imagination bounces around in my brain like bumper cars at Bay Beach until Dr. Ruether finishes her lecture, class is over, and people begin to get up and leave.

November 9, 1983
Dream
I'm in a church basement waiting for a potluck dinner. A man—he seems like Durwood Kirby—puts his hand over my mouth. I bite him—just a little bite at the base of his finger. He doesn't feel it! I bite him again. Then, I just scream for him to get his fucking hand off my mouth. I wake myself up screaming.

Journal: November 12, 1983
Stan and I got into another disagreement last night after I got home. I tried to explain what I've learned about feminist theology. I defined hubris. I got out my notebook and drew a stick man and woman. I drew an ego bubble circle around their heads.

"When men are attacked, they strike out," I explained, "and women turn in. They're passive."

"You're not passive," Stan observes.

"I'm speaking *generally* about the way women ... well, the way I've been enculturated. Anyway," I continue, "the more important thing I learned is that because Jesus didn't fight back, and *looked* passive, women think that being passive is being like Jesus. But that passivity is self-denial. And it is sin."

Stan dropped his head to his chest. To me it was a signal that he felt beaten down.

I don't know how to communicate the way I'm integrating feminist theology. I know I'm angry. I can hear my voice go up several notches in volume when I try to talk with him.

In Field Ed last Monday, I talked about the anxiety attacks I've had for almost twenty years. Curt suggested I reflect on the positive thing that sustains me during the attacks. When Rosie asked, "Is it because you're not able to do something you're supposed to be able to do?" I thought of my father making me perform in the church. The anxiety attacks are always during worship. Perhaps I really don't want to do this whole ministry thing – it's just a big *should*. One gimmick I thought of was somehow to rig a signal to Pastor Glen that I was "into" anxiety. Then I wouldn't feel alone. That's what is distressing. I have such horrible bouts of loneliness. The heating pad on my belly helps and the aching always passes.

Dr. Ruether's question still haunts me. *Can a male savior save women?* I don't have an answer. Dr. Ruether didn't give an answer either. I don't like it when I don't have an answer to a question. So her question falls into a void. I try to *a-void* coming up with an answer, but the question keeps messing with me.

Chapter 18
Mismatched

*You shall know the truth
and the truth shall make you odd.*

- Flannery O'Connor

November 17, 1983

John Huntley hands me my psychological assessment--another form required by the Board of Ordained Ministry. I am seated in his office. He stands about eight feet away from me next to his desk. He says I have 20 minutes to read the results and ask any questions.

I am upset with some of the phrases I read:

She is not satisfied with her social status.

How was that judgment made?

It is highly unusual for a pastor not to want to spend time with the family.

My kids are grown and scattered throughout the country.

She can talk a good game, but she can't deliver.

This hurts! What kind of game? Big game like a rhinoceros? Tough game like chess? And, what keeps me from delivering it? Collapsed uterus? Flat tire? Can't read a map?

"What does this mean?" I ask, pointing to the phrase.

"I didn't write the assessment," he answers.

"Who did?"

"A colleague I have in Indiana."

What? I was psychologically scored—and scarred—by someone

who has never talked with me? The tears that I tried to hold back, spilled over. Dr. Huntley pushed the sleeve of his suit coat up, looked at his watch, indicating my time was up.

He refuses to give me a copy.

His last words to me are, "I'm sorry. You are just not a good match for the parish." Blanched with his searing judgement, I manage to make it back to my room before breaking into sobs. If I'm not fit to be an ordained pastor, what am I doing here?

Journal: November 17, 1983

Jane, my roommate, listened to my distress about my assessment. She sat on the edge of her bed, kept handing me tissue, and let me vent. I told her I should have listened to the women who warned me not to do my assessment with Dr. Huntley. They whispered about his sexual innuendos and his hands brushing across their breasts.

I told her I was afraid that BOOM (Board of Ordained Ministry) would agree with Huntley that I wasn't pastor material.

Jane has been a good roommate. We have a lot in common. Husband. Kids. We both drive hundreds of miles every weekend. But her assessment went well. After I quit crying, she invited me to walk over to Norris for coffee.

"I keep looking for a silver lining in my black cloud of misery," I said. "Maybe the assessment will motivate me to explore my career options more completely."

"Another bright spot is that Huntley didn't make a move on you," Jane said.

"Yeah," I agreed. "Wait a minute. What is wrong with *my* breasts?"

We laughed, and, as we walked back to Loder, I carried a lighter "lode" of inadequacies.

November 30, 1983

Huntley agrees to see me for five minutes.

"I wanted to tell you my reactions to the assessment," I say, standing about two feet into his office with the door *open*.

"My children are grown and on their own, three of them live out of state. I won't be spending much time with them."

"I don't know how the determination was made, but I'm more than satisfied with my social status, and I'm hurt by your colleague's phrase about talking a good game. I infer he means my word isn't any good."

Huntley, seated behind his desk, stretches his arms over some papers he's working on and asks, "What is your reason for being here?"

I tell him about my 1970 religious experience and breakthrough. That I've written about it in my Ministry Project and was easily affirmed and admitted to Level II.

"A psychotic episode is not a good reason to be a pastor," he says, and adds, "Falling in love is a psychotic experience."

While Huntley smirks, I consider his observation and decide there is no comparison between psychosis and falling in love. From newfound strength I ask for what I want.

"May I have a copy of my psychological assessment?"

"I sent it to a psychiatrist."

"Oh." I remain calm and say, "May I have the name and phone number of the psychiatrist?"

I leave Huntley's office with the name and number.

I am not afraid of him anymore.

When I meet with Dr. Samberrien, the psychiatrist who has my assessment, she balks at my request for a copy of the results.

"What do you want it for?" she says, as if I am asking for her firstborn child.

"I want to reread it."

"Your request is highly inappropriate. You are out-of-order even asking for it."

"The report should be shared with me more completely," I argue, getting louder. "I was able to get all my medical records from my earlier hospitalizations."

"I will not give it to you," she says, her voice increasing in volume as well, "but as long as you are here, you can take it back to Dr. Huntley."

She puts the assessment in an envelope, seals it, and hands it to me. A game. I'm not trusted with information about myself, but I'm trusted to deliver it. As soon as I get back to my room I steam the envelope open over my hot pot and reread it before I take it to the Pastoral Counseling office.

I have remembered the negative comments accurately.

December 15, 1983

Dream

Stan and I are in a restaurant. We start to fight. I get very angry. I get caught between feelings: want to leave, but too frightened. I finally decide I'll leave, which means leaving my husband stranded. I get into the car and start out. I turn right down an alley behind the restaurant. At the end of the alley—in the middle of the road, which has become very narrow, there is a plant that looks like a single stalk of asparagus. It's bent over at the top. I don't see how I can get the car past without driving up on a lawn of someone's house or over the plant. A man comes out of the house with a shovel. I am out of the car. He assures me that I can drive past the plant without going up on the lawn. I look at the car. It is smaller. There is just enough room for me to push the car past the plant.

Journal: February 6, 1984

Red letter day. BOOM interview for Deacon's Orders. Three clergy and I met in a small room at one of Camp Lucerne's buildings. Like the picadors at a bullfight, they poked at my self-image.

When I acknowledged my anxiety, Reverend Schmitz asked where it came from. I answered that my father was demanding…nothing I did was good enough for him.

After Pastor Art Farwell reminded me that the bishop lays his hands on ordinands' heads and says, "Take thou authority," he asked me how I would handle an angry male at a council meeting. I answered that I was still learning about my power and that I had been told I needed to develop the masculine side of me. I have no idea how I will act in a male dominated institution.

The worst was when Pastor Sharon Lundquist pointed out that I interpret a personal observation as a value. "If I say 'you have on a brown skirt,' you say 'what's *wrong* with a brown skirt?'" She was right.

I stopped for coffee on my way back to G-ETS. I was too late for supper at Loder, and I didn't feel like eating anyway. My stomach feels as if it's a playground for rabid bats. I expect BOOM will defer me for a year and recommend counseling. It would be okay with me. I still have a lousy self-image.

The more I envision myself in a local parish, the more it feels like "perish."

February 10, 1984

I am in the bedroom at home when Pastor Farwell calls to tell me the Board decided to defer me for a year. "We think you need more time to explore ordination and we're worried about your anxiety," he says. "We also are requiring you to do CPE (Clinical Pastoral Education) and we recommend career counseling."

He promises I'll get a letter confirming the decision.

I put down the telephone, pick up my stomach from the floor, and walk into the living room toward Stan. He is sitting in his green recliner and reading Newsweek. "The phone call was from BOOM—telling me they lowered it. They deferred me for a year."

He stands up and takes me into his arms. I press my head into his plaid flannel shirt and begin to cry. He holds me for a moment and then says, "I've got something for you. It's in the garage. I'll get it."

Stan comes back into the room carrying a plant with red flowers. He says, "This is for Valentine's Day."

"What kind of flower is it?" The flower is ugly. I wish he hadn't bought me anything. I bought him a card, and forgot to bring it home.

"The florist told me it was a cineraria. I thought you could take it back to G-ETS."

"No. I don't want…"

With a sigh, Stan's head falls toward his chest. I have hurt him.

"Thank you," I say. Hoping I can soothe his wound, I add, "I would rather enjoy it here. It wouldn't last long at G-ETS. There's not much light in my room.

"I bought you a valentine, too," I add quickly. "It's still on my desk in Loder. A picture of a young man and woman are on the front. The woman has butterfly wings. The man is standing close at her side. Inside, I wrote, 'Thank you for staying close while I try my wings.'"

Stan raises his eyebrows, nods his head in acknowledgment, and returns to his recliner.

Later he asks, "What do you plan to do?"

"You mean about seminary? I don't know. I'll keep going. I think I'll check out career counseling. Maybe I'll find a real person who can help me identify the things I'm good at."

"Didn't you do that when you were at Oshkosh?"

"Yeah. Funny thing. The inventory indicated I have the same interests as priests."

"Imagine that," Stan says and returns to his magazine.

Journal: September 23, 1984

Last night I finished reading another chapter in *Woman in Therapy* by Miriam Greenspan, one of the recommended books on Dr. Reuther's syllabus. Greenspan's words about how the patriarchal system contributes to female emotional distress, ripped a scab off that terrible, infected St. Elizabeth's psych ward wound.

I shut the door to the one-bedroom apartment I'm subletting for this Fall quarter while another Level III is doing CPE. I walked back and forth stifling sobs. I pounded my pillow with clenched teeth so I didn't scream and prompt neighbors to call 911.

In the psych unit? I must have looked thin and scared. Drugged eyes open wide. Though I tried tried tried to see clearly, my vision blurred by the way I was treated. Kept me in the dark. Kept me infantile.

So many people charted me. Watched me with eyes that supposedly were clear. When I went to the desk to ask permission—like a *baby*—to go for a walk, someone was writing in my chart. Johns, Nagler, Hendricks. That night nurse. They hid the chart when I approached. They knew something I didn't know about me. Kept me ignorant. Helpless, isolated and so very frightened.

For all those years, all I wanted was to be held.

Still in agony for some god or other, I went to bed and while lying there, a soft presence began filling up the room. Aware I was being wrapped in a soft, dark, velvet void like the one I floated in before the men in white cared me off to St. Elizabeth's.

I remember being stunned. *What was it?*

I wasn't afraid. While I didn't know what it was, I knew the presence was definitely feminine.

Journal: September 26, 1984

Evelyn requires journaling for Pastoral Theology. The writing is supposed to include theological reflection. How can I journal about God when the only thing I want to dialog with shows up as an empty void? How can I say I'm comforted by the inside of a soft pocket—the very same place that struck me with lightning and threw me into a locked room?

My reading assignments include more material about the subordination of women built into all our cultural systems. I really thought my independence would be easily won—a process that I could conclude in a few months or a couple of years at most. Ha. My whole way of being is shifting. Cataclysmic.

The biggest personal issue is my relationship with Stan. How am I going to do theology with that?

God whoever, wherever, and whatever you are, are you moving in the midst of my marriage somewhere? If so, I'd like to have more conversation than trying to deal with a black blanket hovering over my head.

I want to be independent, but I don't know what that would look like. There are so few models of freemales.

CHAPTER 19
PASTOR PRACTICE

*Compassion toward others begins with
acceptance of the maligned or wounded inner self.*

- Anonymous

Journal: November 26, 1984

As required by the Board of Ordained Ministry, I am beginning a three-month program in Clinical Pastoral Education at St. Luke's Hospital. After one day, I'm exhausted! On information overload. I feel good about my supervisor, Susan, and the small group I'm in. Ed is a deacon and Gerry a nun. Both Catholic and older than me. Rob is about my age and a burn-out from a Disciples of Christ church. They all seem honest and caring.

I don't know how I'll fit in.

We wear gold jackets that identify us as chaplains. I'm supposed to think of my floor, 6-LM, as my parish and interact with folks as if I'm a pastor. It's more like a rabbit warren with dozens of rooms and padded feet running in and out.

I feel challenged, stimulated, and basically good about myself. But I was frightened when I walked past the Emergency Room and heard a woman groaning.

I'll explore my fear when I meet with my small group.

Journal: December 5, 1984

My first "on call" night was busy. I got about 2 ½ hours of sleep.

Leona died about 11:20 p.m. and at 2:15 a.m. I was called to Janice's room. The family—a husband, sister, and son—saw me in the doorway. I hesitated. Some people see the gold jacket and are frightened. Some angry. Some open and friendly. Susan says when we wear the jacket, we may represent God's presence to some people. Janice's family was glad to see me. I stayed and attended her death with them.

While standing with Janice's family I noticed the gray of her death. Then, in the middle of the grieving, I saw a "light"—kind of a gold aura that filled and transcended the gray room. I thought of my chaplain's jacket and remembered the last time I saw my father and the yellow of his hospital room.

Colors of Death

Janice's skin is gray
stark white sheets
frame her black hair
deep cave mouth
stretched into silent oh.
her husband, sister, son
lean into grief
shake heavy clouds of tears

My father's death was yellow
flowing urine tubes
jaundiced cheeks
sunshine on pillow

still angry at the
male father god
I fled

Now called to dying rooms
I wear chaplain jacket
and stay

an ancient alchemist and I
mix colors, chant incantations
use mortar pestle words and flame
to purify the scenes to precious jewels.

After she died, I helped Janice's family say their goodbyes and offered a prayer without asking. A mistake to my mind. I have made several mistakes these past few days: late for my appointment with Susan, forgot to cover for Fran … I am still learning to be completely present and focused. I try to speak only to respond to a question or with a comment that seems appropriate.

There is much room for improvement.

December 6, 1984

When the elevator opens, there is a person in a wheelchair ready to be pushed off by a nurse. I step out of the way as the nurse pushes the gowned person toward me. I see the woman's hands, folded and lying across a small flannel pad on her lap. Her fingers are bony and bent into arthritic knots. I look toward her face and see it framed with uncombed curls of greasy gray hair. I glance at her cloudy eyes behind glasses, when suddenly, her face is transfigured before me. Like the Virgin Mary, a sky blue scarf falls over her head and cascades past the shoulders of my image. I look quickly to her face as the likeness is wheeled past me. Stunned, I see "Mary" has no mouth.

What *happened*? Is this a Goddess-Mary-who-wants-to-be-heard-but-can't-speak? I think of Stan's face turning into my father's when I met him at the airport. I think of the Ecumenical Institute, St. Elizabeth's and the demons. Am I losing it again?

Am I the one who thinks I'm not being heard?

I remember the benediction I read in one of my theology texts: *May you live until the word of your life is fully spoken.* What would I say if people *were* listening?

December 29, 1984

Stan comes back from Thorson's with beef. I'm reading and as he passes through the great room I feel darkness seep into my bones. I take a deep breath and speak.

"It's hard for me to be home with you. I feel dead here." I put the book down leaning it into the leg of wicker chair I am sitting in.

He doesn't respond until after he has the meat in the freezer. He comes back into the living room, puts some logs in the woodburning stove that heats our solar home.

"I figure when you get your job, you'll split," he says. "You'll have money … be financially independent."

"I've thought about it," I say, "but if I *split,* it won't be because I can support myself. I will leave because of the emptiness in our relationship. We can't seem to nurture each other."

"You seem angry all the time," he said, stoking the fire.

"I am angry," I admit for the umpteenth time. "Sometimes I'm angry with you, but a lot of my anger is diffused. I guess I'm doing my feminist thing twenty years too late."

Stan finishes pushing logs around in the small cast iron stove and sits on the couch across from me. After several moments of a sterile silence, I say, "I wish I wasn't this way. I don't want to beat up on you."

"Do you see why I can't share with you?" he asks.

"Yes," I nod and think about the long years of learning to trust therapists before I could bare my feelings. "I'm probably not the one with whom you can be open," I say and add, "Your feelings are sacred stuff. I don't want to step on your soul."

We sit quietly again until Stan lobs an accusation. "You don't accept anyone's growth unless it's the same as yours."

"You may be right," I say, after considering his observation. "Are you growing?"

He nods and rubs his hands back and forth along his jeans.

"How?" I ask.

"Growing for me means learning new skills … information for problem solving. I like working with machines. Especially the computer."

I'm surprised that he has a specific answer and that we seem to be really talking.

"I grow through relationships," I say, "but you already know that. It's a huge difference between us … and we don't have fun together."

"I liked Larry Stumpf's suggestion," Stan says. "Remember? Every other weekend one of us plans something fun to do?"

I sigh. I know what he'll say next.

"But you didn't like his idea. We never tried it."

"I know. He gave us two options: trade weekend plans or walk through the museum and look at our history. You and Larry thought the weekend trades would work best. I liked the museum thing."

"Why didn't you say something?"

"I don't know. I guess I didn't want to argue."

"Maybe we should try counseling again," Stan says, and leans toward me.

"If you feel we need it and make the appointments, I'll go with *you*."

"But *you* know all the counselors," he argues.

"I don't want to be the 'sick' one any more." I'm careful with my words because I think he is trying to put the responsibility back on me.

"When we were in counseling, you said you were only there to help *me* get better."

He pushes himself back into the couch cushions.

"Well, at least give me the names of people you would consider."

Even though I know he is hitting the ball back into my court, I answer. "Well, I'm okay with Larry."

But when Stan begins citing reasons he can't call Larry, and hopes I will, I shake my head, and mumble, "Uh-uh."

I pick up my book, leave the room, and to quell a rising anger, climb the ladder to the loft. I don't want any more of this shit, I think. I relax into a large velveteen pillow I hauled up into my sacred space.

If he does call a counselor, I will have to deal with "Do I want to stay married?"

Journal: January 1, 1985

It's 1:32 a.m. New Year's Day—1985!

Outside there is a raging blizzard spitting and whipping the night around. Inside I am alert and chewing gum to relax after helping tend the death of Mr. Edmund Stallings—57, cancer. His wife has been on a couch at his bedside since December 17. It was a peaceful, quiet death. His wife is a peaceful together woman. She talked and cried, and was real. I liked her.

Three large, male, friends of Mr. Stallings blew in from the storm, put their arms around her and escorted her (along with a cart full of clothes and Christmas decorations) out into the stinging night. She said, "He *hated* snow. Wouldn't you just know it would be on a night like this?"

Yesterday, I met with my District Committee on Ministry in Green Bay. I was relaxed, and I think the meeting went well. They challenged me regarding my completion of the Board of Ordained Ministry's conditions. I reported I had satisfied the additional requirements and shared my personal growth since being deferred last February. I named specific gifts and skills I have that fit ordained ministry: intelligence, writing, speaking, organizational, and relational skills. I meet with the Board again on February 4.

January 6, 1985

"Luella Nevoraski wants a chaplain," Fran says. "Her chart says she is a 92 year-old Polish woman from Florida."

When I get to Mrs. Nevoraski's room she looks at me and says, "Want male priest."

"I was sent," I say, becoming inured to the overwhelming preference for a clergy*man*. "Is it okay if I stay a few minutes?"

She nods, turns to look out the window and begins to talk. I listen carefully because she speaks with broken English.

"Cancer," she says, pointing at her chest. "Got radiation so she fast don't grow."

"How is the radiation going?"

"Okay, Mrs. As good as can. Have to do."

I smile and ask her if she has children nearby.

"Got daughter. Son in Florida."

"Do you live with your daughter now?"

"When not here, Mrs." Mrs. Nevoraski waves her hand toward the surroundings of the room. I notice the purple blotches of bruises along her arm and remember a friend's comment—that old people are all wrinkled and spotty.

"Is there anything I can do for you?" I ask after a few more minutes of conversation.

Mrs. Nevaroski shakes her head back and forth on the pillow, and says, "No want female priests."

Though she tires me out, I love her. She is an expressive, delightful, woman. Keeps calling me *Mrs.*

As I leave, she says, "I want to die light. Not heavy."

Me too.

January 7, 1985

11:30 p.m. I'm at the bedside of a tiny, curled up woman, who is moaning in agony, "Priest. Priest."

I tell her I'm there.

She says, "Priest. Priest." She doesn't say anything else, just calls for a priest.

At the Morning Report, Father Gerald, one of the resident priests, is angry with me. "Why did you call her parish priest?"

"She kept asking for a priest," I answer, aware that I've evidently made a serious mistake.

"That woman is in the last stages of Alzheimer's. Your referral got the priest from St. Matthew's out of bed, and, when he got here, he couldn't make any sense out of what she wanted him for. He called me this morning, angry."

I can feel my face getting hot and manage to squeak out, "I wasn't sure what to do."

Susan, my supervisor, must see my lips trembling and addresses Father Gerald.

"Nancy is here to learn." She turns to me and says, "If you weren't sure what to do, you can check with the nurse. She can help you decide."

I am supposed to lead the Ecumenical Service right after this meeting. As I begin the worship, I am still dealing with the terrible shame of making a mistake.

Journal: January 22, 1985

This on call seems *too* soon from the last one. I'm burned out. Four more weeks of this and then I go back to G-ETS for my final quarter and degree. Who'll die tonight? Will I get any supper? Any sleep? And, what about my meeting with the Board of Ordained Ministry? The unknown is the pits.

And this morning I was called to those pits. A nurse on 6-LM told me there was a man who really wanted to talk to a chaplain. I knew as soon as I entered his room the man had recently vomited.

He was small, thin, and unshaven. Strings of puke stuck to his whiskers and he stunk heavily of sweat. His uncovered toothpick legs quivered. He wanted me to pray with him. I wanted to run away.

And, then, my savior complex was triggered. "I must love these people, smelly and sour and gross." I gritted my teeth and prayed. Prayed for the man's surgery to go well.

Where is this savior complex from? My mother forcing me to attend suffering?

Nancy Lu, take this casserole to Mrs. Norwalk. The old woman was missing teeth, had a kerosene space heater that made my eyes burn, and gave me a glass of lemonade that had lipstick on it. I gritted my teeth and drank.

Or Susan Miller, a new girl in my third grade class who wiped her boogers in her math workbook. When she came to our church, my mother made me go to her birthday party. My piece of cake had an eggshell in it. I swallowed without gagging.

My jaw now feels as if it's clenched to prevent crunching into an eggshell. I'm a savior with Lockjaw. A taut, taught, mouth.

I swallowed eggshells to please my mother. What's my savior complex now? Do I do this shit out of *love* or a need to please?

February 2, 1985

Stan reaches out to snuggle with me. I pull away, remembering the 100's of times I tried to get out of bed in the morning and he pulled me back in. He is frustrated as I slide out of bed. "Are you getting up?"

"Yes."

"Why?"

I mumble something about still feeling anger after all those years I submitted out of feeling powerless.

"That's all in the past," Stan says. "I know I was a bastard. I've changed. Now is now. Forget that other stuff."

"I'm trying. I don't know why I can't forget." Forgive and forget. Forgive? Has my husband ever asked for forgiveness?

"Are you sorry you were a bastard?" I ask.

"How many times do I have to say I'm sorry?" He is near tears.

I want to say 781 times! Then I picture him starting to say *I'm sorry* 781 times and me counting. I think it's funny, but tighten my lips so I don't grin.

"I don't remember you *ever* saying you were sorry."

"I decided a few years ago I couldn't control you," Stan says, sitting up now, his arms stretched forward and holding his knees. "I could only keep loving you the way you were."

I see myself as a crazy bitch and wonder how this man has put up with me for all these years. With real sympathy, I say, "That must have been hard to deal with."

My husband doesn't respond.

February 5, 1985

Don, a psychotherapist brought in to lead a didactic on alcoholism for our CPE group, explains the process. "As part of our learning, we'll do a sculpturing. I'll arrange you standing physically like a family representation. Come over here," he says, pointing to an empty area in the room. "The five of you will be the family. I'll assign you each a role—one of you will be an alcoholic—and you'll act out what it's like to have an addicted person in the family."

Don asks me to be the alcoholic. As the family members talk about how difficult it is for them to have a daughter and sibling who is addicted, I begin thinking of my hospitalizations. I see patterns of my behavior. I think of my husband. I don't have to play at being sad.

Don says to me, "I am putting you into a 30-day treatment program." He pulls me out of the sculpture and takes me into the corner of the room. After leaving me there for a few moments he leads me back into the family.

"What do you notice?" he asks the group. The mother says she's glad I'm back. The sister says that she can't trust me yet. The father wonders if I'm going to look for a job, and the brother isn't sure if he'll lend me his car again.

Don says, "What do *you* notice, Nancy?"

"The family hasn't *changed*!" I say, startled by what I see. "I'm going right back into the same system!"

Don interrupts my attempt to interpret my observation. He asks, "What would you want to say to them now that you've returned from 'treatment' and they haven't changed?"

"I don't know," I answer. I'm only seeing Stan and the children, huddled together—afraid of me—and standing in front of the dining room drapes on the day I was released from St. Elizabeth's. The first time.

"What are you feeling?" Don asks.

"I think I'm scared. Isolated. And maybe angry."

"Angry? What are you angry about?"

"I don't know."

I wonder why Don assigned me the role of the alcoholic? Did Susan tell him about my psychiatric history? When I picture those times everyone seems so distant. They hadn't changed! My husband and children didn't look at their roles in the drama. I struggled to gain self-worth in the midst of the very same dynamics that fed my sadness and loneliness. How did I *do* it? Will? Desire?

I turned to other people for support. Psychiatrists, Pastors, Friends. And, I turned away from Stan. He and I are emotional eons apart.

If I could do the sculpture over again, I would scream, "Stop it! Stop it! Don't do this to me anymore!" But what was my family *doing* to me? I was the one who was driven, unhappy, controlling.

I wanted to stop all those things then. I'm learning to stop them now.

February 6, 1985

THE CALL comes while I'm sitting at the desk in the CPE office. I'm covering for the office administrator while she is on break, so I answer the phone and the message is for me. Reverend Sumner tells me that BOOM will recommend me for Deacon's Ordination on June 5. He adds that the Board's concern is that I might break down again.

According to Reverend Sumner, another Board member came to my rescue—a recovering alcoholic. The man explained to the Board that of course, I could be psychotic again—just as he could take a drink. He said that people like us know the territory—the pitfalls—better than other folks. He said it was a *gift*. Hoorah! Someone gets it!

I jump up and down. Susan and Rob are here and give me hugs and congratulations. As soon as Fran comes back, I will go to the "on call" room and *call* people.

I pray a silent thanksgiving to the suffering goddess Mary-with-no-mouth. When I see my pain—and the pain of other women—I feel her presence. Women who aren't heard by a patriarchal system.

With no mouth, they can't be fed either.

Journal: February 7, 1985

During the day people kept calling to congratulate me. While I was working with a family of a man who coded, a wrist corsage arrived from Stan. I *hate* corsages. Doesn't he remember after 27 years? His gift—five red rose buds—hooked my sadness. I remembered the dozen red roses he bought when Joan was born, six with Steve's birth, three when Julie was born (364 days after Steve), and a plastic one when Jerry was born.

He thought it was funny. I didn't.

Did he mean for these five roses to symbolize the five others in my family? I think I should feel touched and happy. I don't.

February 9, 1985

I am at the bedside of Mr. Krause, who is scheduled for heart surgery the next morning. He is in a private—and opulent—room that I didn't know existed. I assume the fur coat, thrown carelessly across a leather chair, belongs to his wife. She introduces me to their son, who dismisses me with his eyes and whines about wanting someone to bring him coffee. I restrain myself from kicking him in his balls. When my beeper goes off and I am called to ER, I am glad to leave Mr. Krause and his family.

The death in ER is Mr. Fred Wentworth, an 81 year-old man, who collapsed at an important Masonic event. I introduce myself to Mrs. Wentworth, whose face is drained of color. Two friends are standing close. All three women have gray hair done up in carefully coifed curls. Each is in a floor-length, formal, gown. One of the friends dabs carefully at her eyes with a lacy handkerchief.

Mr. Wentworth, the deceased, is stretched out flat on a gurney. A huge corpse, with a full head of white hair, his feet stretch past the end of the pallet. Still completely dressed, his arms cross over his chest and rest on a rumpled white shirt underneath a formal black suit—like a tux—except there is a red cross on the left sleeve. The edges of his cuffs and lapels are frayed. A frayed death, I think. A-fraid of death.

I am listening to Mrs. Wentworth, the Mason's wife, when the beeper beeps again. Another death. Before I leave, the new widow wants me to pray.

Mr. Wentworth's death scene rides in the elevator with me to 6-L. His black tux could have been a magician's suit. Death. A cruel trick? Like a magician's trick?

I remember my comment to Reverend Holton the cold February, 1970 day after I came back from the Ecumenical Institute. Wild with excitement, I laughed, "The Jesus Story is only a *story*! I've been tricked into joy! The story is a *trick*! A dirty trick so that I will discover there really is *no answer*." I interpreted Reverend Holton's grin as an affirmation that I had been initiated into a conspiracy.

In a few short months, however, I will be ordained. I think clergy play at being shameless shamans. I don't want to be like the guru sitting by the river selling river water.

February 13, 1985

Lena tried to commit suicide this afternoon. She took pills and then called her psychiatrist. I'm at her bedside trying to listen to her without getting caught in my own experience.

"Yesterday, my husband and I were at counseling with my psychiatrist," she says.

"I got angry … and then I got home." Lena, sitting with her feet dangling over the bed's edge, reaches for a tissue and then crumples her body into her tangled sheets.

"That's when you took the pills?" I ask, staying with Lena, but remembering my reckless and raw-with-anger drive home years earlier from the family counseling session in Oshkosh. My wine. My vomiting. My third stint at St. Elizabeth's.

Lena nods, then says, "My husband won't talk with me." (Yup) "I feel like screaming." (Yup) "The floor nurse says I should scream in a pillow." (Yup)

Then Lena tells me about being adopted. An alcoholic mother, who took 14 year-old Lena to the bar, and announced to her drinking buddies, "Look, here's my daughter, the virgin!" Lena's eyes and voice fade into silence.

"Have you made a promise with anyone about calling them *instead* of trying to kill yourself?" I ask.

"My psychiatrist had talked about it once," she answered and plucked at the edge of her hospital gown. "I don't think I made any promise."

My feet feel like they're wearing lead shoes as I leave Lena's room. Around here, my heart goes kaflooey. Arrhythmia. I've got a-rrhythmia. Like Ethel Merman. I try to cheer myself up.

My last day of this work can't come soon enough

Journal: February 18, 1985

During the didactic, Henry the CPE director, said, "What you enjoy doing the most may be your greatest gift. But your greatest gift is also a 'cross' that may become a bridge when you are learning to use and value your gifts."

"When you say *cross*," I asked, ignoring his mixed metaphors, "do you mean a barrier?"

"Not exactly. I mean *fear* of using that gift. I'm saying instead of concentrating on your fears, you should think of all the reasons you *must* use your gifts in order to be true to your emerging self."

My supervision group is helping me see my gifts: relational, public speaking, generosity. But I enjoy writing the most. I can't think of any reasons I *must* write in order to be true to my emerging self.

By July, I may be the pastor of a congregation. I suppose I will use writing some of the time. For sermons and filling out endless reports.

February 19, 1985

The young man is lying on a cot in ER. Another suicide attempt.

"His name is Jeff," a nurse tells me. "He's 27—confused and retarded." I walk over to a man who has a terrible red, flaky rash over his forehead, his ears, around his neck, and into the hospital gown that covers him. His hair looks like greasy straw. He opens his eyes and looks at me. Gray-green eyes. I look directly back into panic.

"Hi Jeff," I smile. "I'm Nancy Ore, Chaplain."

Jeff starts talking immediately. "They're after me. They keep coming and making me do stuff. They tell me I have to do stuff." Jeff shakes his hands as if he is flicking off bugs. "They're at me! They're *at* me!"

"Who is at you?" I ask, as Jeff's agitation increases. I wonder if he has been given any medication.

"My mother and father." He twists his lips into a grimace. His skin looks as if he has shaved it with a potato peeler. He says, "Sometimes I want to die."

"What is happening that you want to die?"

"When they are all at me. My mother and father ... Dr. Berkstaedt."

"Is Dr. Berkstaedt *your* doctor?"

Jeff answers with a slight nod, and says, "He's my dermatologist."

Oh. The poor kid. I can see his mother chasing him down to spread some icky smelling lotion all over him.

"And, the light comes when I want to die," Jeff says, interrupting my image.

The light? *The Light?*

"What does the light do?" I ask, with riveted interest.

"It warns me."

"Does it protect you? Take care of you?"

"Yes."

"Is the light your friend?"

"Yes."

"Can you describe it?"

"It's a bright light. It comes to me when I want to die."

"Is there anything else that would help you?"

"Women," Jeff says, looking at me. "Warm, gentle women who want to care about me."

Does he mean *me*? What can *I* do? I'm relieved to see the ER nurse arriving with a wheel chair. "Here comes a gentle woman to help you, Jeff," I say, and step back out of the way.

Journal: February 19, 1985

Immediately after morning report my beeper went off. I was called to ER and spent the next half hour with Jeff. Jeff—repulsive leper Jeff—is the first person I've met who talks about seeing a light. *The Light.* Even though he didn't describe a *thunderbolt of enlightenment* as the Tibetan Buddhists define it, Jeff's witness affirmed the crashing life-changing zap I experienced on March 16, 1970.

I have read about St. Paul being knocked off his feet on his way to Damascus, Joseph Campbell's "Schizophrenia, the Inward Journey," Anton Boisen's *Out of the Depths*, Andrew Solomon's *The Noonday Demon*, and anything else I could get my hands on.

But Jeff is the only one I've talked with that knows the light. Intimately. Only once was I uncomfortable with his words. When I asked him if there was anything other than the light that helped him, he answered "warm, gentle women who *want to care*." He named *my* condition—my feelings for him. I *wanted* to care. I *desired* caring. I don't know if that desire is enough.

I wanted to feel affection for him. I did not. His exterior was repulsive. But his soul is in the midst of a journey struggle I've been on, although his terrain is most likely different. I don't feel so lonely now.

He probably will never know the gift he gave me.

Journal: February 21, 1985

Susan brushed away tears when she gave me my final evaluation. She had trouble trying to tell me how much she had grown to like me and will miss me. She challenged me to look at gifts I bring to her and the other Pastoral Care Staff.

I reported that I have noticed I am much more centered and focused. I continue to take good care of myself—setting boundaries—going away from that which I don't like and going toward that which I do.

Endings are coming fast. I'm done with CPE. My last quarter at G-ETS starts in a few days. Will I have a pastoral appointment somewhere before June?

Chapter 20
Step Out and Step In

*The place God calls you to is the place where your
deep gladness and the world's deep hunger meet.*
                                                -Frederick Buechner

March 1, 1985

Stan and I are out under a shivering, silver sky by 5:30 a.m. He's jogging laps on this short dead end drive we live on. I'm walking and sliding on the ice puddles in the gravel road by the next-door neighbor's house. The ice is rubbery, gives way and crackles under my shoes. Sounds like crinkling up Saranwrap. If I encased myself in Saranwrap, would decay be thwarted?

Decay. Marriage.

I can hear Stan coming toward me before I can see him as he finishes his first lap. Heavy footfalls and expulsions of breath. The first time he passes me he grunts "Hi." The second time, in the dawning light, nothing. I continue walking until I reach the end of the road, then turn and walk back home. I have coffee perking when Stan comes in, his cheeks frosted red and nose dripping. Without speaking he heads for the back room to change his clothes.

I will drive back to G-ETS on Monday for my final quarter.

March 7, 1985

Mary, a divorced woman in my Theological Ethics class, and I are having supper at The Colorado Company. I tell her about my dying marriage and how much I loved Stan when we got married.

"How does falling *out* of love happen?" she asks.

"I don't know," I answer.

"I didn't expect an answer," she says, "but I've asked myself that question."

"I don't think I ever had an equal love relationship with my husband," I say. "Do you know the Soren Kierkegaard story about the king and the peasant maiden?"

"No."

"I heard it in my Christology course," I say and tell Mary the story. "A powerful king falls in love with a plain peasant woman. He realizes he can't bring her to his palace and shower her with jewels and royal treatment. She would say she loved him, but he wouldn't know if she really did. He didn't want a subject. He wanted a lover. An equal.

"So the king renounces his throne and shows up at her door as a peasant."

"I get it," Mary said. "Like God or Jesus. But they still aren't equal to us."

"I know, and I loved Stan as if I were the young peasant woman. I thought he was like a powerful king. I don't think our love was ever equal … and it's not his fault."

"Whoa. Do you think you can ever get to equal?"

"I don't know. I think it's too late."

Journal: March 15, 1985

Stan and I drove to Central House in Chilton for my 45th birthday dinner. I looked at his profile as he drove, and it was 1959 and our three-day trip to northern Wisconsin, a honeymoon delayed by sixteen months and a two-month-old baby that we left in my mother's care. He was 23. Handsome, chiseled face. I adored him.

As we rode toward Chilton, I noticed the approaching evening sky. Sunlight, diffused by purple and pink clouds, shot one brilliant shaft of gold light to the ground, and moments later several rays created a shimmering fan.

"Look at that spectacular sunset," I said.

"Uh-huh," was the response.

This morning at 5:55 I walked below the cliff and the sun's beams were snagged and tangled by tree limbs, sumac, and bushes. Still golden.

Between that sunset and sunrise, Stan and I again talked about our marital situation.

He started the conversation. "What can we do about your anger?"

"I don't know," I answered, then caught on. "*We?*" I say. "You're going to try and help me fix *my* anger?"

Stan's shoulders sagged in defeat. "I just want to help," he said. "Nothing I say is ever right."

"I'm sorry. I've had so much counseling that I fasten on every word … and I don't want to be the one who *always needs help*."

"Now you're saying I refuse to work on my feelings."

"No. I'm saying I don't *always* want to be the dependent one. I know my anger is an issue. I learned in CPE that my emotional intensities tend to distance people."

"Yes," he agreed quickly. "Your ups and downs have been hard for me."

He is a good man. When I see how his steady work over the years has taken care of his family, I see myself as a small helpless child, bound in white silk ropes. Pretty Nancy. Little ringlets. Nancy, three years old standing by her daddy and reciting the Pledge of Allegiance for the neighbors. Pink starched dress. Smiling. Tied up in holy cords.

Pleasing Daddy.

Is that *still* the issue? It's *wrong* to be angry with my husband?

Unchristian? Nice Nancy wouldn't express her rage. Now what do I do? What *is* holy? What god? No god is telling me anything. I'm only hearing about my anger from *me*.

Do not hurt your husband.

Do not hurt him.

Do not hurt him.

And, the result is:

Dead Nancy.

Dead Nancy.

Dead Nancy.

March 22, 1985

Dream

I am running. I come to a yard in which there is a man, woman and large black dog. The dog runs toward me, goes past me. I am frightened. I turn around to look at the dog. He has turned around as well and is starting to run at me again to attack. I fall down, put out my left arm expecting the dog to bite it. Instead the dog's teeth lock on a pair of sandals I'm carrying.

The woman—large, middle aged, dark haired—stands there. I say, "You could be calling off your dog." She indicates she feels no reason to do so and that I can handle it. I wrest my sandals from the dog. Now I am walking. The dog is in front of me. The dog lifts its back left leg to pee. I start to step over the dog to avoid being hit by urine and knock over the dog. I am afraid he'll be angry, but he rolls over on his back and acts afraid of me.

March 28, 1985

"Something happened last weekend between my husband and me," I say to Evelyn, my seminary advisor. Though her advice is supposed to be about my academic process, she is willing to listen to me about my marriage.

"I leveled with him," I tell Evelyn. "I told him I loved him, but wasn't sure I was *in* love with him anymore. I said I was afraid of his size." I reach for the tissue Evelyn has on her desk.

"How did he respond?"

"He didn't say much. Only that he couldn't do anything about his size. He was sad."

Evelyn nods.

"He called last night to give me a message about my ordination. His voice had a catch in it again. I could tell his lips were tight." I wipe the tears that are trickling down my cheeks. "He didn't say 'I love you' when he hung up."

"How long have you known?"

"Known what?" I'm confused, then understand. "Divorce?"

Evelyn nods.

"I don't know." I'm surprised that Evelyn's question unlocks a door in my mind, and I see Kenneth standing at the threshold. I bring Evelyn further into my confidence.

"A couple years ago, I had a really brief affair. One weekend. Maybe I've known since then."

"Did you tell Stan about your affair?"

"No. He was suspicious. By the time he asked if I was 'getting it somewhere else,' the other man was completely out of my life."

Evelyn hands me another tissue.

"I think I haven't considered divorce seriously because I bought into the belief that God is against it."

"Do you believe that now?"

"I don't think so."

"What do you believe?"

"I think that people in a marriage help each other grow. I think Stan is supporting me and I'm not supporting him." I use another tissue to wipe my nose.

Evelyn pushes the box closer to me. "Your husband has responsibility for your relationship, too," she says. "It doesn't sound as if he has taken it. Or isn't taking it."

"He is beginning to talk with me now, and I'm discovering we don't have much in common. Except our children."

Evelyn smiles. "Your children are an important part of your marriage."

"I know." I shake my head in despair over my failure as a mother. "Since my hospitalizations, I haven't felt like I belonged in the family. Stan kept things going then, and he is the one who communicates with the children now."

I look at my watch. "I need to get to my preaching class," I say, taking one last tissue. "Do I look like I've been crying?"

"You look fine," Evelyn says, "and, you'll be fine. You have a lot of insight about your situation."

"Thank you." I stand up and say, "I owe you a box of Kleenex."

We both smile.

April 16, 1985

Dream:

I am walking at night along Main St. in my home town. As I near the railroad tracks, a man passes me, then stops, turns, and starts to follow me. I know he plans to rape me. As he grabs me, I say "No! Don't rape me." I plead with him. "Please don't rape me." We wrestle. I am putting up a fight. As we are fighting a big dog comes bounding up and distracts the man. The dog gets in the way and stops me from being raped.

Journal: April 18, 1985

Twenty-seven years ago today, Stan and I hopped into his two-toned green '58 push button Rambler and eloped. I remember the trip across the southwestern hills of Wisconsin to Dubuque. His brother, who'd received his driver's license a few weeks earlier, drove. My friend, Ann, sat in the passenger seat.

I wore a white dress. I was 18.

At six-years-old, I was a flower girl at Betty and Bob Bernd's wedding. I wore a white dress and walked down the church aisle tossing red rose petals from the straw basket exactly as I had been taught. After the wedding, my daddy took a picture of me in front of the lilac bushes at our house. The bride gave me the gold heart locket that hangs around my neck in the photo. She gave her heart (and name) to Bob Bernd.

Twenty-seven years ago today, I gave Stan my heart and name. He was strong and handsome and held me tightly all the way home from Dubuque. He has put up with a lot. So have I.

I thought my marriage would last forever.

Three nights after our marriage, my mother found red spots on my sheets. My father hurried across the street to tell the Ore tribe they got a virgin, after all.

On April 18, 1958, my hymen may have been intact, but I was no virgin. My heart, however, had a thick skin around it. Until Kenneth, my ability to let love in had not been penetrated.

April 28, 1985

"When will you hear about an appointment?" Stan asks, as he wipes the last dish from our Sunday supper.

"I don't know. I'll know in the next couple of weeks, I guess." I let the dishwater out of the sink and wipe off the counter.

"I've been thinking about your paycheck," he says, and hangs up the dishtowel. "You'll need money."

"What do you mean?" Of course I'll need money. What is he thinking?

"I thought your paycheck would go into our joint account. We'll have to figure out how much you would need for a month."

"I haven't even thought about a paycheck. I'm still worried about finishing my classes." I turn the light off over the sink. As we walk out of the kitchen, I say, "I won't know what my salary is until I know where I'm appointed and meet with the Pastor Parish Relations Committee."

"Okay," Stan says, "We can talk about it later."

I sit at the trestle table with my 20th Century United Methodist History notes. I am not happy with my husband's plan for *my* paycheck.

May 13, 1985

"What can you tell me about this appointment?" I ask.

"They don't want a woman," Reverend Berg says softly, keeping his hands firmly on the steering wheel and his eyes straight ahead on the highway, "and they don't want someone just out of seminary."

"Oh." I chew on his words in silence.

Reverend Raymond Berg, my district superintendent, is driving me to Oconto to meet with a Pastor Parish Relations Committee. In a couple of weeks, I will graduate from seminary with a Master of Divinity degree. On June 2, I will be ordained a deacon, a three-year probationary status before fulfilling the requirements to be ordained an elder.

"They had a little trouble a few years ago with a woman," Reverend Berg says, his eyes directly ahead on Highway 41. "She was the first woman they had ever had and only stayed a year. There were lots of problems." He doesn't comment about the issues, and I don't ask for further information. I can't do anything about fixing either my schooling or my gender. I'll have to rely on my newfound feminine strength and meet the problems head-on.

In the United Methodist system, the bishop, with the input of the district superintendents, decides the pastoral appointments. The pastor is informed of the decision and, if she or he is agreeable, the first meeting between pastor and people is understood as the introduction of the pastor to the congregation. After an hour or so of conversation, there is a time of discernment during which the pastor and committee meet separately and briefly with the district superintendent. If there are no strong objections by either the people or pastor, the appointment is set.

If my appointment goes through, I will be serving Abrams and Oconto—two churches north of Green Bay. A two-point charge, in the jargon of the United Methodist denomination.

When Reverend Berg turns off Highway 41, my interest in the surroundings increases. We drive two blocks through a small town and pass a general store tucked into the midst of a few well-kept houses. Then Reverend Berg points toward a white frame building with red painted doors that face the main road.

"There is the Abrams church," he says. I look up to see if there is a lighted cross on the roof, remembering what I learned in a workshop for new ministers: major parish problems were often of a logistical nature rather than a theological one. "You have been trained to do exegetics and hermeneutics," the professor said. "But, you are going out to East Rosebud or West Overshoe. In East Rosebud the folks are worried about a leaky roof. And in West Overshoe they are arguing about whether or not to spend the memorial money on a lighted cross for the steeple."

As Reverend Berg drives slowly past the Abrams church, I am relieved to see the *lit cross* decision has already been made and I don't see any holes in the roof.

Twenty minutes later, we pull into the parking lot of the Oconto church. I notice a flat roof on part of the church building and that there is no lit cross anywhere in sight.

My attention is quickly drawn to several faces peering out a front window.

I know when I get out of the car they will see a *woman*. I have carefully chosen my outfit, a beige linen dress with thin blue stripes and buttons up the side. I have put on proper navy blue pumps and tied a matching scarf around my neck. But no matter what I am wearing the people looking out the window are going to know immediately I am a woman.

Shortly after that, they will know I am just finishing seminary. I sigh. 45 years-old and still not adequate.

I pretend I don't see the people scurrying away from the window, and, when I am shown through a door marked *Lounge,* I smile at a group of people staring at me. They are seated on folding chairs around a rectangular, Formica-topped table that is centered in a large carpeted room. The rest of the room is furnished like a living room, with a brown upholstered couch under the front window and several overstuffed beige chairs pushed against adjacent walls. The room includes a piano, a buffet, a large mirror and a variety of religious pictures on pine paneling.

"This is Nancy Ore," Reverend Berg says, walking over to join the people at the table. "She is your new pastor."

My smile feels as if it is traveling through wet flannel.

Reverend Berg and I sit in the only two empty chairs at the table. I am barely settled among the other six people when a frowning woman sitting directly across the table from me stretches her hefty torso over the space between us, shakes her right index finger at me and loudly scolds, "What are you *doing* here? Don't you know you're not supposed to be a minister? Don't you read your Bible? Paul said women aren't supposed to speak in church! 1 Timothy 2.12. Look it up!"

Oh crap! The woman is more familiar with 1 Timothy than I am. My stomach flips over. I decide not to trot out my feminist theology or the scholarly arguments over the authorship of 1 and 2 Timothy. I decide to use my listening skills and respond to the dilemma growing its horns right in the middle of the table.

"I'm sorry you feel that way," I say, hoping my trembling voice doesn't betray my insincerity. "I guess we disagree, but I would be glad to talk more about it with you." Well, kind of glad.

The woman sits back with a disapproving harumph. There are wide-eyed looks and several moments of silence before someone else asks about my family. I am happy with the question and answer that I am married and have four children, all grown and gone from home.

Questions and answers during the next hour do not elicit further controversy.

"Will you live in the parsonage?"

"Yes."

"What about your husband?"

"He will join me during the weekends, and I will spend one night a week at our home north of Appleton."

"When will you start?"

"The last Sunday in June."

"Is the salary okay?"

"Yes."

There are no questions about my theology (off the chart liberal—called an iconoclast) and no further questions about my gender. I am sent into the sanctuary to wait while the committee confers in private with Reverend Berg. He has a big smile on his face when he comes to report their decision. I return with him to the church lounge and tell the committee I am happy to be their new pastor. Mostly I am relieved.

On the drive home, we discuss the large woman's attack. "You handled it well," he says.

"I'm used to the challenge," I respond. "I learned a long time ago I couldn't *be* a pastor because I was a girl."

"Who told you that?"

"Reverend Herschberg at Camp Byron. I was thirteen years old. After a consecration service, the pastor told the boys they could become ministers and girls could be ministers' wives."

Reverend Berg shakes his head in disbelief and asks, "When was that?"

"1953," I answer. "Technically, of course, he was right."

Reverend Berg nods and for the rest of the ride, we talk about the years of struggle before the United Methodist decision in 1956 to grant women full clergy rights. I will soon covenant to be an *itinerant* pastor—willing to be sent anywhere by the bishop.

May 13, 1985

"How did it go?" Stan asks about my meeting.

"In spite of one woman's strong objections, the committee approved my appointment."

"How long a drive will it be from here?"

"About an hour."

"Did you see the parsonage?"

"Yes. People are going to paint it and put down new carpeting."

"How much is your salary?

"$17,500. I also get a travel allowance and money for continuing education."

"Good," he says. "We can pay down some of our debts."

"No! I don't want my paycheck to go into our joint account."

Stan, who is bending over his chair preparing to sit down, straightens up quickly, his eyebrows twisted into surprise.

"I want to see if I can survive on what I make," I explain. "Except for this house, the debts you want to pay down are for things you wanted to buy. For our whole marriage, I haven't known how to argue against your constant use of credit for new things." I move to the end of the trestle table, as if the tangible barrier between my husband and me will give me emotional strength I need to see my decision accepted.

"We have hardly any savings," I continue. "We borrow for emergencies, and there is no money left at the end of the month. I want to see how *I* manage money."

Still staring at me, my husband squints his suspicion, and asks, "What about our joint checking account? Are you going to have access to that money, too?"

"No. That would defeat the purpose. Anyway, your salary is almost three times what mine will be. You'll have *all* that money to spend."

Stan takes a few moments to consider what I've proposed.

"What will you do? Get your own checking account?"

"I guess so. I haven't thought it all through, but it's important for me to see if I can be independent."

"Okay. Let's try it. You know you have a $5,000 student loan to pay off."

"I know."

Why does Stan's agreement to my decision sound like he's giving me permission to take full responsibility for my finances?

May 14, 1985

My friend, Susan, calls at 8:30 a.m. to find out if my appointment had been approved by the Abrams and Oconto Pastor Parish Committee.

"Well, how did it go?" she asks.

"Okay," I answer, reluctant to say more. The appointment process is highly confidential, and I shouldn't have told Susan I was having an introductory meeting. The congregations are supposed to be informed before I share the news publicly.

"Were you approved?"

"Well," I said, trusting my friend, "the appointment went through, but the congregation won't be told until Sunday. I'm not supposed to tell anyone until then."

"How did the meeting go?"

I immediately thought of the angry woman and my gender. "It was okay, but they wanted something I don't have."

"Oh? What's that?"

I answer Susan with one word.

She is silent for a moment, then asks, "Don't they have music up there?"

"I guess not," I say, thinking how the angry woman probably stops all fun.

"But *you* can play!"

I'm confused for a moment, then quickly realize my friend heard my earlier one-word answer as *pianist.*

Journal: May 16, 1985

"You're different," Jane said. "You have a grace about you." We hugged goodbye. Jane and I have been roommates for most of our seminary residency. We've been good friends. Our daily conversations are over. She has an appointment in Michigan. I'll be in northern Wisconsin with Lake Michigan between us and I have not mastered walking on water yet.

"You have a good presence in the pulpit," Milly said, and Rodney, who will take an appointment in Indiana, told me he would be happy to have me as a colleague.

The words of my friends swirled around and settled in my gut. It is nice to know others see in me something that is graceful and powerful. And, although I am not consciously in touch with such potential of a grace and power-filled being, I know I am different from September of 1982.

But what happened?

I changed a tire, arranged a checking account, and got mostly A's. I learned how to exegete and herminate. I lived in a dorm for the first time in my life. I maintained my Presidential Scholarship, articulated my own theology, and earned an Master of Divinity. My Credo—my required statement of belief—was affirmed. Instead of carrying home a bag of medication from St. Elizabeth's, I head to Abrams and Oconto equipped with boxes of books, techniques, and resources.

During these three years, I also managed a *really late* adolescence. Jane and I found a ladder and put up the "No Bullshit" sign in room 205. I took Jesus' broken digit lying at the base of his neglected statue on the third floor and gave different folks Jesus' finger. But most importantly, I fell in love—lost a love—and discovered the love that I give to others is okay.

V
From Seminary to Service

Chapter 21
Ordination

The master's sermon that day consisted of one enigmatic sentence. With a wry smile he said, "All I do is sit by the bank of the river selling river water."
-Anthony de Mello

Journal: June 2, 1985

7:30 a.m. This year's Wisconsin Annual Conference of the United Methodist Church is being held at the University of Wisconsin at Stevens Point. The marquee outside announced the event:

UNTIED METHODIST CONFERENCE.

The Ordination Service is scheduled for this morning, and I am feeling like the marquee description. Unraveled.

At 6:30 a.m. I did my regular practice in my dorm room: scripture, meditation, journal, and prayer. I never know which god I'm talking to. This time I wanted to talk with someone who has a *real* ear about how nervous I am. I keep thinking about Kenneth and thinking that I shouldn't be ordained.

During my February interview, without naming him, I told the three reps from the Board about that weekend and how important it was to my spiritual growth. One of the pastors reminded me of the story from Luke's gospel about the woman who interrupted Jesus' supper with Simon the Pharisee. The woman had broken several religious rules. She cried for forgiveness. She dried her tears off Jesus' feet with her hair, which should stay covered in public. She kissed his feet and poured out expensive perfume on him. Simon was outraged, but Jesus upbraided him.

The pastor quoted Jesus to me. "She who loves much, her sins, which are many, are forgiven, for she loved much."

I think of me passionately pouring out love. I am confused. Does it mean my behavior is excused because it's "love?" Or are my sins some kind of other sins (not adultery)—that are cancelled *because* I love? Does loving atone for sinning?

Was my loving Kenneth eternal sin? I didn't intend to hurt anyone, although my relationship with Stan is blocked and obviously hurts him. I feel sad about that. I think of the early years we had—how hard he worked. How steady he was when I was unhinged.

The lectionary for today included a covenant between Abram and God. Abram trembled in the Lord's presence. As soon as I read Genesis 15.12: *a deep and terrifying darkness fell upon Abram,* the lid blew off the cauldron of dread that bubbles in my stomach during worship. So far I have been able to tamp down the fire, but today? How can I have hands laid on me when I've been unfaithful?

How can I pastor two rural churches, one of which has Abram's name?

For some reason, Grandma Field's farmhouse filled the screen in my mind. I stood near the granary, looking at the house. The pump was there, the black handle pushed down after Grandpa had filled the pail for the kitchen water. The yard I was standing on is peppered with little black and white swirls of chicken shit. I longed to be barefoot, but I kept my shoes on at Grandma's ever since the horrifying morning that chicken poop squished between my toes.

The sun was shining and the sky was blue with long wisps of clouds like horsetails flicking off flies. Grandpa and Grandma were sitting on the porch in the white Adirondack chairs that needed paint. Sally, the dog that fetched the cows, was at Grandma's feet. When I asked Grandma why Sally had cream-colored spots—one over each eye on her black head, Grandma said, "When a dog has those spots, it's smart."

I believed her.

Why is my grandmother showing up in this journal on my ordination day? God-whoever-you-are, what am I supposed to see at Grandma's house? My rural roots? Ah yes. The Grandma who nagged at me. The Grandma whose conditional love squelched me. The Grandma who showed up at St. Elizabeth's as a goat demon. Why Grandma's farm now? Am I about to relive childhood sights, sounds, and smells at Abrams and Oconto? A and O. Alpha and Omega. The beginning and the end. Grandma was at my beginning. Will this rural church appointment be my ending?

Now I think of my other grandmother. Grandma Bauer. "As long as you have your sense of humor, Nancy," she said, "you'll be okay." Small, well-groomed. Calm, accepting, genteel, but no touching. Grandma Bauer was my model and I am nothing like her.

Grandma Field. Fat, sweaty, critical. She wiped my mouth with a sour dishrag. But, she touched me.

Both grandmothers were strong women who handed down love to me as surely as they gave their DNA. These stories of my unfolding… Mythstory, Mythstical God. You—through countless people—touch me.

I am scared. The dread is there in the pit of my gut. My bowels are roiling. I started my period, of course. My body seems to need to emphasize my gender at every important rite of passage.

In an hour the bishop will lay hands on my head and …What will happen? Will I be ordained while impure?

June 2, 1985

Along with several other ordinands, I am in the long procession of clergy to be led into the gym where over a thousand people from around the state have gathered for this special service. My husband, my mother, two of my children and several of my friends are among the crowd somewhere.

As we make our way slowly to the front of the worship space, I am calmed and then overwhelmed when I see smiling, supportive, friends: Brenda, Wesley, Bruce, Thad, Lu, Charlie, Jan, Mary, Dave, Carly, Martha, Lois. It is *good* to be here.

During the entire event, my stomach and mind behave. I sing the hymns, listen to the sermon, and step confidently to the kneeler, remembering to put the 3"x5" card printed with my name on the ledge in such a way that the bishop announces the correct name of the one he is ordaining. I leave the service with a stole around my neck—a symbol of the towel that Jesus used to wash his disciples' feet. The sign of a servant.

As the organ blasts out the postlude and the service ends, I am ecstatic. My family and friends greet me with hugs and laughter. A clown, part of the "untied" people for the conference, hands me a balloon.

Stan has arranged a celebration luncheon for my friends and family in the Holiday Inn. After we eat, I open cards and gifts. I thank the giver and raise each gift high enough for people to see. There is a message inside the card from my friends, Susan, Barb, and Rusty. I read the words aloud:

"Now you have everything you need to be their pastor."

Curious, and in front of a room full of family and friends, I open the tiny package attached to the card. Lying between two small squares of cotton is a pink, inch-long eraser, shaped like a male body part. I immediately recognize the *thing* I told Susan I needed to be a pastor. Red-faced, I don't know whether I should explain this x-rated gift.

With 30 people watching and waiting, I take a deep breath, hold up the tiny eraser phallus and tell the story of Susan's phone call.

Everyone laughs, of course, and I am delighted with the gift.

"I plan to stick this piece of power in the pocket of my alb," I announce, "and have it with me every Sunday."

Journal: June 12, 1985

I met Rusty for lunch. She had two photographs of my ordination. The first is a shot of the ordinands standing and facing the crowd. The photo is taken from the top of the gym bleachers and though I'm hard to identify from such a distance, I think I see myself with the others getting ready to be ordained.

Because the second photo is taken from a closer vantage point, Rusty had to have made her way down from the bleachers and into the aisle near the stage. I am kneeling in my White-Alb-Holy-Ghost outfit in front of Bishop David Lawson. His right hand is on my head and sometime during the brief ritual, he says, "Take thou authority …"

I notice the same phrase is in Rusty's snapshot, printed across a white cloth that covers a large makeshift altar behind the bishop. In the photo my kneeling body blots out the last three letters of the bishop's order.

The command I see in the photo is: "Take thou author."

I look at Rusty and grin. Her eyebrows are raised as if waiting for a response from me. This may be a sign, I think. But from where or whom? Another question to which I will never have the answer. I thank Rusty for the snapshot, take it home and frame it.

The command has a permanent home on my desk.

Epilogue

You start by writing to live.
You end by writing so as not to die.

--Carlos Fuentes

Though I didn't have the "extra finger" (the piece of male anatomy I lacked), my ministry at Abrams and Oconto was rich and fulfilling. With the exception of a few people who didn't want a "lady pastor," the folks accepted me and taught me a lot about being a spiritual servant. I ministered in four more churches in Wisconsin before retiring in 2003.

During my ordination process, when asked about why I was pursuing ministry, I said, "I want to be close to holy things." Though I was referring to administering the sacraments, which included rituals reserved for ordained clergy, I was surprised by many sacred moments through the years that included the delight of children, the grieving of bereaved, and even moments within the interminable meetings. My prayers were granted over and over.

In 1986, my husband and I separated. Our divorce was final on May 6, 1987. Coincidently, that day was also the fiftieth anniversary of the Hindenburg disaster. However, our twenty-nine years of marriage had good times, so the comparison doesn't stand.

Another pastor, Charles King, supervised my seminary field ed requirement, and helped me with administrative demands in my first few years of ministry. Also divorced, Charles and I began dating in 1989 and married in 1990. When it came time to decide if I would change my name, I jokingly lobbied for "Nancy Queen," but we both liked the hyphenated name of Bauer-King and the contradictory social status the two combined names implied.

At the time we married, the children Charlie and I had from our first marriages were grown and gone. Some had children of their own. Today, with the exception of one son, all our children, most of our grandchildren (and three great-grandchildren), live in states other than Wisconsin. We enjoy visiting in the many places they have settled.

After our retirements, Charlie and I continued to serve five more churches in an interim capacity. I retired for the fifth time (completely) in 2009. We presently live (and love) in a condo in Racine, Wisconsin, that has a great view of Lake Michigan. My desk is shoved up against the east window of our office where my muse often comes riding in on a wave.

I have a long-time friend who recently commented about her life: "I cry when I have to, and laugh when I can."

These days I am laughing much more and much longer than crying.

-Nancy Bauer-King
March 14, 2017

Acknowledgements and Thank Yous

What is love?
Gratitude.
What is hidden in our chests?
Laughter.
What else?
Compassion.

-Rumi

How do I thank the dozens of persons who loved me while I searched for the laughter and compassion hidden within my heart?

I am grateful for those who stayed present during some of the messiest moments I experienced: Rusty, Thad, Brenda, Dorothy, Marge, Gerry, Hazelyn, Jack, Jim, Paul, Bruce, Emma, Rosemary.

Thank you to Carolyn Kott Washburne who asked the initial question that motivated me to write this story and supported my early attempts. And a special thank you to Linda Angel, my Tuesday morning breakfast friend for many years, who has heard most of the "rest" of my stories.

I am especially grateful for Robert Vaughan and the Friday morning Round Table Group at Red Oak Studio, who listened, critiqued, and encouraged me to persevere. And, thank you to Kim Suhr, Director of Red Oak Studio, whose sharp eye edited the manuscript and whose writing acumen suggested welcome improvements.

A big thank you to Shannon Ishizaki and the staff at TEN16 Press, whose admirable patience with this technologically challenged woman brought this book into being.

Finally, boundless gratitude and love to Charles, who has lived with me for twenty-seven years and still loves me. Amazing!

www.ingramcontent.com/pod-product-compliance
Lightning Source LLC
Chambersburg PA
CBHW020923090426
42736CB00010B/1018